From Start to Finish

dBASE IV 1.1

Carol Elston and Sue Orrell

PITMAN PUBLISHING
128 Long Acre, London, WC2E 9AN

A Division of Longman Group UK Ltd

© Carol Elston and Sue Orrell 1993

First published in Great Britain 1993

British Library Cataloguing-in-Publication Data
A catalogue record for this book is available from the British Library

ISBN 0 273 03816 8

Printed in England by Clays Ltd, St Ives plc

Contents

Introduction

As the title states, this book is designed to take the new user of dBASE IV from start to finish. Starting by creating a simple computerised database system, the tasks and activities progress in complexity until, at the finish, the user is a competent dBASE programmer.

dBASE IV has three main working environments; the *Control Centre*, the *Dot Prompt* and the *Programming* environment. This book is divided into four parts dealing with each of these working environments. Parts 3 and 4 cover the programming environment through to an advanced stage.

The topics covered in Parts 1 and 2 of this book correspond approximately to the material required for the RSA, PEI, City & Guilds and BTEC examination levels. Since examination syllabuses vary in content and are constantly under revision, the order of topics may not align exactly to any given syllabus. It is important to note that Parts 2, 3 and 4 cover topics and material beyond the current scope of most examination syllabuses. These topics have been included to provide an appreciation of all the sophisticated features of dBASE IV.

About the accompanying diskettes

There is a pack containing three diskettes, available from Pitman Publishing, to accompany this book (*see* order form at the end of the book). For those familiar with DOS, each diskette contains a sub-directory for every chapter requiring new files. Each sub-directory is named by chapter number eg C4 for Chapter 4.

Throughout this book it is assumed that all files are accessed from the hard disk and are stored in a sub-directory with the path C:\DBASE\DATA. The appropriate files are copied into this sub-directory from the floppy disk by means of a simple batch file. The batch files have the same names as the sub-directories. The process of copying the necessary files is explained below.

If you are working through the entire book you may not need to copy any files from the floppy disk as you will be creating them as you go. However, if you need to complete the text quickly, you may want to miss out some of the consolidation exercises. In this case you can move on to the next chapter by copying the required files from disk.

The text is designed so that you can work at your own pace. You may decide to complete one Part, or a number of chapters, and then practice your new skills for several months before moving on. Alternatively, you can use the text as a "crash course", working through the chapters consecutively. By using the disks you can always repeat chapters by copying the necessary files for that chapter from the floppy disk.

Icons used throughout the book

The *diskette* icon is used to indicate exercises which may require you to copy new files from disk. It is also used to indicate information that is important to disk users.

The icon of the *person seated at the computer* is used to indicate exercises or information that is of importance to readers who have not purchased the diskettes. Exercises indicated in this way will include the creation or modification of a file or files that will be referred to in later chapters.

The *bomb* icon is used as a warning. Wherever you see the icon take special care and read the information carefully.

The *arrow* icon indicates an exercise or activity.

Setting-up a data directory

Follow the instructions below before starting Part 1 to ensure that your system is configured in line with the examples given.

1   If your computer screen shows the DOS prompt, a letter followed by a colon (:) ie C:, C:\ ,C:\DOS or A:, go to instruction 3.

2   If your screen shows a menu, select the option that allows you to exit to DOS. You should now see the DOS prompt.

You are going to create a new sub-directory (area of the hard disk) to hold the databases and related files that you will create throughout this text.

3   If the DOS prompt does not start with the letter C type **C:** and press the Enter key.

4   Type **CD \DBASE** and press the Enter key.

5   Type **MD DATA** and press the Enter key.

6   Type **CD DATA** to change to the newly created sub-directory.

Using the diskettes

For those using the disks that accompany this book, you will need to refer to the following instructions whenever you want to copy files from the floppy disk to the data sub-directory on the hard disk. Although the instructions will have little meaning at this stage, by including them at the beginning of the book, rather than when they are first required, it will make it easier when you need to refer back.

If working through the book, you will first need to refer to these instructions at the beginning of Chapter 5.

1 Before copying files from disk, it is important to make sure that those files are not currently open (in the memory of the computer). When using the Control Centre, make sure that all listed files are below the line in the panels (*see* 5.3 Closing a database, page 30). If using the dot prompt, type **CLOSE ALL**, to close all files before copying from disk (*see* 16.4 Using a database and modifying the data, page 118).

2 Put the disk for the appropriate Part in drive A of your machine.

3 Press **Alt + T** to access the **Tools** menu.

4 Select the **Dos utilities** option. A list of all the files in the C:\DBASE\DATA subdirectory will be displayed.

5 Press **Alt + D** to select the **DOS** menu.

```
Perform DOS command
Go to DOS

Set default drive:directory   {C:\DBASE\DATA}
```

6 Select the **Perform DOS command** option. A prompt will appear for you to type a DOS command. For those not familiar with DOS (Disk Operating System) do not worry too much about this process. You are simply copying the files from the floppy disk drive, called A to your working sub-directory on the hard disk, called C, by means of a batch file. A batch file contains a number of DOS commands that run one after another. The batch files used in this process contain a command to copy the appropriate files from one destination to the other.

7 Type **A:** followed by the batch file name. For example, to copy the files for Chapter 5, type **A:\C5** (each time you need to copy files you will be given the name of the batch file). Press **Enter** to complete the command.

8 The disk drive light should flash and the message *File(s) copied* will appear at the bottom of the screen with the prompt; *Press any key to return to dBASE IV.* Press a key and you will be returned to the sub-directory listing.

9 To exit from the **DOS utilities** menu press **Alt + E** and press **Enter** to select the only option, **Exit to Control Centre.**

10 Remove the disk from drive A but keep it somewhere safe as you will need it again later.

Working without the disks

 If you decide to use this book without the disks it is recommended that you start at the beginning of each Part and follow the topics through. As each Part progresses, files created earlier in that Part are referred to and may need to be used.

At the beginning of each part you will find a list of the files needed to complete the Part and a reference to the number of the chapter where the files were initially created. By referring back, you can create all the necessary files and then work your way through the Part.

If you begin with Part 1 and complete all the examples and all the consolidation exercises indicated by the icon of the figure at the computer, you will have generated all the files necessary for the next chapter. Each chapter starts with a check-list of files so that you can make sure that you have completed all necessary exercises and are ready to continue.

Consolidation exercises

Consolidation exercises have been included at the end of some Chapters and Parts. These are designed to give extra practice without step-by-step guidance. It is recommended that you initially attempt these exercises without referring to the current Chapter or Part. If you do incur difficulties, refer to the appropriate section in the book. If still unable to complete the task, refer to the appropriate Appendix at the back of the book for more detailed help.

The Appendices numbered 1 to 3 contain step-by-step help on the consolidation exercises in the respective Part.

Part 1

The Control Centre

1   Scenario and objective

This Part will introduce the terminology used to describe the storage and manipulation of data on a computer. You will take an existing recording system and transpose the details onto a computer.

1.1   Scenario

You will computerise a system used by an estate agent in the fictitious town of Greenoak. This estate agent is an independently-run family business and only sells properties in the local area. For every property on their books they record the following information:

- Property address - the house/flat name or number and the street

- The area of Greenoak in which the property is situated - this can either be Farley, Lumley or Old Town - properties in the centre of town do not have an area

- The town - which in most cases is Greenoak

- The type of property - the type is categorised as:
  T - terraced
  C - cottage
  S - semi-detached
  D - detached
  F - flat

- The age of the property - the age is categorised as:
  O - Old (pre Victorian)
  V - Victorian
  E - Edwardian
  PR - Pre-war
  PO - Post-war
  M - Modern (1960 - 1985)
  N - New (1986 onwards)

- Number of bedrooms

- Number of reception rooms

- Garden - this is recorded as yes or no depending on whether the property has gardens

- Garage - again, recorded as yes or no

- Freehold - recorded as yes if the property is freehold, no if leasehold

- The asking price of the property

- The date taken onto the estate agent's books

- The name of the owner of the property

- The telephone number of the owner

- The agent dealing with the property - the agents are referenced as A1, A2 etc

- The commission rate charged for selling the property

- Amount owing for advertisements placed in the local paper

- The date that the property is sold

- Any other comments

In addition to keeping records on the properties for sale, they also keep records on customers looking to purchase properties. They record the following information:

- The full name of the customer including their title, Mr, Mrs, Miss, Ms and their first name and surname

- The customer's full address including post code

- Contact telephone number

- The date the customer enrolled with the agency

- The type of property they are looking for using the same abbreviations used when recording properties e.g C for cottage, S for semi - a customer looking for a semi or detached house would be entered as S D - customers with no preference are entered as ANY

- The maximum price they are willing to pay

- The minimum number of bedrooms required

- The preferred area, e.g. Lumley, Farley etc - entered as ALL for no preference

- Applicant type - recorded as follows
  HOT - customer who does not have a property to sell
  WARM - customer who has sold their property subject to contract
  COLD - customer who has a property to sell

- Agent - recorded as A1, A2 etc

- General comments

The objective of Part 1 is to take the estate agent example and create a computerised system that will enable any of the agents working for the estate agents to:

- Add a new property or customer

- Make changes to property or customer details

- Delete information on properties or customers that are no longer registered

- Produce lists and reports in alphabetical or numeric order

- Quickly match properties to customers

This can be achieved by using dBASE IV working within the Control Centre.

2   Database concepts

As with all computer applications, a wealth of jargon has developed to describe the storage and manipulation of data, the term *database* being the most commonly used. Prior to computers, manual databases were in use. It was accepted office practice to file away documents rather than pile them up on a desk or stack them in the corner of the office. By storing these documents in categories a database system has been created.

On a day-to-day basis we all use databases; the telephone directory, an address book, consumer catalogues, any list of related information can be termed a database.

This chapter will look at a number of terms used to describe data stored on a computer, giving parallel examples from manual information storage systems.

2.1   Database

A database, or *database file* as it is often called, is a collection of information stored in the same place. Examples include a telephone directory or address book; another analogy is the card box. In any office, next to the telephone you may find a box containing cards; each card holding information on an individual customer. This is a manual database. A similar system could be set up on the computer with the customer information being stored in a database file.

2.2   Field

A *field* can be described as one item of information within the database. So, by definition, a database is made up of a number of fields. In general terms, each database is broken down into categories of information. With a card box the data may be categorised as name, address, telephone number etc. Each category of information is a field.

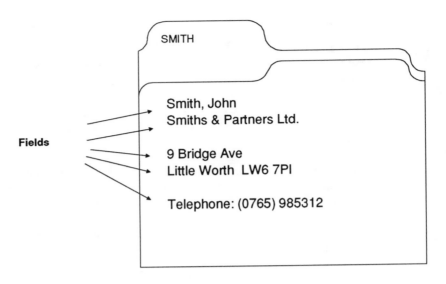

Fields

SMITH

Smith, John
Smiths & Partners Ltd.

9 Bridge Ave
Little Worth LW6 7Pl

Telephone: (0765) 985312

2.3 Record

Record is the term used to describe a group of fields relating to the same subject. Each card in the card box would be a record. So, taking our analogy a stage further, the card box is the database, each card in the box a record and the information detailed on the cards, fields.

2.4 Database system

A business would also hold information on the products they sell and the orders taken for those products. This information may be stored in a filing cabinet; one drawer for customer information, one for products and one for orders. Such a collection of information, uniformly stored, is a type of *database system*.

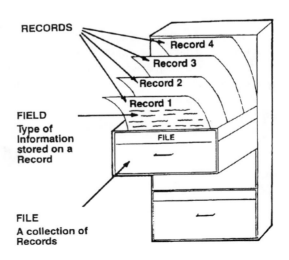

RECORDS

Record 4
Record 3
Record 2
Record 1

FIELD
Type of
Information
stored on a
Record

FILE

FILE
A collection of
Records

2.5   Relational Database System

If the database files can be linked together on common information, the database system is referred to as a *relational database system* i.e. there is a relationship between the information in the database files. With the example of the customer, product and order files, the information could be related in the following way:

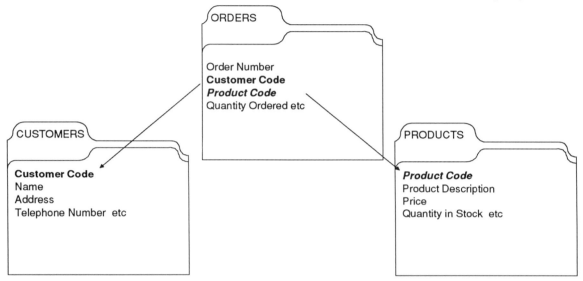

Every time an order is placed a new card is added. The code for the customer placing the order is included on the card as well as the code for the product ordered. If, at a later stage, further information is required on the customer or product the appropriate card can be found in the customer or product card box. To make this task easier, the cards in the customer card box are ordered by customer number and the cards in the product card box by product number. It is then fairly easy to flick through the cards and locate the required information. This is exactly the same principal used by a computerised relational database system, the only difference being that the related information is searched for by the computer and found very quickly!

2.6   Database Management System (DBMS)

A *database management system* is just as it says, a system to manage data. Some products can only manipulate data within a single database file whereas more sophisticated products can manipulate data from within several related databases. These products are referred to as *relational database management systems*.

2.7   dBASE IV defined

dBASE IV is a relational database management tool incorporating a storage facility, report generator, text editor and programming facility. dBASE is designed to enable the user to create, store, maintain and report on information.

Manual databases are part of every-day life, the telephone directory being one database probably used by everyone. dBASE, as with all computerised databases allows the user more flexibility for manipulating the data. With manual databases the view of the data is static; with a computerised database the information can be sorted or searched in as many ways as required. Computerised databases are useful in today's working environment because of their versatility and speed.

dBASE is one of the most popular packages available. In the initial stages it is easy to use and as your needs grow so do the capabilities of dBASE IV. Common routines can be developed into *programs* to be used over and over again and for the more technically inclined there is a sophisticated programming language allowing users to develop their own applications.

Typical dBASE IV systems:

- Telephone and Address Directory system

- Financial Ledger system

- Stock Control system

- Customer Information system

- Equipment Maintenance Record system

- Loan and Hire Tracking system

3   Getting started with dBASE IV

3.1   Powering up the computer

The start-up procedure for the IBM XT/AT personal computers or the PS/2 range (and compatible machines) is as follows:

- check there is no floppy disk in the disk drive

- switch on your screen if it has a separate power source

- switch on your system unit

The fan and hard disk drives will start to hum and the computer will go through a self-checking routine. You will either end up at the C: (DOS prompt) or some form of front end menu. Most computers have their own built-in clocks so it should not be necessary to key in the date and time. If you are prompted, simply type the date and time in the format indicated.

3.2   Starting the program

When a program is started or accessed, the software is loaded into the computer's memory.

1   Make sure you have completed the Setting-up a data directory instructions on page viii.

2   If you have just completed the Setting-up a data directory instructions you will already be accessing the DBASE\DATA sub-directory and can miss out this step. If you are not accessing the directory, type:

C:
CD \DBASE\DATA

Press Enter to complete each command. You have now changed to the directory where the data is to be stored.

3   To load the dBASE program, type the following remembering to press the Enter key to complete the command.

DBASE

If you receive the error message *Bad command or filename* it is because dBASE is not included in the *DOS path* (dBASE is usually added to the path during the installation procedure). To change the path on a permanent basis you will need to refer to your DOS manual. To change the path for this session only, type **PATH C:\;C:\DBASE** and press the | **Enter** | key. If you now type **DBASE** and press the | **Enter** | key you should successfully access the package.

The copyright message appears. Either press | **Enter** | or wait a few seconds and the dBASE IV Control Centre is displayed. If your screen is blank apart from the word "Command" at the bottom, your system has been set up to by-pass the Control Centre. To access the Control Centre type **ASSIST** and press the | **Enter** | key.

3.3   The Control Centre

The Control Centre allows the use of many of the features of dBASE IV without the need for detailed command entry in the *dot prompt* environment. The following operations can be performed using the Control Centre:

- Creating database files

- Displaying and changing data

- Designing data entry forms

- Creating reports and labels

- Designing and running applications

- Managing files and catalogs

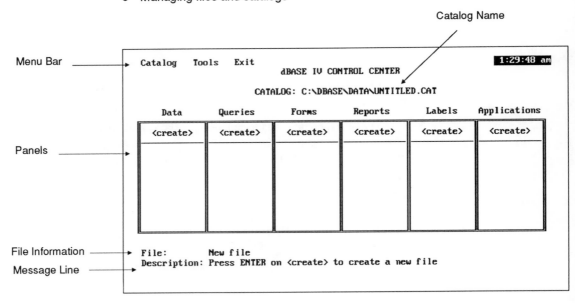

The Control Centre is divided into six basic areas:

The **menu bar** displays three menu options, **Catalog**, **Tools** and **Exit**. A selection of commands to manipulate the data can be accessed from these menu options.

The **catalog name** indicates the catalog or group of files currently selected. Catalogs are looked at in detail in Chapter 4.

The **control panel** is made up of six panels each used to create, select or modify files of a particular type. The six file types are data, queries, forms, reports, labels & applications.

The **file information lines** are directly under the panels - they show the name and description of the selected file.

The **message line** shows prompts or descriptions of menu items. This line will change as different options are chosen.

3.4   Using Control Centre menus

The menu bar can be accessed by the following methods:

| F10 | accesses the most recently used menu option.

| Alt + C | accesses the **Catalog** menu.

```
Use a different catalog
Modify catalog name
Edit description of catalog

Add file to catalog
Remove highlighted file from catalog
Change description of highlighted file
```

| Alt + T | accesses the **Tools** menu.

```
▶ Macros
▶ Import
▶ Export
  DOS utilities
  Protect data
  Settings
```

| Alt + E | accesses the **Exit** menu.

```
Save changes and exit
Abandon changes and exit
```

Once a menu has been selected other menus can be selected by using | → | and | ← |. Menu options can be selected by using the | ↑ | and | ↓ | keys to highlight the required option and pressing the | Enter | key.

| Esc | exits from the menu bar and returns to the Control Centre.

Help is available from almost anywhere within dBASE IV.

| F1 | accesses help.

| F4 | moves to the next help screen.

| F3 | moves to the previous help screen.

| Esc | leaves help.

The dBASE help facility is *context sensitive*. That is, help is given on the current task. In addition, the following options can be selected from the bottom of the screen:

- **Contents** accesses the help table of contents

- **Related topics** accesses a window of topics related to the current topic

- **Backup** retraces steps through the help system

- **Print** prints the current help page

1   Access the **Catalog** menu, highlight the **Use a different catalog** option and press | F1 | to call up help. Read the help screen and exit from help.

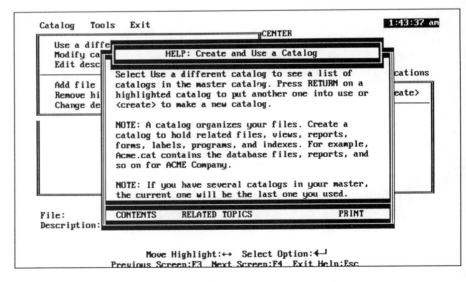

2   Experiment with accessing help on a selection of the options available from the menus.

3.6　　　Exiting from dBASE IV

Exit to dot prompt Quit to DOS

To leave dBASE and return to the operating system or front end menu, access the **Exit** menu. Select the **Quit to DOS** option.

If you accidentally choose the **Exit to dot prompt** option press $\boxed{\text{F2}}$ or type **ASSIST** to return to the Control Centre.

 Always leave dBASE by accessing the **Exit** menu. By doing this you can be sure that all files are closed. If you just turn off the computer data can be lost.

4 Creating a database system

Designing the database file structure(s) is the most important step when creating a database system. It is worth spending time talking with everyone who will be using the system to make sure that you have considered all the requirements. Take the time to jot down all the information that will be needed in your database. This is another way of saying decide what fields you need in the database.

Once you have determined your requirements, the next stage is to create your database files using dBASE IV.

4.1 Using catalogs

A *catalog* is used to group all the files relating to a database system. By forming a catalog, dBASE keeps track of which files on disk are part of the database system, which reports and data entry screens belong to which database file and so on. Catalogs make life easier!

You are going to create two separate database systems - one to contain the files relating to the business of the Estate Agency and another for storing personal information such as details on friends and family. Initially you will create the catalog for the agency files.

1　Press $\boxed{\text{Alt + C}}$ to select the **Catalog** menu. Select the first option, **Use a different catalog**.

```
 Catalog   Tools   Exit
┌───────────────────────────┐
│ Use a different catalog    │
│ Modify catalog name        │
│ Edit description of catalog│
├───────────────────────────┤
│ Add file to catalog        │
└───────────────────────────┘
```

A pop up menu appears containing the options to create a new catalog or select an existing catalog.

```
┌──────────────┐
│   CATALOG    │
├──────────────┤
│ <create>     │
│ UNTITLED.CAT │
└──────────────┘
```

2　You need to create a new catalog so highlight the **Create** option and press $\boxed{\text{Enter}}$.

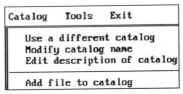
```
Enter name for new catalog:  ESTATE
```

3　Type **ESTATE** as the catalog name and press $\boxed{\text{Enter}}$. The file extension CAT will be added automatically by dBASE. A file extension is an optional three characters that can be added to the end of a filename. dBASE uses an assortment of file extensions to identify the different types of files created. The catalog name line will now read:

CATALOG: C:\DBASE\DATA\ESTATE.CAT

4.2   Structuring the database

Once you have determined the fields that will make up the database file the next stage is to decide on *field names*, *types* and *lengths* for all the fields in the database file.

Field name

Each field must be allocated a name. This name should be meaningful and can be up to 10 characters in length. The name must not include spaces or hyphens but the underscore character can be used for two part names eg EMP_NO for a field containing employee numbers.

Field type

Once you have decided on the fields that you need in the database, the next stage is to determine the type of data that is to be stored in the field. The following choices are available:

A field should be defined as **character** type if it is to hold information made up of a combination of letters, digits or other characters. You can not carry out any type of arithmetic operation on a character field. Examples of character fields are surname, address and telephone number.

Numeric fields utilise *binary coded decimal* numbers which, in simple terms means that decimal information is not subject to rounding errors. This field type should be used when accuracy to a fixed decimal place is essential. Examples of numeric fields are salary, rent, price, quantity in stock.

Floating fields are similar to numeric except *floating point arithmetic* is used - ideal for quick calculations but rounding errors can occur.

In general, you should always define a field that is going to contain date information as a **date** field. By doing this you will be able to search for records on or between specified dates. For example, if you had a database containing the names, addresses and birthdays of family and friends you would be able to list everyone who had a birthday in the current month.

A **logical** field can be used to hold true/false information. For example, with the Estate Agency database you may need to determine whether a property has a garden. This could be set as a logical field as the contents will be either yes or no.

A **memo** field should be used when storing character-type data that varies a great deal in length. For example, if you have a customer database you may need a comments field where you can enter information on contacts made with that customer. For a new customer you may only have to enter a few words. For an established customer you may want to include a couple of paragraphs of information. If a database contains a memo field, dBASE automatically creates a text file with the same name as the database file and an extension of .DBT. Each time a memo field is accessed you are given access to the part of the text file containing the information relevant to the current record. You can add or delete information using basic editing commands.

Field width

You must specify the field width for character and numeric fields. This is the maximum number of digits and characters you intend to enter in the field. Character fields can be up to 254 characters; numeric fields can have a maximum length of 20 digits, including the minus sign (for negative numbers) and the decimal point. Logical fields are automatically given a length of 1, for T or F and date fields a length of 8 eg 01/01/92. dBASE will automatically assign a width of 10 characters to a memo field to store pointer information to a dBASE text file (DBT file).

Index

Indexing will be looked at in detail in Chapter 10. Leave the default as No.

4.3   Creating a database

It is useful to spend time designing the structure of your databases before diving in!

The database system you will be using in this part of the text is designed for an estate agent. There will be three databases making up the system, two relating to the properties available for sale and another for the internal staff records.

The first database you are going to create will hold the details on the properties for sale. Remember the steps:

- decide which fields are needed - write a list

- give the fields suitable names

- decide on the field types

- decide on the field lengths

- make sure that the appropriate catalog is open

You are then ready to create the database structure. (You may find it useful at this stage to refer back to Chapter 1.1 to remind yourself of the fields needed to create this database.)

1 Highlight the **Create** option from the **Data** panel of the Control Centre and press Enter . The following screen will appear:

```
 Layout   Organize   Append   Go To   Exit                        2:00:37 am

┌─────┬────────────┬─────────────┬───────┬─────┬───────┐ Bytes remaining:   4000
│ Num │ Field Name │ Field Type  │ Width │ Dec │ Index │
├─────┼────────────┼─────────────┼───────┼─────┼───────┤
│  1  │    ▄▄▄▄     │  Character  │  ▄▄   │ ▄▄  │   N   │
│     │            │             │       │     │       │
│     │            │             │       │     │       │
│     │            │             │       │     │       │
│     │            │             │       │     │       │
│     │            │             │       │     │       │
│     │            │             │       │     │       │
│     │            │             │       │     │       │
│     │            │             │       │     │       │
│     │            │             │       │     │       │
├─────┴────────────┴─────────────┴───────┴─────┴───────┤
│Database  C:\dbase\data\<NEW>         Field 1/1                  Num
          Enter the field name. Insert/Delete field:Ctrl-N/Ctrl-U
```

2 Add the following field information using the Enter key to move to the next field and the Spacebar to toggle through the available field types. If in doubt, always refer to the help information displayed at the bottom of the screen.

Num	Field Name	Field Type	Width	Dec	Index
1	PROP_ADD	Character	25		N
2	AREA	Character	20		N
3	TOWN	Character	10		N
4	POSTCODE	Character	10		N
5	TYPE	Character	1		N
6	AGE	Character	2		N
7	NO_BEDS	Numeric	2	0	N
8	RECEPT	Numeric	2	0	N
9	GARDEN	Logical	1		N
10	GARAGE	Logical	1		N
11	FREEHOLD	Logical	1		N
12	PRICE	Numeric	10	2	N
13	DATE_TAKEN	Date	8		N
14	OWNER	Character	25		N
15	TELEPHONE	Character	12		N
16	AGENT	Character	4		N

Num	Field Name	Field Type	Width	Dec	Index
17	COMMISSION	Numeric	4	2	N
18	ADVERTS	Numeric	8	2	N
19	DATE_SOLD	Date	8		N
20	COMMENTS	Memo	10		N

4.4   Saving the structure

When the structure of the database has been entered it must be saved or cancelled. Press $\boxed{\textbf{Alt + E}}$ to access the **Exit** menu and select the option to save the changes made. The other option, abandon will do just that, you will loose any changes you have made to the structure.

If the structure is saved, you will be prompted to give the database a name. DOS restrictions apply; filenames must be 8 or less characters in length and must not contain a space or punctuation character.

⊃   Save the completed database structure with the name **PROPERTY**.

4.5   Adding records to a database

Once the structure of the database is saved, data can be added. In general, the steps to do this are as follows:

- highlight the name of the database in the **Data** panel by using $\boxed{\uparrow}$ and $\boxed{\downarrow}$ to move between the databases in the catalog;

- select the file by pressing the $\boxed{\textbf{Enter}}$ key;

- highlight and select the **Modify structure/order** option;

```
Use file    Modify structure/order    Display data

     Press ENTER to select or ESC to cancel
```

- use $\boxed{\rightarrow}$ to move across to the **Append** menu and select the **Enter records from keyboard** option;

```
  Enter records from keyboard
  Append records from dBASE file
▶ Copy records from non-dBASE file
```

- a blank *data entry template* will be displayed allowing you to enter the data for the next record in the database.

---

1 Select the **PROPERTY** database from the **Data** panel.

2 Select the **Modify structure/order** option.

3 Select the **Enter records from keyboard** option from the **Append** menu.

4 A blank template is displayed allowing you to enter the details for the first record. Enter the following data pressing the Enter key to move to the next field when necessary (if the field is full dBASE will automatically move to the next field, if not you need to manually move to the next field by pressing the Enter key. Be careful with the use of upper and lower case, the dBASE querying commands are *case sensitive*. To dBASE, Lumley is different to LUMLEY. Stop when you reach the memo field.

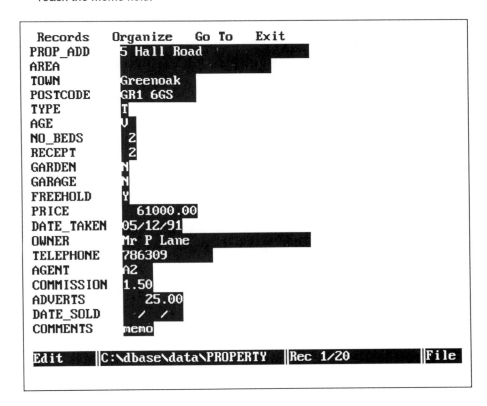

4.6 Accessing a memo field

To access the memo field:

* position the cursor on the memo field and press F9;

* an empty screen will appear. Type the memo text in the usual way, correcting any mistakes using the Delete or Backspace keys;

- to save the data press $\boxed{\textbf{Alt + E}}$ to access the **Exit** menu and select the **Save** option. You will be returned to the record template. The word *MEMO* will now be in upper case indicating that there is information stored in the memo field.

 1 Access the memo field for the first property and type the following:

Property in need of general modernisation but retaining many original features. Price reflects potential.

2 Save the memo text and return to the record template.

4.7 Adding further records

At this stage you can either add the remaining 19 records to the PROPERTY database, or, if you are working with the disks you can copy the completed version of the PROPERTY database at the beginning of the next chapter.

 If you have decided to copy the PROPERTY file from the disk, continue from 4.8 Exiting from append, page 26.

If you are not working from the disk, press the $\boxed{\textbf{Enter}}$ key to display a blank template for the second record. Add the records detailed on the following pages to the database being consistent with case.

FIELD NAME	RECORD 1	RECORD 2	RECORD 3	RECORD 4
PROP_ADD	5 Hall Road	89 Cliff Road	6 Brook Road	4 Hever Court
AREA		Lumley	Farley	Old Town
TOWN	Greenoak	Greenoak	Greenoak	Greenoak
POSTCODE	GR1 6GS	GR6 5TA	GR7 6EW	GR3 6SA
TYPE	T	F	T	D
AGE	V	N	V	M
NO_BEDS	2	2	4	4
RECEPT	2	1	2	3
GARDEN	F	F	F	T
GARAGE	F	F	F	T
FREEHOLD	T	F	T	T
PRICE	61000	51000	55000	150000
DATE_TAKEN	05/12/91	05/01/92	10/01/92	11/11/91
OWNER	Mr P Lane	Gerald Tims	Mr H Jones	Karen Bright
TELEPHONE	786309	654219	753216	456821
AGENT	A2	A2	A3	A1
COMMISSION	1.5	1.5	1.5	1.25
ADVERTS	25		50	75
DATE_SOLD				

COMMENTS	Property in need of general modernisation but retaining many original features. Price reflects potential.		A larger than average terrace house. Ideal as an investment property.	This property is 20 years old, situated at the end of a cul-de-sac. Set in large landscape gardens to 3 sides.

FIELD NAME	RECORD 5	RECORD 6	RECORD 7	RECORD 8
PROP_ADD	6 Elm Road	90 Primly Rise	43 Trewitt Ave	23 Yew Bank Drive
AREA	Lumley	Lumley	Farley	Lumley
TOWN	Greenoak	Greenoak	Greenoak	Greenoak
POSTCODE	GR6 6HS	GR4 3ER	GR9 6TY	GR5 4RW
TYPE	T	C	D	D
AGE	E	O	PR	PO
NO_BEDS	3	2	3	4
RECEPT	2	1	2	2
GARDEN	F	T	T	T
GARAGE	F	T	T	T
FREEHOLD	T	T	T	T
PRICE	89000	92000	125000	167000
DATE_TAKEN	15/02/92	12/01/92	21/10/91	01/03/92
OWNER	Fred Collins	Ms H Green	Graham Drew	Mr H Lewis
TELEPHONE	456298	324786	678543	834652
AGENT	A2	A3	A5	A3
COMMISSION	1.25	1.5	1.5	1.5
ADVERTS		25	75	
DATE_SOLD				

COMMENTS	A well maintained Edwardian terrace retaining many original features.	A pre-Victorian cottage in need of some modernisation - listed building in conservation area.	A classic detached property within easy access to junction 21 of the M1.	A substancial property. Price reflects need for general improvements both external and internal.

FIELD NAME	RECORD 9	RECORD 10	RECORD 11	RECORD 12
PROP_ADD	32 Leder Road	8 Oak Lane	76 Ruin Grove	9 Bookers Ave
AREA	Old Town	Farley	Old Town	Lumley
TOWN	Greenoak	Greenoak	Greenoak	Greenoak
POSTCODE	GR3 9YU	GR9 5TR	GR3 6YU	GR4 9IU
TYPE	C	S	T	S
AGE	V	PO	V	PR
NO_BEDS	2	3	5	3
RECEPT	1	2	2	2
GARDEN	T	T	F	T
GARAGE	F	T	F	F
FREEHOLD	T	T	T	T
PRICE	80000	99000	63000	65000
DATE_TAKEN	08/01/92	21/01/92	02/12/91	17/11/91
OWNER	Miss L Price	Mr T Hill	John Franks	Helen Smith
TELEPHONE	987321	768451	546987	453981
AGENT	A1	A3	A3	A3
COMMISSION	1.25	1.5	1.25	1.5
ADVERTS	25		50	50
DATE_SOLD				

COMMENTS	A delightful cottage situated back from the road in this much sought after area.	A traditional semi with large gardens to both front and rear.	This property is currently let as 4 self-contained flats realising in excess of £500 per month.	A larger than average semi with new conservatory built on the rear.

FIELD NAME	RECORD 13	RECORD 14	RECORD 15	RECORD 16
PROP_ADD	56 Rainforest Way	7 Kelly Park Drive	6 Kirk Way	90 Otway Road
AREA	Farley	Lumley		Farley
TOWN	Greenoak	Greenoak	Greenoak	Greenoak
POSTCODE	GR8 5RQ	GR7 5TB	GR1 8UX	GR7 4RT
TYPE	D	S	F	D
AGE	N	M	M	E
NO_BEDS	5	3	1	5
RECEPT	3	2	1	3
GARDEN	T	T	F	T
GARAGE	T	F	F	T
FREEHOLD	T	T	T	T
PRICE	340000	83000	48000	450000
DATE_TAKEN	19/03/91	05/10/91	13/01/92	21/03/92
OWNER	Mr D Swan	Mrs Franks	Mrs T Ring	Mr Young
TELEPHONE	651803	546843	987342	567349
AGENT	A1	A5	A6	A1
COMMISSION	1.5	1.5	1.5	1.5
ADVERTS		75	25	
DATE_SOLD				

COMMENTS	This property is 18 months old and is being sold fully equipped with carpets, curtains and a full range of kitchen appliances.	Situated in a quiet position overlooking farmland.		An imposing Edwardian property situated in 2 acres of land on the outskirts of Greenoak.

FIELD NAME	RECORD 17	RECORD 18	RECORD 19	RECORD 20
PROP_ADD	4 Garden Terrace	12 Lewis Mount	6 Taper Ave	13 May Lane
AREA	Old Town	Lumley	Old Town	Lumley
TOWN	Greenoak	Greenoak	Greenoak	Greenoak
POSTCODE	GR2 6TY	GR4 5RW	GR2 4TC	GR6 5TB
TYPE	T	S	F	C
AGE	V	M	V	O
NO_BEDS	2	3	1	3
RECEPT	2	2	1	2
GARDEN	T	T	T	T
GARAGE	F	T	T	T
FREEHOLD	T	T	F	T
PRICE	67000	81000	67000	105000
DATE_TAKEN	19/02/92	12/12/91	02/03/92	24/03/92
OWNER	Keith Perry	Miss Davis	Miss J Tailor	Mr Martin
TELEPHONE	(072) 459231	762543	(081) 876402	345876
AGENT	A2	A3	A4	A5
COMMISSION	1.25	1.25	1.5	1.5
ADVERTS	50	25	25	
DATE_SOLD				

COMMENTS	Although this property requires a degree of modernisation it is in the unusual position of being set in large gardens to both the front and rear.	This property has planning permission for an extension to the rear.	As part of an imposing Victorian residence, this executive flat has access to the grounds surrounding the house.	A larger than average cottage property situated close to all amenities.

4.8　Exiting from append

To exit from the **Append** screen:

```
Exit
Transfer to Query Design
Return to Database Design
```

press [**Alt + E**] and select the **Exit** option from the menu;

```
Save changes and exit
Abandon changes and exit
```

press [**Alt + E**] again and select the **Save changes and exit** option from the menu.

⊃ Exit from **Append** saving your record(s).

4.9　Consolidation exercises

1 Write down the field name, type and width you would use to hold the following data (the agent number will be entered as A followed by up to three digits - at the moment you only employ six agents but you hope to expand!):

NAME	TYPE	WIDTH
Agent number		
Surname		
First name		
Title		
Street		
Area		
Town		
Postcode		
Date of birth		
Telephone number		
Base salary		
Commission		
Holiday entitlement		

2 Using this database structure designed in step 1 of the exercise, create a database called **STAFF**. Append the following records.

	RECORD 1	RECORD 2	RECORD 3
Agent number	A1	A2	A3
Surname	Smith	Jones	Brown
First name	David	Clare	Barry
Title	Mr	Mrs	Mr
Full address	10 Old Lane	23 The Drive	10 Southbank
	Lumley	Stoketon	
	Greenoak	Newford	Greenoak
	GR5 7YT	NE1 9IU	GR1 4ER
Date of birth	12/12/56	30/06/65	22/09/67
Telephone no	743421	986143	768543
Base salary	15000	12500	13750
Commission (%)	11	10	10
Holiday (days)	25	21	21

	RECORD 4	RECORD 5	RECORD 6
Agent number	A4	A5	A6
Surname	Chapman	Greeves	Levin
First name	Mary	Alex	Linda
Title	Mrs	Mr	Miss
Full address	45 Layburn Road	1A Central Ave	12 Aintree Walk
	Lumley	Farley	
	Greenoak	Greenoak	Greenoak
	GR5 5MT	GR3 8KP	GR1 9WR
Date of birth	09/10/52	22/05/60	18/12/63
Telephone no	769032	874109	896412
Base salary	15500	11500	12750
Commission (%)	11	10	10
Holiday (days)	25	21	21

This exercise is optional and is not crucial for future activities. However, it will serve to reinforce topics as we progress through this section.

1   Create a new catalog called **PERSONAL**. Create your own personal database to hold the names, addresses, telephone numbers, birthdays and any other relevant information for your friends and family.

2   Add at least 10 records. When you have finished entering the data change the active catalog back to **ESTATE**.

Use this space to design your database:

Personal Records:

Field Name	Field Type	Field Width

See Appendix 1, page 244 for solutions.

5   Viewing the database

Once the database structure has been created and the records added, you are
going to want to view the data. Taking the PROPERTY database, you will need to
look through the records to match prospective purchasers with suitable properties.
At the moment the database is very small and you will be able to just list the records
on the screen and scroll through them. As databases grow, this is not as
satisfactory. You will need to specify certain criteria so that only a subset of records
are displayed. For example, you may have a prospective buyer who wants a
two-bedroom flat in Lumley. By setting up these criteria you will be able to display
the appropriate records. This is termed *querying a database* and will be looked at in
Chapter 8. This chapter will concentrate on displaying all the records in a database
and the techniques available for moving around and searching for particular records.

5.1   Preparing for this chapter

In order to complete this chapter you need the following files:

File name	File type	Chapter
ESTATE	Catalog	4
PROPERTY	Database	4
STAFF	Database	4

 If you have not created these files in the previous chapters you will need to refer
back to the chapter number listed above and create the files.

 If you have purchased the disks that accompany this book you can copy the
necessary files from the appropriate floppy disk. To do this, complete the following
instructions:

1   Make sure you have created a sub-directory on the hard disk called
DBASE\DATA (*see* Setting-up a data directory, page viii).

2   Load dBASE (*see* 3.2 Starting the program, page 9).

3   Follow the instructions for Using the diskettes on page viii. The batch file is
called **C5**.

Opening a database

In order to display the records in a database it must firstly be opened for use. Before opening the database the appropriate catalog should be activated. By accessing the catalog the databases which make up the database system are displayed in the **Data** panel.

Once the catalog is open, you can move through the list of databases using $\boxed{\uparrow}$ and $\boxed{\downarrow}$. To use a database, highlight the database name, press $\boxed{\text{Enter}}$ and select the **Use file** option from the menu.

```
Use file    Modify structure/order    Display data

      Press ENTER to select or ESC to cancel
```

The selected database name will appear above the line in the **Data** panel, indicating that this database is in use.

1   Open the database called **PROPERTY** by highlighting the name in the **Data** panel, pressing the $\boxed{\text{Enter}}$ key and then selecting the **Use file** option. The database name should now appear above the line in the **Data** panel.

Only one database can be in use at any one time. As soon as you open another database the current database is closed.

2   Open the **STAFF** database. You should find that the STAFF database is displayed above the line and PROPERTY has returned to below the line. Open the **PROPERTY** database again.

Closing a database

To close the active database, highlight the database name (which will be above the line in the **Data** panel), press $\boxed{\text{Enter}}$ and select the **Close file** option from the menu.

```
Close file    Modify structure/order    Display data

      Press ENTER to select or ESC to cancel
```

It is advisable to close the active database before leaving your computer, even if only for a short period. If a database is active and the machine turned off, dBASE will mark the end of the file as the current record. So, if you have 100 records in your database and dBASE happens to be pointing to record number 25 when you turn off the machine, next time you use the database it will appear to only have 25 records! By closing the active database, the pointer is moved to the end of the file so, if your machine is switched off, no harm will be done.

5.4   Working with the database

Once a database is in use there are two options available, **Modify structure/order** and **Display data**. These options are referred to as *design* and *data*. The options can be selected from a menu by highlighting the database name in the **Data** panel and pressing the Enter key.

Both options can also be selected by keyboard shortcuts as indicated at the bottom of the screen.

```
Help:F1  Use:◄┘  Data:F2  Design:Shift-F2  Quick Report:Shift-F9  Menus:F10
```

By pressing F2 you will be able to display and change the information stored in the active database.

By pressing SHIFT + F2 you can change the structure of the active database; add, delete or change field specifications.

Both options allow you to add records to the database (you used the **Modify structure/order** option in the last chapter to add records to the PROPERTY database) and also change the order of the records by grouping them in alphabetical, numerical or date order.

5.5   Viewing records

By pressing F2 you can display the records in the current database in what is termed, *browse* mode. You can also zoom in on a particular record by switching to *edit* mode. You do this by pressing F2 a second time. In fact F2 acts as a *toggle* key. When pressed from the Control Centre you access either browse or edit mode, depending on which mode was last accessed. When pressed from browse mode F2 accesses edit mode. When pressed from edit mode F2 accesses browse mode again. This *zooming* feature is very handy when you have located the record you want. You can then *zoom* in on the record so that you can see all the fields at a glance.

Browse mode

The following keys can be used to move through the data in browse mode.

| `F4` | moves to the next field (the `TAB` key can also be used). |
| `F3` | moves to the previous field (`SHIFT + TAB` can also be used). |

If `F3` or `F4` are used to move to a memo field the field will automatically be opened.

`←`	moves left a character.
`→`	moves right a character.
`↑`	moves up a record.
`↓`	moves down a record.
`End`	moves to the last field in the current record.
`Home`	moves to the first field in the current record.
`Page Up`	moves up 17 records, or to the top of the database.
`Page Dn`	moves down 17 records, or to the bottom of the database.
`Ctrl+PgUp`	moves to the first record in the database.
`Ctrl+PgDn`	moves to the last record in the database.
`F9`	displays information in a memo field. If pressed from within the memo screen, returns to browse mode.

1 With **PROPERTY** as the active database press `F2` to view the data.

PROP_ADD	AREA	TOWN	POSTCODE	TYPE
5 Hall Road		Greenoak	GR1 6GS	T
89 Cliff Road	Lumley	Greenoak	GR6 5TA	F
6 Brook Road	Farley	Greenoak	GR7 6EW	T
4 Hever Court	Old Town	Greenoak	GR3 6SA	D
6 Elm Road	Lumley	Greenoak	GR6 6HS	T
90 Pinly Rise	Lumley	Greenoak	GR4 3ER	C
43 Trewitt Ave	Farley	Greenoak	GR9 56Y	D
23 Yew Bank Drive	Lumley	Greenoak	GR5 4RW	D
32 Leder Road	Old Town	Greenoak	GR3 9YU	C
8 Oak Lane	Farley	Greenoak	GR9 5TR	S
76 Ruin Grove	Old Town	Greenoak	GR3 6YU	T
9 Bookers Avenue	Lumley	Greenoak	GR4 9IU	S
56 Rainforest Way	Farley	Greenoak	GR8 5RQ	D
7 Kelly Park Drive	Lumley	Greenoak	GR7 5TB	S
6 Kirk Way		Greenoak	GR1 8UX	F

If the screen does not resemble the previous illustration press F2 again. F2 will either access *browse* mode or *edit* mode, depending on which was accessed last. By pressing F2 a second time you will access browse mode if in edit mode and vice versa.

2   Experiment with these keyboard shortcuts by moving around the **PROPERTY** database. Open the **STAFF** database and *browse* the data. Open the **PROPERTY** database again.

Editing mode

The majority of the keys used to move around the database in browse mode are the same in edit mode. There are a few differences though and these are listed below:

↑   moves up a field.

↓   moves up or down a field.

Page Up   moves up a record.

Page Dn   moves down a record.

End   moves to the end of the field.

Home   moves to the beginning of the field.

 1   Open the **PROPERTY** database and press F2 (once or twice) to take you into edit mode. Practice moving around the database and toggling from edit to browse and back to edit.

| 5.6 | **Searching for a specific record** |

```
Top record
Last record
Record number        {1}
Skip                 {10}

Index key search
Forward search        {}
Backward search       {}
Match capitalization  YES
```

Although the majority of the options covered in the next sections can be accessed from both browse and edit modes, examples given will be from within browse mode.

In addition to the *quick keys* shown for the edit and browse modes, you can also move around the database by selecting options from the **Goto** menu. This is accessed by pressing **Alt + G**.

Top record moves the cursor to the first record in the database (same as **Ctrl +Pg Up**).

Last record moves to the last record in the database (same as **Ctrl +Pg Dn**).

Record number allows you to type the number of the record you want to go to. You may need to use the **BACKSPACE** key to delete the current number before typing the new number.

Skip allows you to specify the number of records you want to skip. If you are pointing to record 5 and you specify 10 as the skip number you will be pointing to record 15.

The **Index key search** option is not available at the moment as you have not yet indexed the database.

Forward search allows you to search forward through the current column (field) of the database for a given value.

Backward search searches backwards for a given value.

Match capitalization is used when searching. The default is set to **Yes** but it can be changed to **No**, eg if searching for Green as a surname dBASE would find GREEN, Green or green if capitalization is set to **No**, but would only find Green if set to **Yes**.

Sometimes there may be more than one record in your database with the same field value. For example, there could well be more than one Smith in a customer database. There are two keyboard shortcuts available to continue a search to the next or previous occurrence of a value.

| Shift + F4 | finds the next occurrence of the value.

| Shift + F3 | finds the previous occurrence of the value.

1 Using the **PROPERTY** database, make sure that you are in browse mode. Use the **Goto** menu to move directly to record 5. Use the **Skip** option to skip 6 records.

2 Move to the first field of the first record of the database. You need to find details on the property at *6 Taper Ave*. Access the **Goto** menu and select the **Forward search** option (remember to press | Enter | to select the menu option). Type **6 Taper Ave** and press| Enter | again to confirm. The cursor should move directly to the selected record.

3 Move the cursor to the **AREA** field in the first record. Select the **Forward search** option from the **Goto** menu. Backspace out the current search value and type **Old Town**. Once you press the | Enter |key the cursor will point to the first property in Old Town. To continue searching through the database press| Shift + F4 |. To search backwards press| Shift + F3 |.

5.7   Using wildcards when searching

Wildcards come in very handy when you are not quite sure what you are searching for. For example, you may want to find the record for the property owned by Mr. Downs or maybe it is Downes or even Downing? By using the| * | wildcard dBASE will find all three, you simply need to type **Down*** as your search value. The | * | represents any characters. The other wildcard that can be used is the | ? |.

The ? represents any one character. So, for example if you were not sure whether a customer spelt their name Smith or Smyth you could enter the search value as **Sm?th**.

You have a property on your books owned by a client with the surname of Davis. You are not sure whether it is a Mr, Miss or Mrs Davis. By using a wildcard you can search for all occurrences.

1 Move the cursor to the **OWNER** field of the first record. Access the **Goto** menu and select the **Forwards search** option. Backspace out the previous entry and type *Davis as the search value.

5.8 Locking fields

```
Lock fields on left  {1}
Blank field
Freeze field         {}
Size field
```

If using a database with more than a few fields it becomes quite frustrating when comparing fields that cannot be displayed on the screen at the same time. To solve this problem, you can *lock* the fields at the left of the database so they remain on the screen as the remaining fields scroll to the right.

To lock fields, select the **Fields** menu by pressing **Alt + F**. Select the **Lock fields on left** option. Type a number corresponding to the number of fields (columns) you want to lock.

You want to display the address of the property along with the name and telephone number of the owner. You need to lock the first field in the database (PROP_ADD) so that when you scroll across the fields the address is still displayed.

1 Make sure that the **PROP_ADD** field is displayed at the left of the screen. Select the **Fields** menu and set the **Lock fields on left** option to **1**. Scroll across the database to display the three required fields.

PROP_ADD	OWNER	TELEPHONE	AGENT	COMMISS
5 Hall Road	Mr P Lane	786309	A2	1.50
89 Cliff Road	Gerald Tims	654219	A2	1.50
6 Brook Road	Mr H Jones	753216	A3	1.50
4 Hever Court	Karen Bright	456821	A1	1.25
6 Elm Road	Fred Collins	456298	A2	1.25
90 Pimly Rise	Ms H Green	324786	A3	1.50
43 Trewitt Ave	Graham Drew	678543	A5	1.50
23 Yew Bank Drive	Mr H Lewis	834652	A3	1.50
32 Leder Road	Miss L Price	987321	A1	1.25
8 Oak Lane	Mr T Hill	768451	A3	1.50
76 Ruin Grove	John Franks	546987	A3	1.25
9 Bookers Avenue	Helen Smith	453981	A3	1.50

2 To unlock the fields, access the **Fields** menu, select the **Lock fields on left** option and change the value to **0**.

5.9   Resizing the display width of a field

When in browse mode it is possible to change the display width of one or more fields. This can be handy when you need to see more fields on the screen at the one time. You could solve this problem by switching to edit mode if you are only interested in the one record. If interested in a number of records, change the display width of the fields by moving the cursor to each field in turn and selecting the **Size field** option from the **Fields** menu. Use the ⟶ and ⟵ keys to resize the field, pressing **Enter** to confirm.

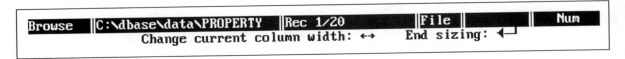

```
Browse    C:\dbase\data\PROPERTY   Rec 1/20              File              Num
          Change current column width: ↔      End sizing: ↵
```

1   You need to display the address of the property, the owner's name and telephone number and the amount they have spent on advertising. Lock the **PROP_ADD** column at the left of the screen (*see* 5.8 Locking fields). Scroll across so that the owner's name and telephone number is displayed.

2   In order to display the advert column as well, you need to resize one or more columns. Move to the **OWNER** field, access the **Fields** menu and select the **Size field** option. Use the ⟵ to decrease the display width of this field so that you can also see the **ADVERT** field. Press **Enter** to confirm.

PROP_ADD	OWNER	TELEPHONE	AGENT	COMMISSION	ADVERT
5 Hall Road	Mr P Lane	786309	A2	1.50	25.
89 Cliff Road	Gerald Tims	654219	A2	1.50	0.
6 Brook Road	Mr H Jones	753216	A3	1.50	50.
4 Hever Court	Karen Bright	456821	A1	1.25	75.
6 Elm Road	Fred Collins	456298	A2	1.25	0.
90 Pimly Rise	Ms H Green	324786	A3	1.50	25.
43 Trewitt Ave	Graham Drew	678543	A5	1.50	75.
23 Yew Bank Drive	Mr H Lewis	834652	A3	1.50	0.

5.10   Exiting from browse or edit

To exit from browse or edit mode access the **Exit** menu by pressing **Alt + E**. There are only two options available, **Exit** and **Transfer to Query Design**. Select the **Exit** option. You will return to the Control Centre.

Exit to the Control Centre.

Consolidation exercise

1 Create a database called **CUSTOMER** with the following structure:

Num	Field Name	Field Type	Width	Dec	Index
1	SURNAME	Character	20		N
2	FIRSTNAME	Character	15		N
3	TITLE	Character	4		N
4	STREET	Character	20		N
5	AREA	Character	20		N
6	TOWN	Character	10		N
7	POSTCODE	Character	8		N
8	TELEPHONE	Character	12		N
9	ENROLED	Date	8		N
10	TYPE	Character	10		N
11	MAX_PRICE	Numeric	10	2	N
12	MIN_BEDS	Numeric	2	0	N
13	REQ_AREA	Character	18		N
14	APP_TYPE	Character	4		N
15	AGENT	Character	4		N
16	COMMENTS	Memo	10		N

2 The **CUSTOMER** database will be referred to throughout Parts 1 and 2 of this book. If working without the disk, it is recommended that you append the following records at this stage (*see* next page).

FIELD NAME	RECORD 1	RECORD 2	RECORD 3	RECORD 4
SURNAME	Jones	Kemp	Jones	Samuels
FIRSTNAME	Peter	Mary	Fred	Diane
TITLE	Mr	Miss	Mr	Ms
STREET	22 Layburn Street	38 Fairfield Lane	12 Portland Road	32 Lemming Lane
AREA	Old Bridge	Lumley	Chapelford	Lumley
TOWN	London	Greenoak	Leeds	Greenoak
POSTCODE	EC2 5TY	GR5 6RW	LS4 5TO	GR4 6TD
TELEPHONE	(081) 345621	982176	(0532) 33921	567432
ENROLED	01/02/92	01/01/92	12/09/91	01/01/92
TYPE	C D S	F	T S C	D S
MAX_PRICE	150000	45000	68000	100000
MIN_BEDS	2	1	2	3
REQ_AREA	ALL	4 5 6	1 2 3	4 5 6
APP_TYPE	HOT	HOT	WARM	COLD
AGENT	A5	A6	A1	A4

COMMENTS	Mr Jones is relocating from London in March - only able to view properties at weekends.		Mr Jones is relocating from Leeds. He has a property to sell in Leeds which is currently under offer.	Diane Samuels is interested in receiving information on available properties but has not yet put her house on the market.

FIELD NAME	RECORD 5	RECORD 6	RECORD 7	RECORD 8
SURNAME	Hughes	Smith	Price	Kelly
FIRSTNAME	Linda	John	Jill	P
TITLE	Miss	Mr	Mrs	Mr
STREET	12 The Avenue	45 Hargarth Road	32 Wayside Ave	6 Levin Way
AREA	Farley		Old Town	Lumley
TOWN	Greenoak	Bradford	Greenoak	Greenoak
POSTCODE	GR8 5RT	BD4 5TB	GR3 6UP	GR5 6TY
TELEPHONE	654921	(0274) 976491	456365	987341
ENROLED	03/12/91	05/01/92	15/12/91	17/11/91
TYPE	F	C D	F T S	D
MAX_PRICE	50000	190000	60000	300000
MIN_BEDS	1	3	2	4
REQ_AREA	ALL	ALL	7 8 9	4 5 6 7 8 9
APP_TYPE	HOT	WARM	COLD	WARM
AGENT	A3	A2	A3	A1

COMMENTS	Linda Hughes is a first time buyer looking at properties in Greenoak, Carvley and Little Howden.	Mr Smith is retiring to the area. Although he has accepted an offer on his property he is in a chain situation.	Mrs Price has put her house on the market but has not received any offers to date.	Although involved in a chain, Mr Kelly has discussed taking a bridging loan if a suitable property becomes available.

3   Add at least another four records using appropriate data. These 12 records will give you enough data to use in examples. If however, you have the time, you may want to add several more records at this stage.

4   Access browse mode and search for a customer with the surname **Smith**. Toggle to edit mode to view the customer details. Return to browse mode.

5   Move to the top of the database. Find the first customer who is assigned to **Agent 1**. Are there any other customers assigned to this agent?

6   In browse mode, display the full name of the customer, their telephone number and the date they enrolled.

7   Unlock any locked fields and close the database.

See Appendix 1, page 245 for solutions.

Changing, adding & deleting data

You have already seen that the browse and edit modes can be used to display the records in a database. These modes can also be used to change (edit) information, delete records and add records.

6.1 Preparing for this chapter

In order to complete this chapter you need the following files:

Filename	File Type	Chapter
ESTATE	Catalog	4
PROPERTY	Database	4
CUSTOMER	Database	5

If you have not created these files in the previous chapters you will need to refer back to the chapter number listed above and create the files.

If you have purchased the disks that accompany this book you can copy the necessary files from the appropriate floppy disk. To do this, complete the following instructions:

1   Make sure you have created a sub-directory on the hard disk called DBASE\DATA (*see* Setting-up a data directory, page viii).

2   Load dBASE (*see* 3.2 Starting the program, page 9).

3   Follow the instructions for Using the diskettes on page viii. The batch file is called **C6**.

6.2 Changing text

The next exercise requires you to open the CUSTOMER database and display records. In Chapter 5, you did this by selecting from the appropriate menus. In this chapter you will use a shortcut to open and display a database in one step. To do this, simply highlight the database name in the **Data** panel (it doesn't matter whether it is above or below the line) and press F2 . The database is opened and the records displayed in either browse or edit mode. Remember, F2 will toggle between the two modes.

⮑ Highlight the **CUSTOMER** database name in the **Data** panel and press `F2`.

You can edit data in both browse and edit modes. Move to the required field and use the following editing keys:

`Backsp`   deletes the character to the left of the cursor.

`Delete`   deletes the character at the cursor position.

`Ctrl + T`   deletes from the cursor to the beginning of the next word.

`Ctrl + Y`   deletes from the cursor position to the end of the current field.

`Insert`   acts as a toggle. If **Insert** is **On**, the **Ins** indicator will be displayed at the bottom of the screen and, as you type, characters will be inserted at the cursor position. If **Insert** is **Off** you will type over existing characters.

⮑ 1 Linda Hughes has changed her phone number. Move to the **TELEPHONE** field in record 5. Make sure that **Insert** is **Off** and type the new phone number, **875643**.

2 Move to the **AREA** field in record 3 and change the area from Chapelford to **Chapelforth**.

3 You have discovered Ms Samuel's first name to be **Deborah**. Amend this information in the **FIRSTNAME** field.

4 You have misspelt the street name in the record for Mr Jones (record 1). It should read **Layeburn** instead of Layburn. Move the cursor to the *b* in Layburn. Make sure **Insert** is **On** and type **e**.

5 The address for John Smith (record 6) should read **45 Hargarth Street**, not Hargarth Road. Move the cursor to the beginning of the word *Road* and press `Ctrl + Y` to delete to the end of the field and type **Street**.

6.3   Deleting records

```
Undo change to record

Add new records
Mark record for deletion
Blank record
Record lock
Follow record to new posit
```

With dBASE, the deleting of records is a two stage process. In the first instance you *mark a record for deletion*. At this stage, if you change your mind, you can recall the record; in other words, unmark it. The second stage is called *packing*. When you pack the database the records that are currently marked for deletion are permanently removed from the database.

Records can be marked for deletion by positioning the cursor on the record, in either edit or browse modes, accessing the **Records** menu with `Alt + R` and selecting the **Mark for deletion** option.

```
Undo change to record

Add new records
Clear deletion mark  ◄───
Blank record
Record lock
Follow record to new posit
```

Once a record is marked for deletion it can be unmarked by following the same procedure. Press ⎡Alt + R⎤ and select the option that will now read, **Clear deletion mark**.

You can tell at a glance whether or not a record is marked for deletion by looking at the status bar at the bottom of the screen. The **Del** indicator will be displayed if the record is marked.

```
Browse   ‖C:\dbase\data\CUSTOMER‖Rec 3/10        ‖File‖        ‖DelNum      Ins
         Position selection bar: ↑↓    Select: ◄┘   Leave menu: Esc
                   Mark/unmark this record for deletion
```

```
Create new index
Modify existing index
Order records by index
Activate .MDX index file
Include .MDX index file
Remove unwanted index tag

Sort database on field list
Unmark all records     ◄───
Erase marked records   ◄───
```

The keyboard shortcut for marking or unmarking a record for deletion is ⎡Ctrl + U⎤. Press this combination once to delete the current record and press it again to unmark the record.

If you want to unmark all the records in the current database you can do this by selecting the **Unmark all records** option from the **Organise** menu.

The records marked for deletion can be permanently removed by selecting the **Erase marked records** option from the **Organise** menu. This is known as *packing* the database.

The **Organise** menu is not available from within the browse and edit modes with earlier versions of dBASE IV. To unmark all deleted records or pack the database, exit from the current mode by accessing the **Exit** menu, highlight the database name in the **Data** panel and press ⎡Shift + F2⎤. This will take you directly to the **Modify structure/order** screen. The **Organise** menu will be displayed and you will see the required options.

Mark a couple of records in the **CUSTOMER** database for deletion using both the menu and keyboard shortcut outlined above. Unmark the records.

6.4   Undoing a change

```
Undo change to record  ◄───

Add new records
Clear deletion mark
Blank record
Record lock
Follow record to new posit
```

You can undo any changes you make to a record as long as you have not moved your cursor off of the record. As soon as you move your cursor to another record the changes are saved and cannot be automatically undone.

To undo changes to a record access the **Records** menu and select the **Undo change to record** option.

1   Position the cursor on the record for **Fred Jones** and press ⎡F2⎤ to take you into edit mode. Change some of the data in the record but do not page up or down. If you do, you will save the changes.

2   Press ⎡Alt + R⎤ to access the **Records** menu and select the **Undo Changes to record** option. The data should be returned to how it was before you made the changes.

6.5 Blanking a record

```
Undo change to record
Add new records
Clear deletion mark
Blank record       ◄────────
Record lock
Follow record to new posit
```

The entire contents of a record can be deleted if you need to replace all the details. It is not a good idea to use this method simply to delete a record as you will end up with blank records in your database. To delete the record you must mark the record for deletion and then pack the database as seen in an earlier section. To blank a record place the cursor on the record to be blanked, access the **Record** menu and select the **Blank record** option.

1 Move the cursor to the first record in the database (in either browse or edit mode) and select the **Blank record** option from the **Records** menu. The data should disappear leaving a blank record.

2 In a real situation you could type your new data at this stage. But, as you do not want to lose the data for Mr Jones, access the **Records** menu again and select the **Undo change to record** option to replace the data.

6.6 Adding records

When in browse or edit modes there are two methods of adding new records to the database. The first method is to move to the bottom of the database by pressing **Ctrl + Pg Dn**. If you then press **Page Dn** (if in edit mode) or **↓** (if in browse mode) you will see the following prompt at the bottom of the screen:

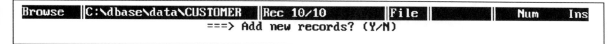

```
Browse     C:\dbase\data\CUSTOMER   Rec 10/10        File                 Num     Ins
                  ===> Add new records? (Y/N)
```

By typing **Y**, for yes, you will be able to add records to the database.

The other method, is to select the **Add new records** option from the **Records** menu.

When entering a number of records, you may well find that the data in a particular field is the same as in the previously entered record. If this is the case the ditto key, **Shift + F8** can be used to repeat the information from the same field in the previous record.

1 Use one of the above methods to add two records to the **CUSTOMER** database (*see* next page). When you reach the **TOWN** field in the first record press **Shift + F8** to copy the town data from the previous record.

2 Use the ditto key to enter both the **TOWN** and **AREA** fields for the second record.

3 Access the **Exit** menu to save the new records and exit to the Control Centre.

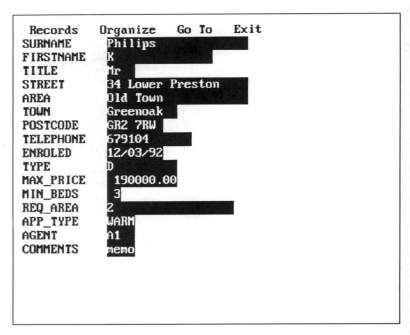

```
   Records    Organize    Go To    Exit
SURNAME        Morris
FIRSTNAME      Lesley
TITLE          Miss
STREET         19 Lands Lane
AREA           Old Town
TOWN           Greenoak
POSTCODE       GR2 8PL
TELEPHONE      219543
ENROLED        12/03/92
TYPE           F T
MAX_PRICE         40000.00
MIN_BEDS          2
REQ_AREA       ALL
APP_TYPE       HOT
AGENT          A3
COMMENTS       memo
```

Use the ditto key to copy the town data from the previous record.

```
   Records    Organize    Go To    Exit
SURNAME        Philips
FIRSTNAME      K
TITLE          Mr
STREET         34 Lower Preston
AREA           Old Town
TOWN           Greenoak
POSTCODE       GR2 7RW
TELEPHONE      679104
ENROLED        12/03/92
TYPE           D
MAX_PRICE        190000.00
MIN_BEDS          3
REQ_AREA       2
APP_TYPE       WARM
AGENT          A1
COMMENTS       memo
```

Use the ditto key to copy the town and area data from the previous record.

7 Modifying the database structure

You have now seen how you can change the contents of a database. In this chapter you will look at how you can change the structure of the database. You will consider the following:

- adding new fields

- deleting fields that are no longer required

- changing field names

- changing field types

- changing the field width

7.1 Preparing for this chapter

In order to complete this chapter you need the following files:

File name	File type	Chapter
ESTATE	Catalog	4
PROPERTY	Database	4
CUSTOMER	Database	5

 If you have not created these files in the previous chapters you will need to refer back to the chapter number listed above and create the files.

 If you have purchased the disks that accompany this book you can copy the necessary files from the appropriate floppy disk. To do this, complete the following instructions:

1 Make sure you have created a sub-directory on the hard disk called DBASE\DATA (*see* Setting-up a data directory, page viii)

2 Load dBASE (*see* 3.2 Starting the program, page 9).

3 Follow the instructions for Using the diskettes on page viii. The batch file is called **C7**.

1   When the **Modify structure** option is selected, dBASE makes a copy of the database file with the same name as the database but with the extension BAK. This is called a *backup* file. After the structure modifications are completed, dBASE appends the contents of the backup file to the modified database file. It is important to make sure that there is enough room on the disk for the two copies of the database - the backup version and the modified version. You must also be careful not to interrupt dBASE while it is appending the backup records as you may lose data.

2   You should not change the name of a field and the width or type at the same time. If you need to change the name and the width or type, change the name first and save the changes and then access the **Modify structure** option again and change the width or type.

3   You should not insert or delete fields and change field names at the same time. Again, do one change, save the structure and then access the **Modify structure** option a second time.

4   If you convert a field from numeric to character, dBASE will convert numeric characters to digits until it encounters a non-numeric character. If the first character is non-numeric the converted field will contain 0. For example, 123AB will convert to 123 whereas, AB123 will convert to 0.

5   Numeric fields will convert to character fields without any problems.

6   Logical fields can be converted to character fields and vice versa. Logical fields cannot be converted to numeric fields.

7   Date fields can be converted to character fields. Character fields that are correctly formatted (for example, dd/mm/yy) can also be converted to date fields.

 In a nut shell be very careful when modifying the structure of a database. If in any doubt, make a copy of the database before making any changes. You can then always use the copied version if things go wrong. To find out more about copying files refer to Chapter 21, File management.

7.3   Changing the structure of a database

To change the structure of a database, highlight the database name in the **Data** panel of the Control Centre and press $\boxed{\text{Shift + F2}}$.

Modify the structure of the **CUSTOMER** database. The **Organise** menu will automatically be displayed. Press $\boxed{\text{Esc}}$ to remove it from the display. The following screen will appear (*see* next page):

Layout	Organize	Append	Go To	Exit		

Num	Field Name	Field Type	Width	Dec	Index
1	SURNAME	Character	20		N
2	FIRSTNAME	Character	15		N
3	TITLE	Character	4		N
4	STREET	Character	20		N
5	AREA	Character	20		N
6	TOWN	Character	10		N
7	POSTCODE	Character	8		N
8	TELEPHONE	Character	12		N
9	ENROLED	Date	8		N
10	TYPE	Character	10		N
11	MAX_PRICE	Numeric	10	2	N
12	MIN_BEDS	Numeric	2	0	N
13	REQ_AREA	Character	18		N
14	APP_TYPE	Character	4		N
15	AGENT	Character	4		N
16	COMMENTS	Memo	10		N

7.4   Adding, deleting and changing fields

To insert a new field, position the cursor below where you want the field to go and press Ctrl + N . A blank line appears in the database structure. Enter the details for the new field in the usual way.

Field names can be deleted by placing the cursor on the field and pressing Ctrl + Y .

The entire field can be removed from the structure by pressing Ctrl + U . If you accidentally press Ctrl + U instead of Ctrl + N access the **Exit** menu and select the **Abandon** option. You can then start again.

The field type can be changed by placing the cursor on the field type and pressing the Spacebar until the required field type is displayed.

The field width can be changed by over-typing the current value.Changes can be saved or abandoned by accessing the **Exit** menu.

At the moment the **CUSTOMER** database does not have a field to record whether the customer has a preference regarding the age of the property. You can add a *character* type field into which you can add the codes O, V, E, PR, PO, M and N. You can also enter ANY for customers with no real preference. For example, a customer requiring a property built in Edwardian times or earlier would be entered as O V E.

1   Move the cursor to below the **TYPE** field and press Ctrl + N . Enter the following details (*see* next page):

Num	Field Name	Field Type	Width	Dec	Index
1	SURNAME	Character	20		N
2	FIRSTNAME	Character	15		N
3	TITLE	Character	4		N
4	STREET	Character	20		N
5	AREA	Character	20		N
6	TOWN	Character	10		N
7	POSTCODE	Character	8		N
8	TELEPHONE	Character	12		N
9	ENROLED	Date	8		N
10	TYPE	Character	10		N
11	AGE	Character	14		N
12	MAX_PRICE	Numeric	10	2	N
13	MIN_BEDS	Numeric	2	0	N
14	REQ_AREA	Character	18		N
15	APP_TYPE	Character	4		N
16	AGENT	Character	4		N

2   Access the **Exit** menu and select the **Save changes and exit** option. You will
    be asked to confirm this change. Select **Yes**.

3   Browse the data and add the following **AGE** field data (codes) for the customers
    on the books. Save the changes.

TYPE	AGE	MAX_PRICE
C D S	O V E	150000.00
F	M N	45000.00
T S C	ANY	68000.00
D S	PO M N	100000.00
F	M N	50000.00
C D	O V E	19000.00
F T S	ANY	60000.00
D	ANY	300000.00
S T	ANY	80000.00
T	O V E PR	35000.00
S T	PR PO	70000.00
S D	ANY	120000.00
F T	ANY	40000.00
D	N	190000.00

8

Query by example

You have already seen that you can find a selected record in browse or edit modes by searching for a value in a particular field. This method is only suitable for the simplest of queries. As soon as the searching criteria becomes more complex you will need to use the dBASE built in *Query by Example* feature. Query by example is just as it sounds; you give an example of the type of records you want to find and dBASE finds them for you.

8.1 Preparing for this chapter

In order to complete this chapter you need the following files:

File name	File type	Chapter
ESTATE	Catalog	4
PROPERTY	Database	4

 If you have not created these files in the previous chapters you will need to refer back to the chapter number listed above and create the files.

 If you have purchased the disks that accompany this book you can copy the necessary files from the appropriate floppy disk. To do this, complete the following instructions:

1 Make sure you have created a sub-directory on the hard disk called DBASE\DATA (*see* Setting-up a data directory, page viii).

2 Load dBASE (*see* 3.2 Starting the program, page 9).

3 Follow the instructions for Using the diskettes on page viii. The batch file is called **C8**.

8.2 Creating a query

In general terms, when you create a query, you are presented with a *database skeleton* which looks similar to the browse screen but without the records. You can then select the fields that you want included in your query. The fields you choose are displayed in a *view skeleton*.

The next step is to specify a criteria which will determine the records that feature in the query. dBASE then filters out all the fields that are not included in the view skeleton and all the records that do not match your criteria. So, for example, if you were only interested in the address and prices of the properties in the Old Town area of Greenoak you would add the PROP_ADD and PRICE fields to the view skeleton and set the criteria as the AREA field being Old Town. The following examples will show the steps involved in detail.

To create a query highlight the **Create** option in the **Queries** panel and press the `Enter` key. If a database is in use at the time of creating the query it is assumed that the query is based on that database. If there is not a database in use, the **Layout** menu will be displayed.

To open the appropriate database select the **Add file to query** option. A list of available databases will appear to the right of the screen. Highlight and select the appropriate database. The database skeleton will be displayed.

The following keys can be used to scroll across the fields.

`Tab`   moves the cursor right a field

`Shift + Tab` moves the cursor left a field

You cannot use `F3` and `F4` to move left and right when creating a query. These keys have different uses as you will see later.

1   Making sure that there is no database open, move to the **Queries** panel and select the **Create** option. The **Layout** menu will be displayed.

2   Select the **Add file to query** option and choose the **PROPERTY** database.

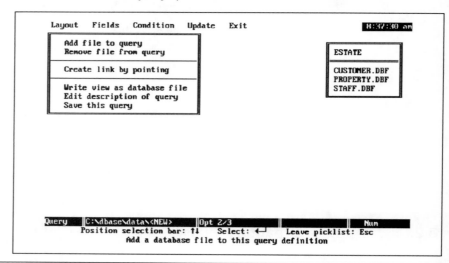

3   The **PROPERTY** database skeleton is displayed. Use `Tab` and
    `Shift Tab` to move across the fields.

8.3   Adding fields to a query

When creating a query you do not need to include all the fields. Initially the query is
empty; there are no fields included. To include a field move the cursor so that it is
under the required field name and press `F5`. The field will be added to the view
skeleton at the bottom of the screen. `F5` works as a toggle. If pressed again the
field will be removed from the view skeleton.

1   Move to the **PROP_ADD** field and press `F5` to add it to the view skeleton.
    Repeat the process to add the **OWNER**, **TELEPHONE** and **ADVERTS** fields.

```
View
<NEW>        Property->    Property->    Property->    Property->
             PROP_ADD      OWNER         TELEPHONE     ADVERTS
```

8.4   Activating a query

To activate a query press `F2`. You will be taken to browse mode where you will
see the fields and records specified in the query. So far, you have not selected
which records to display, so all records are shown.

Press `F2` to activate the query. The fields that were not included in the view have
been filtered out of the query.

```
Records    Organize    Fields    Go To    Exit

PROP_ADD               OWNER              TELEPHONE    ADVERTS

5 Hall Road            Mr P Lane          786309       25.00
89 Cliff Road          Gerald Tims        654219       0.00
6 Brook Road           Mr H Jones         753216       50.00
4 Hever Court          Karen Bright       456821       75.00
6 Elm Road             Fred Collins       456298       0.00
90 Pimly Rise          Ms H Green         324786       25.00
43 Trewitt Ave         Graham Drew        678543       75.00
23 Yew Bank Drive      Mr H Lewis         834652       0.00
32 Leder Road          Miss L Price       987321       25.00
8 Oak Lane             Mr T Hill          768451       0.00
76 Ruin Grove          John Franks        546987       50.00
9 Bookers Avenue       Helen Smith        453981       50.00
56 Rainforest Way      Mr D Swan          651803       0.00
7 Kelly Park Drive     Mrs Franks         546843       75.00
6 Kirk Way             Mrs T Ring         987342       25.00
90 Otway Road          Mr Young           567349       0.00
4 Garden Terrace       Keith Perry        (072)459231  50.00

Browse    C:\dbase\data\<NEW>      Rec 1/20      View           Num
```

8.5   Returning to query design

To return to the query design screen you can either select the **Return to query design** option from the **Exit** menu or use the keyboard shortcut, **Shift +F2** .

➧ Press **Shift + F2** to return to query design

8.6   Changing a query

The fields included in the query can easily be changed. In this example you want a list of all records including the property address, the price, the agent selling the property and the commission rate. You can remove the fields that you no longer want in the query by moving to the field in the database skeleton and pressing **F5** . You can then add the new fields in the same way.

➧ 1   Change the view skeleton so that it includes the following fields:

View <NEW>	Property-> PROP_ADD	Property-> PRICE	Property-> AGENT	Property-> COMMISSION

2   Activate the query and then return to query design.

8.7   Including criteria on a character field

At the moment the query just filters out the *fields* that you are not interested in. What you now want to do is to filter out the *records* that you are not interested in. You can do this by including appropriate criterion under the field names in the database skeleton. For example, if you only wanted to include properties managed by Agent 1 you could enter this as a criteria under the AGENT field name. The only thing to remember when entering a criterion on a character-type field, is that you must enclose the text in quotes. For example to specify Agent 1 as the criteria you would type "A1".

➧ 1   Move to the **AGENT** field in the database skeleton and type **"A1"**.

Property.dbf	↓PRICE	DATE_TAKEN	OWNER	TELEPHONE	↓AGENT	↓COMMISSION	ADV
					"A1"		

2   Activate the query and then return to query design.

Records	Organize	Fields	Go To	Exit

PROP_ADD	PRICE	AGENT	COMMISSION
4 Hever Court	150000.00	A1	
32 Leder Road	80000.00	A1	
56 Rainforest Way	340000.00	A1	
90 Otway Road	450000.00	A1	

8.8   Removing criteria and fields from the view

To remove a criteria from the database skeleton move to the entry and press
Ctrl + Y .

You have already seen that you can add and remove fields from the view by
pressing F5 . As a shortcut for adding or removing all the fields to or from the
view, position the cursor under the database name (1st column of the database
skeleton) and press F5 . By pressing F5 once, all the fields will be added to the
view. By pressing F5 a second time, all the fields will be removed from the view.

1   Move to the **AGENT** field criteria and press Ctrl + Y . The criteria **"A1"** should
be deleted.

2   Move the cursor to under the database name in the database skeleton and press
F5 . Even though you cannot see them on the screen, all the fields from the
PROPERTY database have been added to the view.

8.9   Moving between skeletons

The F4 key moves the cursor to the next skeleton currently displayed on the
screen. For example, if the cursor is currently placed within the database skeleton,
by pressing F4 the cursor will move to the view skeleton.

The F3 key moves the cursor to the previous skeleton.

If you want to check which fields are included in the view skeleton, you can move to
the skeleton and scroll across the fields. The following example shows this.

⟳   1   Press **F4** to move to the view skeleton and use **Tab** and **Shift + Tab** to scroll across the fields.

     2   Press **F3** to move back to the database skeleton and, with the cursor under the database name, press **F5** to remove all the fields from the view.

8.10   Including criteria on numeric fields

You have already seen how to include a criterion on a character field. You typed the required value under the appropriate field name surrounded by quotes ("A1"). The quotes are not necessary when including a numeric criterion. For example, if you wanted to find all properties with 1 bedroom, you could simply type 1 under the NO_BEDS field. It is also possible to use mathematical operators as part of the criterion. If you wanted to find properties with more than 2 bedrooms you could enter the criterion as >2. The following operators can be used:

>   Greater than ie **> 2** more than 2 bedrooms

<   Less than ie **< 60000** less than £60,000

<>   Not equal to (# can also be used) ie **<> 1** not one bedroomed

>=   Greater or equal to ie **>= 2** two or more bedrooms

<=   Less than or equal to ie **<= 3** three or less bedrooms

⟳   1   Include the criterion **>3** in the **NO_BEDS** column and add the following fields to the view skeleton.

Property.dbf	↓PROP_ADD	AREA	TOWN	POSTCODE	TYPE	AGE	↓NO_BEDS	RECEPT
		███					>3	

View			
<NEW>	Property-> PROP_ADD	Property-> PRICE	Property-> NO_BEDS

     2   Press **F2** to activate the query and return to query design.

```
Records    Organize   Fields   Go To   Exit
┌─────────────────────────┬───────────────┬──────────────────────────────┐
│PROP_ADD                 │PRICE          │NO_BEDS                       │
├─────────────────────────┼───────────────┼──────────────────────────────┤
│6 Brook Road             │   55000.00    │                            4 │
│4 Hever Court            │  150000.00    │                            4 │
│23 Yew Bank Drive        │  167000.00    │                            4 │
│76 Ruin Grove            │   63000.00    │                            5 │
│56 Rainforest Way        │  340000.00    │                            5 │
│90 Otway Road            │  450000.00    │                            5 │
│                         │               │                              │
└─────────────────────────┴───────────────┴──────────────────────────────┘
```

8.11   Including criteria on date fields

To include a value as a criterion for a *date type* field, you must enclose the date in curly brackets. For example, to find all properties taken onto the books on 10th January 1992, you would type {10/01/92} in the DATE_TAKEN column of the database skeleton. It is more likely that you would want to find all properties taken on before or after a certain date. You can do this by using the same operators as used with numeric criteria.

1   Remove the current criteria and fields and set up the example below. Activate the query and return to query design.

Property.dbf	RECEPT	GARDEN	GARAGE	FREEHOLD	PRICE	↓DATE_TAKEN	OWNER
◄						>{1/1/92}	

View				
<NEW>	Property-> PROP_ADD	Property-> AREA	Property-> TYPE	Property-> DATE_TAKEN

2   This example would "miss" any properties actually taken onto the books on 1/1/92. Change the criterion so that it reads >={1/1/92}. Activate the query and return to query design.

8.12   Including criteria on logical fields

The values held in logical fields are either T for true or F for false. To identify these values as logical place a dot either side of the logic letter ie .T. or .F. (you could also use .Y., .N., .y., .n., .t. or .f.). So, to search for all properties with garages you could type .T. or .Y. as the criteria in the GARAGE field column.

Create the example below, activate the query and then return to query design:

Property.dbf	RECEPT	GARDEN	↓GARAGE	FREEHOLD	PRICE	DATE_TAKEN	OWNER
			.Y.				

View				
<NEW>	Property-> PROP_ADD	Property-> AREA	Property-> TYPE	Property-> GARAGE

8.13   Using AND criteria

So far you have specified a single criterion when querying the database. This is just the tip of the iceberg - dBASE allows you to create extremely complex multiple queries to extract the data you need.

You may want to find all the properties in Lumley with 3 or more bedrooms. You can do this quite simply by typing the criteria into the two appropriate columns. This is referred to as an *AND criteria*. A record must meet the first *and* second criteria to be included.

1 Enter the following criteria in the database skeleton and select the **PROP_ADD**, **AREA**, **TYPE**, **PRICE** and **NO_BEDS** fields.

Property.dbf	↓PROP_ADD	↓AREA	TOWN	POSTCODE	↓TYPE	AGE	NO_BEDS	REC
		"Lumley"					>2	

2 Activate the query and return to query design.

PROP_ADD	AREA	TYPE	PRICE	NO_BEDS
5 Elm Road	Lumley	T	89000.00	3
23 Yew Bank Drive	Lumley	D	167000.00	4
9 Bookers Avenue	Lumley	S	65000.00	3
7 Kelly Park Drive	Lumley	S	83000.00	3
12 Lewis Mount	Lumley	S	81000.00	3
13 May Lane	Lumley	C	105000.00	3

You can take this a stage further and include three criteria; properties in Lumley, with 3 or more bedrooms, costing less than £90,000.

3   Modify the query to include the third criterion and activate the query.

Property.dbf	↓AREA	T	P	↓TYPE	AGE	↓NO_BEDS	RECEPT	G	G	F	↓PRICE
	"Lumley"	■				>=3					<90000

In this case the record must meet the first *and* second *and* third criteria to be included. (>=3 is the same as >2)

8.14   Using OR criteria

An *OR criteria* is where a record must meet the first *or* second criteria to be included. For example, you may want to find all terrace *or* semi detached properties. To do this you need to create two separate queries in the database skeleton. dBASE will process both queries for each record in the database and if one *or* the other criteria is met the record will be included.

Create and activate the following query. Include the **PROP_ADD**, **PRICE**, **AREA** and **TYPE** fields.

Property.dbf	↓AREA	TOWN	POSTCODE	↓TYPE	AGE	NO_BEDS	RECEPT	GARDEN
				"T"				
				"S"				

```
┌─────────────────────────────────────────────────────────────────────────────┐
│  Records   Organize   Fields   Go To   Exit                                   │
├─────────────────────────────┬─────────────┬───────────────┬──────────────────┤
│ PROP_ADD                    │ PRICE       │ AREA          │ TYPE             │
├─────────────────────────────┼─────────────┼───────────────┼──────────────────┤
│ 5 Hall Road                 │ 61000.00    │               │ T                │
│ 6 Brook Road                │ 55000.00    │ Farley        │ T                │
│ 6 Elm Road                  │ 89000.00    │ Lumley        │ T                │
│ 8 Oak Lane                  │ 99000.00    │ Farley        │ S                │
│ 76 Ruin Grove               │ 63000.00    │ Old Town      │ T                │
│ 9 Bookers Avenue            │ 65000.00    │ Lumley        │ S                │
│ 7 Kelly Park Drive          │ 83000.00    │ Lumley        │ S                │
│ 4 Garden Terrace            │ 67000.00    │ Old Town      │ T                │
│ 12 Lewis Mount              │ 81000.00    │ Lumley        │ S                │
│                             │             │               │                  │
├─────────────────────────────┴─────────────┴───────────────┴──────────────────┤
│ Browse   C:\dbase\data\<NEW>      Rec 1/20        View           Num          │
└─────────────────────────────────────────────────────────────────────────────┘
```

8.15   Using OR and AND criteria

It is also possible to include both an OR and AND criteria in the same query. For example, you may want to find all terraced or semi detached properties which cost less than £70,000. Breaking this down there are two criteria; terraced *and* less than £70,000, *or* semi *and* less than £70,000. This can be entered in the following way:

Property.dbf ↓TYPE	AGE	NO_BED	REC	GARDEN	GARAGE	FREEHOLD	↓PRICE	DA
"T"							<70000	
"S"			▉				<70000	

⟳   Create and activate the above query using the same fields as the previous query.

8.16   Saving a query

All the queries that you have created so far have been one off. There may well be some queries that are repeated on a regular basis. Rather than creating these queries over and over again they can be saved and accessed from the Control Centre.

```
┌──────────────────────────────┐
│ Add file to query            │
│ Remove file from query       │
├──────────────────────────────┤
│ Create link by pointing      │
├──────────────────────────────┤
│ Write view as database file  │
│ Edit description of query    │
│ Save this query        ◄──── │
└──────────────────────────────┘
```

To save a query access the **Layout** menu and select the **Save this query** option. Give the query a suitable name applying the DOS rules for naming files. The query file will be saved to disk with the extension .QBE (Query By Example). You can also name the query file by selecting the **Save changes and exit** option from the **Exit** menu.

1 Create a query that includes the **PROP_ADD, AREA, TYPE, AGE, NO_BEDS** and **PRICE** fields. Include the criteria **"Lumley"** in the **AREA** field. Test the query to make sure that it is correct and then return to query design.

2 Access the **Layout** menu and select the **Save this query** option.

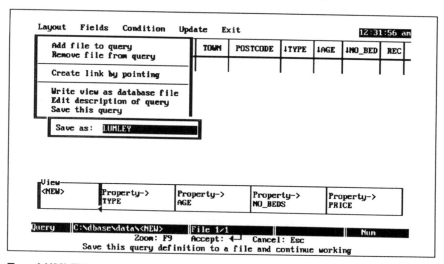

3 Type **LUMLEY** as the query name.

4 Change the criteria to **"Farley"**. Test and save the query as **FARLEY** (you will need to backspace out the current file name).

5 Change the criteria to **"Old Town"**. Test and save the query as **OLDTOWN** (remember spaces are not allowed in a file name).

The remainder of our properties do not have any data entered in the AREA field. The next section will look at one of the methods available for selecting these records.

8.17   Searching for part of a string

You have created query files for three areas of Greenoak. The fourth area in the town centre can be identified as having a post code starting with GR1. If you include the value **"GR1"** as the POSTCODE field criterion you will not find a match as GR1 is only part of the post code. You need to use the **$** operator which searches for part of a string. For example $ **"GR1"** will look for the string GR1 within the field so will find any string containing the characters GR1. It does not matter where they are positioned within the string so long as they are grouped in the given order ie TYGR123 would be found but not G5R123.

1 Remove the criterion from the **AREA** field and type the criterion $ **"GR1"** in the **POSTCODE** column.

2 Remove the **AREA** field from the view and add the **POSTCODE** field.

Property.dbf	AREA	TOWN	POSTCODE	↓TYPE	↓AGE	↓NO_BED	REC	GARDEN	GARAG
			$"GR1"						

PROP_ADD	TYPE	AGE	NO_BEDS	PRICE	POSTCODE
5 Hall Road	T	U	2	61000.00	GR1 6GS
6 Kirk Way	F	M	1	48000.00	GR1 8UX

Records   Organize   Fields   Go To   Exit

⊃ 3   Save this query as **CENTRE**.

8.18   Exiting from query design

To exit from query design access the **Exit** menu. Two options are available, **Save changes and exit** or **Abandon changes and exit**. If the query has already been saved, you can safely use the **Abandon changes and exit** option.

⊃   Exit from query design.

8.19   Using a query

To use a saved query position the cursor on the query name in the **Query** panel and press **F2**.

Queries
<create>
CENTRE
FARLEY
LUMLEY
OLDTOWN

So, using our examples, if a client entered the office and wanted to know what properties are available in Lumley you could highlight the query called LUMLEY and press **F2**. The appropriate records are displayed.

⊃   Access each query in turn. Select the **Exit** option from the **Exit** menu to return to the Control Centre.

8.20   Changing a saved query

To return to query design once a query has been saved, highlight the query in the **Query** panel and press **Shift + F2**.

1　You have included the **AREA** field in the queries **LUMLEY**, **FARLEY** and **OLDTOWN**. As each query filters out records from other areas the inclusion of this field is not really necessary. Modify each of the three queries in turn and remove the **AREA** field from the view skeleton.

2　Create a new query called **ALL**. There are no criteria attached to this query but you only want to include the **AREA**, **PROP_ADD**, **TYPE**, **AGE**, **NO_BEDS** and **PRICE** fields (add fields in this order) . This query will be used in the next chapter so be sure to save it. Exit from query design.

8.21　　Consolidation exercises

1　Using the **PROPERTY** database, create a query to include the following fields:

View─ <NEW>	Property-> PROP_ADD	Property-> TYPE	Property-> AGE	Property-> PRICE

2　Activate the query and return to query design.

PROP_ADD	TYPE	AGE	PRICE
5 Hall Road	T	U	61000.00
89 Cliff Road	F	M	51000.00
6 Brook Road	T	U	55000.00
4 Hever Court	D	M	150000.00
6 Elm Road	T	E	89000.00
90 Pimly Rise	C	O	92000.00
43 Trewitt Ave	D	PR	125000.00
23 Yew Bank Drive	D	PO	167000.00
32 Leder Road	C	U	80000.00
8 Oak Lane	S	PO	99000.00
76 Ruin Grove	T	U	63000.00
9 Bookers Avenue	S	PR	65000.00
56 Rainforest Way	D	M	340000.00
7 Kelly Park Drive	S	M	83000.00
6 Kirk Way	F	M	48000.00
90 Otway Road	D	E	450000.00
4 Garden Terrace	T	U	67000.00

3　List all terraced properties.

Property.dbf	TOWN	POSTCODE	↓TYPE	↓AGE	NO_BEDS	RECEPT	GARDEN	GARAGE
			"T"					

PROP_ADD	TYPE	AGE	PRICE
5 Hall Road	T	U	61000.00
6 Brook Road	T	U	55000.00
6 Elm Road	T	E	89000.00
76 Ruin Grove	T	U	63000.00
4 Garden Terrace	T	U	67000.00

4   List all properties in Lumley.

Property.dbf	↓PROP_ADD	↓AREA	TOWN	POSTCODE	↓TYPE	AGE	NO_BEDS	REC
		"Lumley"						

PROP_ADD	AREA	TYPE	PRICE
89 Cliff Road	Lumley	F	51000.00
6 Elm Road	Lumley	T	89000.00
90 Pimly Rise	Lumley	C	92000.00
23 Yew Bank Drive	Lumley	D	167000.00
9 Bookers Avenue	Lumley	S	65000.00
7 Kelly Park Drive	Lumley	S	83000.00
12 Lewis Mount	Lumley	S	81000.00
13 May Lane	Lumley	C	105000.00

5   List all properties priced at less than £80,000.

6   List all properties taken onto the books in 1991.

7   List all properties with gardens.

8   List all properties in Old Town which have a garden.

9   List all semis with a garden and a garage.

10 List all semis or terraces with 2 or more bedrooms.

See Appendix 1, page 245 for solutions.

9 Producing simple reports

You have already seen that you can display records by accessing the *browse* facility. This can be used to view the entire database or a subset of records as specified by a query. In this chapter you will look at the methods available for producing printed lists and reports using both the *quick report facility* and the use of the dBASE *Report Generator*.

The dBASE Report Generator is useful for the production of more complex reports, especially when requiring group or summary reports. This chapter will provide an introduction to the reporting feature available. Including dBASE functions in reports is covered in Chapter 20.

9.1 Preparing for this chapter

In order to complete this chapter you need the following files:

File name	File type	Chapter
ESTATE	Catalog	4
PROPERTY	Database	4
CUSTOMER	Database	5
ALL	Query	8
LUMLEY	Query	8
FARLEY	Query	8
OLDTOWN	Query	8
CENTRE	Query	8

If you have not created these files in the previous chapters you will need to refer back to the chapter number listed above and create the files.

If you have purchased the disks that accompany this book you can copy the necessary files from the appropriate floppy disk. To do this, complete the following instructions:

1   Make sure you have created a sub-directory on the hard disk called DBASE\DATA (*see* Setting-up a data directory, page viii).

2   Load dBASE (*see* 3.2 Starting the program, page 9).

3   Follow the instructions for Using the diskettes on page viii. The batch file is called **C9**.

The Control Centre has a facility for producing what is termed the **quick report**. The resulting report contains all the records in the current database or query file presented in column format. All numeric fields are totalled and the date and page numbers appear at the top of each page.

The quick report is produced by pressing <u>Shift + F9</u> whilst in the Control Centre. The quick report will be produced for whichever database or query is currently active (above the line in the panel). This type of report is rarely suitable for use with a database file unless the database only has a small number of fields.

The report created will contain all the fields in the database and unless you are using a wide carriage printer or can access your printer in landscape mode (sideways) you will find that the fields wrap round onto the next line of the report. You will see an example of this later on. The other alternative is to print the report in *condensed* mode (smaller print) but with large databases you may still have problems with the text wrapping round if printing on standard A4 size paper.

1   For this example you will use the **LUMLEY** query file. Move your cursor to the **LUMLEY** query in the **Query** panel and press <u>Enter</u>. Select the **Use view** option. If you look at the bottom of the screen you will see the command for producing a quick report. Press <u>Shift + F9</u>.

Help:F1   Use:◄┘   Data:F2   Design:Shift-F2   Quick Report:Shift-F9   Menus:F10

Once the **Quick report** option has been selected the **Print** menu will be displayed.

```
Begin printing      ◄──
Eject page now
View report on screen ◄──

Use print form   {}
Save settings to print form

Destination
Control of printer
Output options
Page dimensions
```

2   Before printing it is always advisable to view your report on the screen. To do this select the **View report on screen** option from the **Print** menu.

3   Press <u>Esc</u> to exit followed by any key key to continue.

You will notice that some of the information is not applicable. You are not likely to be interested in the total number of bedrooms or price of the properties. This type of report is ideal for a quick listing of information but is not sophisticated enough for many uses.

```
Page No.    1
01/09/92

PROP_ADD                    TYPE   AGE   NO_BEDS      PRICE

89 Cliff Road                F      N        2      51000.00
6 Elm Road                   T      E        3      89000.00
90 Primly Rise               C      O        2      92000.00
23 Yew Bank Drive            D      PO       4     167000.00
9 Bookers Avenue             S      PR       3      65000.00
7 Kelly Park Drive           S      M        3      83000.00
12 Lewis Mount               S      M        3      81000.00
13 May Lane                  C      O        3     105000.00
                                            23     733000.00
```

To print a quick report you follow the same steps but select the **Begin printing** option from the **Print** menu.

1   If you have a printer attached to your computer make sure it is switched on and has a supply of paper. Make sure that the **LUMLEY** query is still active and press | **Shift + F9** |. Select the **Begin printing** option from the **Print** menu to produce a printed report containing the records in this query.

2   Open, and either view to screen or print a quick report for the queries **OLDTOWN**, **FARLEY** and **CENTRE**.

9.3   Setting condensed print

If you need to produce a quick report for a query file or database file that is too wide for the printer paper you can change the options so that the report is printed in *condensed* format.

Standard A4 paper has a width of 80 characters whereas the wider computer paper can hold up to 132 characters. By specifying condensed print you can print almost twice as many characters across the paper. If your report is still too wide for the paper you will have to either produce a query (if reporting on the entire database) or, if already using a query, change the query to include less fields. The other option is to modify the report using the dBASE Report Generator and change the display widths of the fields.

```
Begin printing
Eject page now
View report on screen

Use print form   {}
Save settings to print form

Destination
Control of printer  ◀────
Output options
Page dimensions
```

Condensed printing can be set by changing the **Text pitch** option within the **Control of printer** option of the **Print** menu.

```
Text pitch              CONDENSED
Quality print           DEFAULT

New page                BEFORE
Wait between pages      NO
Advance page using      FORM FEED

Starting control codes  {}
Ending control codes    {}
```

The following are some of the other options that can be changed:

Text pitch

Text pitch can be set to **Condensed** (smaller type face) or; **Pica** or **Elite** which are type styles.

Quality print

If your printer has the capability to print **Letter quality**, which simply means produce a higher quality output, you can set this to **Yes** for final copies. Printers which have printer ribbons usually over-print the text a second time when set to letter quality. So, although the output is better the printing time is longer.

New page

You can tell dBASE to force a new page **Before**, **After** or **Before and after** (both) printing your document. You can also set this option to **None**.

Wait between pages

If set to **No** dBASE will assume you have continuous stationery (paper with perforations between each page) or a paper tray so that the pages can be automatically fed through the printer. If you need to feed the paper manually you will need to set this option to **Yes**.

To change any of these settings select the appropriate option from the menu and either type the required entry or use the | **Spacebar** | or | **Enter** | key to scroll through the available settings. When complete press | **Esc** | to exit.

1   Open the **ALL** query and display the quick report to the screen. Notice the text wraps round onto the next line because the report is greater than 80 characters in width. Assuming that you are using standard A4 paper this will cause a problem when printing the report. Press | **Esc** | to exit.

2   Access the **Print** menu for the **ALL** query. Select the **Control of printer** option and change **Text pitch** to **Condensed** and **New page** to **After**.

3   Print the report.

9.4	Customised reports

The quick report is adequate for your own use but if you need to send the information to a client or another member of staff you may want to tidy it up. The dBASE Report Generator contains a number of sophisticated features many out of the scope of this chapter. However, it is fairly simple to use the Report Generator to produce the equivalent of the quick report and then make a few changes to the layout.

To create a report select the **Create** option from the **Report** panel. If you have a database or query open, dBASE will assume that you are creating the report for that data. If you do not have a file open dBASE will prompt you for a file name.

The next screen to appear contains the empty report structure with the **Layout** menu displayed.

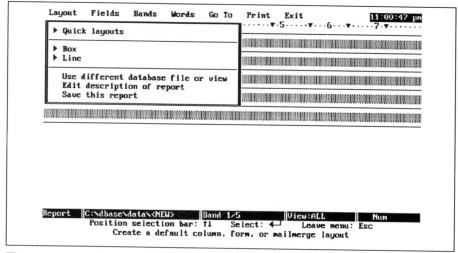

There are several options available. You can enter each field into the report one by one or you can let dBASE create a *quick layout* for you. If you choose the **Quick layout** option from the menu, you are given three choices:

Column layout

The column layout is the same as the quick report layout, field names at the top of columns, numeric fields totalled with date and page number at the top of each page.

Form layout

The form layout looks very much like the edit or append screen with each record on a page of its own with the field data in a list. The fields can be moved around to the required layout.

Mailmerge layout

A mailmerge report is where each record appears on its own page. Initially the field layout looks similar to the form layout. In most cases the majority of the fields may be deleted leaving just the fields that need to be included in a letter. For example, name and address. If the same field needs to be displayed more than once the field can be included wherever needed.

As soon as you select the required layout the fields from the current database or view are added to the report template. With this example the fields included in the ALL query are brought into the template in a column format. If you were to print the report at this stage, it would be identical to the quick report produced earlier.

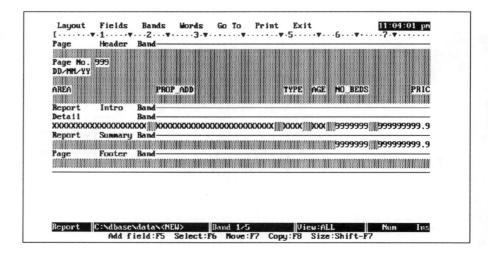

1   Making sure that the **ALL** query is still open, move to the **Report** panel and
    select the **Create** option.

2   Select the **Quick layout** option from the **Layout** menu. Select **Column report**.

9.5	**Report bands**

Header band

All the information in the header band will appear at the top of each page. Initially
the information included in this band is the page number, date and field names.

Report intro band

This band appears at the top of the report and is initially empty. It can contain
information which only appears on the first page of the report eg a covering letter or
a report title.

Detail band

This band contains the fields that make up the report.

Report summary band

Numeric fields are totalled in this band. The information in this band will print at the
end of the report.

Page footer band

All information in this band will appear at the bottom of each page of the report.
This band is initially blank.

9.6   Changing text on the report

Text can be added anywhere within the report. To insert text make sure that **Insert** is **On** (check for the **Ins** indicator on the status line at the bottom of the screen). If the **Ins** indicator is not displayed, press Insert to turn **Insert** to **On**, position the cursor and type. To overtype text press the Insert key again so that **Insert** is **Off**. Text can be deleted using the Delete or Backspace keys.

1   Make sure that **Insert** is **On**, position the cursor at the beginning of the date in the header band and type **Report printed on**:

```
   Layout   Fields   Bands   Words   Go To
   [·······▼·1·····▼···2···▼·····3·▼·······▼··
   Page        Header   Band
   Page No. 999
   Report Printed on: DD/MM/YY
```

By default the column headings are displayed as the field names. In many cases this is not ideal. The column headings can be changed to contain more suitable text.

2   Change the field headings as outlined in the following example:

```
   [·······▼·1·····▼···2···▼·····3·▼······▼·······▼·5····▼···6···▼·····7·▼·······
   Page        Header   Band
   Page No. 999
   Report Printed on: DD/MM/YY

   Area of Greenoak        Property Address        Type & Age   Number of    Property
                                                   of Property  bedrooms      Price
   Report      Intro    Band
   Detail               Band
   XXXXXXXXXXXXXXXXXXXXX   XXXXXXXXXXXXXXXXXXXXXXXXX  XXXX  XXX  9999999  999999999.9
```

9.7   Changing band size

The height of any of the bands can be increased or decreased by inserting or deleting lines.

Lines can be inserted into the band by either inserting a carriage return by pressing the Enter key at either the beginning or the end of a line or by pressing Ctrl + N.

Lines can be deleted by pressing Ctrl + Y. The line at the cursor position will be deleted.

To move around the report template use a combination of the arrow keys and the
[End], [Home] and [Tab] keys.

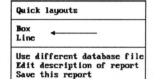

Make sure that **Insert** is **On**. Move to the end of the header band so that the cursor
is following the word "Price" and press [Enter] to insert a new line.

9.8   Drawing lines and boxes

The general appearance of a report can be improved by drawing *lines* and *boxes*
around text or field data.

To include a line or box on the report, access the **Layout** menu by pressing
[Alt + L] and select the **Line** or **Box** option.

Whether you have selected **Box** or **Line** you will now be given the option to draw a
single or double line or to choose your own character. Once you have selected the
draw character it is simply a case of following the instructions at the bottom of the
screen. Position the cursor where you want the line to begin or the left-hand corner
of the box to be and press [Enter] to confirm. Use the arrow keys to size the box or
line. When the box or line is the required size press [Enter] to confirm.

In this exercise you will draw a double line under the column headings.

1   Select the **Line** option from the **Layout** menu. Select **Double line**.

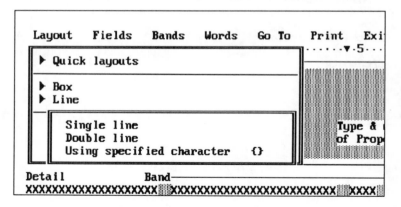

2   Your cursor should now be at the beginning of the blank line under the column
headings. If it is not, move it to this position. Press [Enter] to confirm the start
of the line.

3   Use the [→] to draw a line across the full report width and press [Enter] to
confirm the completion of the line.

Deleting fields

As you have already seen, dBASE automatically produces a summary field for all numeric fields in the report. In many cases some of these summarised fields are irrelevant. With this report you will need to delete the summarised fields for both the number of bedrooms and price fields. Summary fields can be deleted by positioning the cursor on the field and pressing Delete .

```
Area of Greenoak       Property Address          Type & Age    Number of    Property
                                                 of Property   bedrooms      Price
Report     Intro   Band────────────────────────────────────────────────────────────
Detail             Band────────────────────────────────────────────────────────────
XXXXXXXXXXXXXXXXXXXXX  XXXXXXXXXXXXXXXXXXXXXXXXXX  XXXX    XXX  9999999   999999999.9
Report     Summary Band────────────────────────────────────────────────────────────
                                                              9999999   999999999.9
```

➲ Move to the summary band and delete the summary fields for the **NO_BEDS** and **PRICE** fields.

Printing the report

The **Print** menu is accessed by pressing Alt + P . The options are similar to those displayed with the quick report.

➲ Access the print menu and view the report to screen. You will notice that the report is wider than 80 characters. If you are using standard A4 paper you will need to set the text pitch to condensed from within the **Control of printer** option. If you have a printer attached print the report.

Page No. 1

Report Printed on: 23/10

Area of Greenoak	Property Address	Type & Age of Property		Number of bedrooms	Property Price
	5 Hall Road	T	V	2	61000.00
Lumley	89 Cliff Road	F	N	2	51000.00
Farley	6 Brook Road	T	V	4	55000.00
Old Town	4 Hever Court	D	M	4	150000.00
Lumley	6 Elm Road	T	E	3	89000.00
Lumley	90 Pimly Rise	C	O	2	92000.00

Changing page settings

Page settings can be changed by accessing the **Page dimensions** option from the **Print** menu.

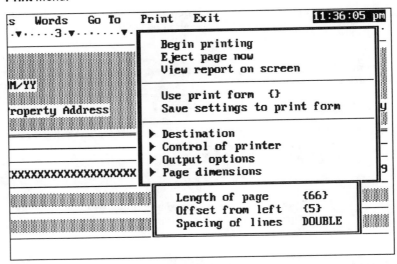

The length of the page can be adjusted. The default **Length of page** is **66** lines which is the required setting for A4 paper. The **Offset from left** (left margin) is set to **0**. This can be changed if your report is too close to the left of the page. **Spacing of lines** is set to **Single**. This can be changed to **Double** or **Triple** if required.

Change the page dimensions so that the **Offset from left** is set to **5** and **Spacing of lines** is set to **Double**. Remember to exit from the menu with Esc .

9.12   Including the £ symbol in a report

```
▶ Add field
  Remove field
▶ Modify field  ◀——
▶ Change hidden field
```

If there are currency fields within a report the presentation may be improved by including the currency symbol in front of the field values. To do this you need to change the *picture* of the field. Part 2 will look at all the various ways you can change the way the data is displayed, referred to as *changing the picture*. Following is an example incorporating the currency symbol.

1   Move your cursor to the **PRICE** field in the detail band and press Alt + F . Select **Modify field**.

The keyboard shortcut, F5 can also be used to modify existing fields or add new fields to a report.

There are two ways in which you can change the way the field is displayed referred to as **Template** and **Function**. **Template** is used to change an individual character or number within a field whereas **Function** is used to change the whole field. The feature you want, currency, is a Function.

2   Select the **Picture functions** option. The following screen will appear:

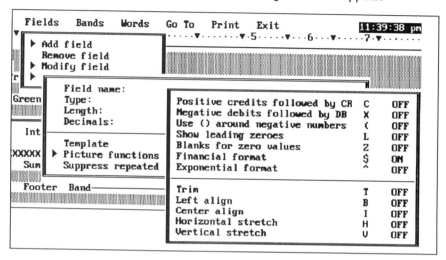

3   Move the cursor down to the **Financial format** option and press the Enter key to toggle the option to **On**.

4   Again, it is always important to read the information at the bottom of the screen. It tells you to press Ctrl + End to save the **Function** options. Press Ctrl + End again to return to the report template. Print the report again to observe the changes.

9.13   Saving a report

If you are making a number of changes it is a good idea to save your report at regular intervals. To save and continue select the **Save this report** option from the **Layout** menu. To save and exit from the Report Generator select the **Save changes and exit** option from the **Exit** menu. In either case you will be asked to give your report a name if you are saving it for the first time. If you have made any changes to the print settings you will be asked if you want to save those settings.

```
 ┌─────────────────────────────────────────────────────────────────┐
 │ Fields   Bands   Words   Go To   Print   Exit      11:49:24 pm   │
 │ 1·····▼···2···▼····3·▼······▼······▼·┌──────────────────────────┐│
 │ Header  Band────────────────────────│ Save changes and exit     ││
 │ ▓▓▓▓▓▓▓▓▓▓▓▓▓▓▓▓▓▓▓▓▓▓▓▓▓▓▓▓▓▓▓▓▓▓▓▓│ Abandon changes and exit  ││
 │ ▓99                                  └──────────────────────────┘│
 │ nted on: DD/MM/YY ▓▓▓▓▓▓▓▓▓▓▓▓▓▓▓▓▓▓▓▓▓▓▓▓▓▓▓▓▓▓▓▓▓▓▓▓▓▓▓▓▓▓▓▓▓▓▓▓│
 │ ▓▓▓▓▓▓▓▓▓▓▓▓▓▓▓▓▓▓▓▓▓▓▓▓▓▓▓▓▓ge  Number of   Property │
 │ ┌──────────────────────────────────────┐ rty bedrooms    Price  │
 │ │ Print form settings are new or changed.│                       │
 │ │ Do you want to save them?              │  ─────  ────────  ─────│
 │ │                                        │                       │
 │ │         Yes            No              │XXX 9999999 9999999999.│
 │ └──────────────────────────────────────┘                       │
 │ ▓▓▓▓▓▓▓▓▓▓▓▓▓▓▓▓▓▓▓▓▓▓▓▓▓▓▓▓▓▓▓▓▓▓▓▓▓▓▓▓▓▓▓▓▓▓▓▓▓▓▓▓▓▓▓▓▓▓▓▓▓▓▓▓ │
 │ Footer  Band─────────────────────────────────────────────────── │
 │ ▓▓▓▓▓▓▓▓▓▓▓▓▓▓▓▓▓▓▓▓▓▓▓▓▓▓▓▓▓▓▓▓▓▓▓▓▓▓▓▓▓▓▓▓▓▓▓▓▓▓▓▓▓▓▓▓▓▓▓▓▓▓▓▓ │
 └─────────────────────────────────────────────────────────────────┘
```

⟳ Select the **Save changes and exit** option from the **Exit** menu. Name the report **ALL**. Save the changes to the print settings with the default name, **ALL.PRF**.

9.14 Accessing a report from the Control Centre

To access a report that you have created within the Report Generator, position the cursor on the report name within the **Report** panel and press ⎣ **Enter** ⎦.

You are given three choices. You can print the report, modify it or display the data in the report in browse mode.

```
 ╔═════════════════════════════════════════════════════════╗
 ║                                                         ║
 ║   Print report    Modify layout    Display data         ║
 ║        Press ENTER to select or ESC to cancel           ║
 ║                                                         ║
 ╚═════════════════════════════════════════════════════════╝
```

9.15 Consolidation exercise

⟳ 1 Create a query for the **CUSTOMER** database to include the following fields; **FIRSTNAME**, **SURNAME**, **TELEPHONE** and **COMMENTS**.

2 Save the query as **COMMENTS**.

3 Create a customised report based on the **COMMENTS** query.

4 Select **Column report** as the report type. Use the **Quick layout** option to bring in the fields from the query.

5   Underline the column headings.

6   Print the report.

7   Save the report as **COMMENTS**.

See Appendix 1, page 248 for solutions.

1   If you require additional practice, produce a report from your personal database to show the names and birthdays of friends and family.

10 Organising the database

In most cases data is entered into a database file in date order. For example new customers are added to the CUSTOMER database as they enrol and properties are added as to the PROPERTY database as they become available for sale. Occasions will arise when you need to output the data in a different order. For example, you may want a print out of all customers in order of name.

Databases can be ordered in two ways, by sorting or indexing.

10.1 Preparing for this chapter

In order to complete this chapter you need the following files:

File name	File type	Chapter
ESTATE	Catalog	4
PROPERTY	Database	4
CUSTOMER	Database	5

 If you have not created these files in the previous chapters you will need to refer back to the chapter numbers listed above and create the files.

 If you have purchased the disks that accompany this book you can copy the necessary files from the appropriate floppy disk. To do this, complete the following instructions:

1 Make sure you have created a sub-directory on the hard disk called DBASE\DATA (*see* Setting-up a data directory, page viii)

2 Load dBASE (*see* 3.2 Starting the program, page 9).

3 Follow the instructions for Using the diskettes on page viii. The batch file is called **C10**.

10.2 Sorting a database

When a database is *sorted* another database is created containing exactly the same information as the first database but with the records in a different order.

Database in natural order	
1	Jones
2	Samuals
3	Green
4	Taylor
5	Adams
6	Smith
7	Richards

Sorted Database	
1	Adams
2	Green
3	Jones
4	Richards
5	Samuals
6	Smith
7	Taylor

Although the **Sort** option has its uses, there are two distinct disadvantages:

- a new database is created taking up valuable disk space;

- if new records are added the database must be sorted again.

10.3 Indexing

By *indexing* a database, records can be displayed with respect to any field or group of fields. As long as the indexes are held as *tags* in the database's *multiple index file*, the indexes will reflect any changes if the data is changed (by adding or deleting records).

There are very definite advantages to indexing:

- The index tag does not contain a copy of the whole database. It simply contains the record numbers in the required order, thus saving disk space, ie if the tag is ordering the database by surname, the record for Adams which could be record no 5, would be the first record in the index tag:

Database in natural order	
1	Jones
2	Samuals
3	Green
4	Taylor
5	Adams
6	Smith
7	Richards

Indexed Database	
5	Adams
3	Green
1	Jones
7	Richards
2	Samuals
6	Smith
4	Taylor

- If records are added or deleted from the database the index tags will automatically be kept up to date.

Every database is automatically given a multiple index file as soon as an index tag is created. This multiple index file is given the same name as the database with an extension of .MDX ie the PROPERTY database will have an associated index file called PROPERTY.MDX. The default MDX file is automatically opened whenever the database is opened. Additional MDX files can also be created but these would need to be opened manually. An MDX file can contain up to 47 index tags so, in most cases one default MDX file will be sufficient to hold the required tags.

A tag holds the information to tell dBASE how to index the data. For example, a tag could be set-up to order the database on the SURNAME field. It all sounds very complicated but in fact, with practice it becomes quite logical!

In this first example you will create an index tag to order the records in the CUSTOMER database by surname. At the moment the records are displayed in what is termed *natural order*, the order they were entered. If a database is opened in the usual way the records will always be displayed in the natural order. To display the records in any other way the appropriate tag must be opened.

Open the **CUSTOMER** database by highlighting the database name in the **Data** panel and pressing F2 to access browse/edit mode. Toggle to browse mode if necessary. The records are displayed in their natural order, for example:

SURNAME	FIRSTNAME	TITLE	STREET	AREA
Jones	Peter	Mr	22 Layeburn Street	Old Bridge
Kemp	Mary	Miss	38 Fairfield Lane	Lumley
Jones	Fred	Mr	12 Portland Rd	Chapelforth
Samuals	Deborah	Ms	32 Lemming Lane	Lumley
Hughes	Linda	Miss	12 The Avenue	Farley
Smith	John	Mr	45 Hargarth Street	
Price	Jill	Mrs	32 Wayside Ave	Old Town
Kelly	P	Mr	6 Levin Way	Lumley
Hill	David	Mr	12 Young Street	Lumley
Summers	Kevin	Mr	45 Lowham Road	Kingley

10.4   Creating a tag

```
Create new index      ◄———
Modify existing index
Order records by index
Activate .MDX index file
Include .MDX index file
Remove unwanted index tag

Sort database on field list
Unmark all records
Erase marked records
```

To create an index tag select the **Create new index** option from the **Organise** menu.

If you have an earlier release of dBASE IV the **Organise** menu is not available from within the browse or edit environments. To create and activate index tags, highlight the database name from within the **Data** panel of the Control Centre. Press Enter and select the **Modify structure/order** option. The **Organise** menu should be displayed.

Once you have selected to create a new tag the next stage is to give the tag a meaningful name. This could be the same name as the field you are ordering on.

You now need to provide an expression. This can be just a field name or a more complicated expression involving a number of fields and dBASE functions. The following examples involve only simple index expressions. For more complex indexing see Chapter 00.

By pressing $\boxed{\textbf{Shift + F1}}$ dBASE presents a list of available fields, operators and functions that can be used to make up an index expression.

To generate the defined index press $\boxed{\textbf{Ctrl + End}}$. The index tag will be generated and added to the multiple index file (MDX). The records will now be displayed in the required order.

1　Select the **Create new index** option from the **Organise** menu. Press $\boxed{\textbf{Enter}}$ to access the **Index name** option and type **NAME** as the index name. Press $\boxed{\textbf{Enter}}$ to complete.

```
┌─────────┬───────────────────────────────────────────────────────────┐
│ Jones   │  Name of index                          {NAME}             │
│ Kemp    │  Index expression                       �█████████████████  │
│ Jones   │ ┌─────────────────┬─────────────┬─────────────────┐        │
│ Samual  │ │ Fieldname       │ Operator    │ Function        │ DING   │
│ Hughes  │ │                 │             │                 │        │
│ Smith   │ │ SURNAME         │ #           │ ABS             │        │
│ Price   │ │ FIRSTNAME       │ $           │ ACCESS          │        │
│ Kelly   │ │ TITLE           │ *           │ ACOS            │        │
│ Hill    │ │ STREET          │ **          │ ALIAS           │        │
│ Summer  │ │ AREA            │ +           │ ASC             │ r, numeric │
│         │ │ TOWN            │ -           │ ASIN            │   fields in │
│         │ │ POSTCODE        │ ->          │ AT              │        │
│         │ │ TELEPHONE       │ .AND.       │ ATAN            │ meters, │
│         │ │ ENROLED         │ .OR.        │ ATN2            │ SC to canc │
│         │ └─────────────────┴─────────────┴─────────────────┘        │
└─────────┴───────────────────────────────────────────────────────────┘
```

2　The cursor is moved to the **Index expression** option. Press $\boxed{\textbf{Enter}}$. Press $\boxed{\textbf{Shift + F1}}$ for a field list and select **SURNAME**. Press $\boxed{\textbf{Enter}}$ to complete.

3　Generate the index by pressing $\boxed{\textbf{Ctrl + End}}$. The index is built and the records displayed in surname order.

SURNAME	FIRSTNAME	TITLE	STREET	AREA
Hill	David	Mr	12 Young Street	Lumley
Hughes	Linda	Miss	12 The Avenue	Farley
Jones	Peter	Mr	22 Layeburn Street	Old Bri
Jones	Fred	Mr	12 Portland Rd	Chapelf
Kelly	P	Mr	6 Levin Way	Lumley
Kemp	Mary	Miss	38 Fairfield Lane	Lumley
Price	Jill	Mrs	32 Wayside Ave	Old Tow
Samuals	Deborah	Ms	32 Lemming Lane	Lumley
Smith	John	Mr	45 Hargarth Street	
Summers	Kevin	Mr	45 Lowham Road	Kingley

Notice in this example, record 12 (David Hills) is now the first record in the list. Depending on whether you have added additional or different records to the CUSTOMER database, your indexed database may be different.

10.5 Including a secondary index field

Looking at the ordered CUSTOMER database you can see that you have two customers with the surname of Jones; Peter and Fred. You could include the FIRSTNAME field as part of the index so that the record for Fred Jones is displayed before the record for Peter Jones. This is referred to as a *secondary index* field. When creating an index containing a secondary (or even *tertiary*) field the expression must contain the field names separated by the ⊞ symbol. The following examples are valid expressions:

SURNAME+FIRSTNAME
BRANCH+DEPARTMENT+SURNAME

With the second example you are taking the index to a third level. You could take it even further by including the FIRSTNAME field as the fourth part of the index. dBASE simply adds the text together to do the comparisons. So when comparing JONESPETER and JONESFRED, Jones Fred will come first in the order.

You can only add together fields of the same type. For example if you tried to create an expression AREA+PRICE for the PROPERTY database, dBASE would return an error. This is because AREA is a character field and PRICE a numeric field. dBASE does come equipped with functions to solve these problems (*see* Chapter 20)

```
Create new index
Modify existing index ◄──
Order records by index
Activate .MDX index file
Include .MDX index file
Remove unwanted index tag

Sort database on field list
Unmark all records
Erase marked records
```

To make changes to an existing index, access browse or edit mode, select the **Modify existing index** option from the **Organise** menu. Select the appropriate index tag from the list and make the required changes to the expression or name.

1   From within browse mode, select the **Modify existing index** option from the **Organise** menu. Select **NAME** as the index to be modified.

2 Move to the **Index expression** option and press $\boxed{\text{Enter}}$ and either type the new expression or use the $\boxed{\text{Shift + F1}}$ feature to choose the $\boxed{+}$ operator and the **FIRSTNAME** field. The expression should read **SURNAME+FIRSTNAME**. Press $\boxed{\text{Enter}}$ followed by $\boxed{\text{Ctrl + End}}$ to complete.

```
Name of index                        {NAME}
Index expression                     {SURNAME+FIRSTNAME}
FOR clause                           {}
Order of index                       ASCENDING
Display first duplicate key only     NO
```

Fred Jones is now displayed before Peter Jones.

Records	Organize	Fields	Go To	Exit

SURNAME	FIRSTNAME	TITLE	STREET
Hill	David	Mr	12 Young Street
Hughes	Linda	Miss	12 The Avenue
Jones	Fred	Mr	12 Portland Rd
Jones	Peter	Mr	22 Layeburn Street
Kelly	P	Mr	6 Levin Way
Kemp	Mary	Miss	38 Fairfield Lane

10.6   Accessing an index tag

To use an index tag that has already been created access the **Organise** menu and select the **Order records by index** option. A list of available index tags will be displayed. Select the required tag and the records will be ordered accordingly.

1 Display the **CUSTOMER** database in its natural order by selecting the **Order records by index** option from the **Organise** menu. Select **Natural order**.

2 Repeat this process to display the records in order of name.

3 Exit from browse mode.

10.7   Creating a descending index

For this example you will index the PROPERTY database using the PRICE field. When indexing on a numeric or date field you may want to order your data in *descending order*, highest to lowest price or most recent to earliest date. This can be achieved by selecting the **Descending** option when generating an index tag.

1 Display the **PROPERTY** database in browse mode. Move across to the **PRICE** field (so that you can easily see the result of the index). Access the **Create new index** option from the **Organise** menu. Enter **PRICE** as the index tag name and select the **PRICE** field as the expression.

The order option has two choices, **Ascending** or **Descending**. The Enter key toggles between the two.

```
Name of index                     {PRICE}
Index expression                  {PRICE}
FOR clause                        {}
Order of index                    DESCENDING
Display first duplicate key only  NO
```

2 Select the **Descending** option and press Ctrl + End to complete. The properties should now be displayed in order of price, highest to lowest.

3 Exit from browse and close the database.

10.8 Consolidation exercises

1 Produce a new index tag for the **PROPERTY** database based on the **DATE_TAKEN** field. Call the index tag **DATE_TAKEN** and set the order to **Ascending**.

```
Name of index                     {DATE_TAKEN}
Index expression                  {DATE_TAKEN}
FOR clause                        {}
Order of index                    ASCENDING
Display first duplicate key only  NO
```

The records should be ordered by date, for example:

GARDEN	GARAGE	FREEHOLD	PRICE	DATE_TAKEN	OWNER
Y	N	Y	80000.00	08/01/91	Miss L Price
Y	Y	Y	99000.00	21/01/91	Mr T Hill
Y	Y	Y	340000.00	19/03/91	Mr D Swan
Y	N	Y	83000.00	05/10/91	Mrs Franks
Y	Y	T	125000.00	21/10/91	Graham Drew
Y	Y	Y	150000.00	11/11/91	Karen Bright
Y	N	Y	65000.00	17/11/91	Helen Smith
N	N	Y	63000.00	02/12/91	John Franks
N	N	Y	61000.00	05/12/91	Mr P Lane
Y	Y	Y	81000.00	12/12/91	Miss Davis
N	N	N	51000.00	05/01/92	Gerald Tims
N	N	Y	55000.00	10/01/92	Mr H Jones

2 View the **PROPERTY** database in its natural order.

3 View the **PROPERTY** database by price.

4 Create a new index tag for the **CUSTOMER** database based on the **ENROLED** field. Order the records as **Ascending**.

5 Access the **CUSTOMER** database and view the records by name.

6 Close the **CUSTOMER** database.

See Appendix 1, page 249 for solutions.

11 Producing mailing labels

dBASE can be used to automatically produce labels from either an entire database file or from the records included in a query. For example, you could produce labels for all the clients in the CUSTOMER database or you could produce labels from our LUMLEY query file if you needed to send a letter to the owners of properties in the Lumley area of Greenoak.

11.1 Preparing for this chapter

In order to complete this chapter you need the following files:

File name	File type	Chapter
ESTATE	Catalog	4
PROPERTY	Database	4
CUSTOMER	Database	5
NAME	Index tag	10

 If you have not created these files in the previous chapters you will need to refer back to the chapter number listed above and create the files.

 If you have purchased the disks that accompany this book you can copy the necessary files from the appropriate floppy disk. To do this, complete the following instructions:

1   Make sure you have created a sub-directory on the hard disk called DBASE\DATA (*see* Setting-up a data directory, page viii).

2   Load dBASE (*see* 3.2 Starting the program, page 9).

2   Follow the instructions for Using the diskettes on page viii. The batch file is called **C11**.

11.2 Creating labels

To create labels firstly make sure that the appropriate database or query file is opened and then select the **Create** option from the **Labels** panel. The label screen will be displayed allowing you to add the fields that are to appear on the label.

In this example you will produce labels for all the records in the CUSTOMER database, displaying the following details (*see* next page):

TITLE SURNAME STREET AREA TOWN POSTCODE	Mr Jones 10 Little Brook Ave Lumley Greenoak GR5 7YP
TITLE SURNAME STREET AREA TOWN POSTCODE	Miss Andrews 23 The Drive Lumley Greenoak GR5 8TY
TITLE SURNAME STREET AREA	Mr Peters 54 Dover Road Old Town

 1   Browse the data in the **CUSTOMER** database.

2   Access the **Organise** menu and select the **Order records by index** option. Select **NAME**. Exit from browse.

3   Move to the **Labels** panel and select the **Create** option. The following blank label should appear in the centre of the screen:

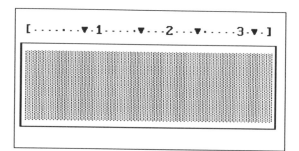

11.3   Adding fields to a label

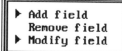

Fields can be added to the label by positioning the cursor at the starting position of the field and selecting the **Add field** option from the **Fields** menu. A list of available fields appear. Choose the required field from the list and press Ctrl + End to accept the format for the field.

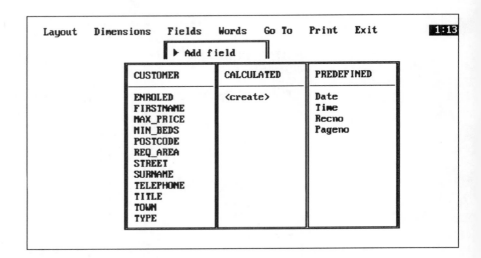

The keyboard shortcut for this menu selection is F5. By pressing F5 the field list will automatically be displayed and the required field can be selected.

1 Position the cursor in the top left-hand corner of the label, press F5 and select the **TITLE** field (you will need to scroll down the list of fields to display the **TITLE** field). Press **Enter** to select the field followed by **Ctrl + End** to accept the format.

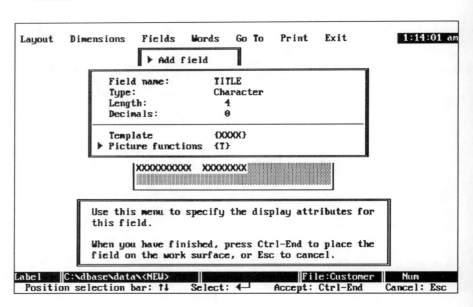

2 Leave a space after the title and add the **SURNAME** field by pressing F5 and selecting from the list. Add the remaining fields as illustrated in the following example (*see* next page).

```
TITLE  SURNAME
STREET
AREA
TOWN  POSTCODE
```

11.4   Setting the label dimensions

Once you have set up the fields that are to appear on the labels, the next stage is to
enter the correct dimensions for the label stationery on hand. dBASE has several
built in label sizes but if none of these are correct you can set your own dimensions.

When you access the **Dimensions** menu and select the **Predefined size** option,
the following screen will appear:

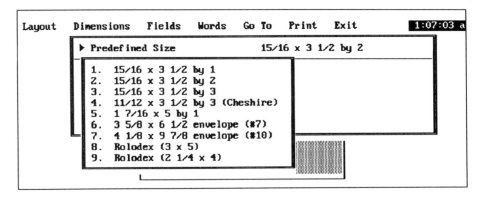

If your label size is listed type the appropriate menu number. If not, enter the
dimensions manually.

 Access the **Dimensions** menu. Select option number **2** from the **Predefined size**
option, 2-across labels.

11.5   Displaying and printing labels

To view the labels on the screen select the **View labels on screen** option from the
Print menu.

```
Mr  Jones                    Miss  Kemp
22 Layeburn Street           30 Fairfield Lane
Old Bridge                   Lumley
London  EC2 5TY              Greenoak  GR5 6AW

Mr  Jones                    Ms  Samuels
12 Portland Rd               32 Lemming Lane
Chapelforth                  Lumley
Leeds  LS4 5TO               Greenoak  GR4 6TD

Miss  Hughes                 Mr  Smith
12 The Avenue                45 Hargarth Street
Farley                       Bradford  BD4 5TB
Greeoak  GR8 5RT
```

Begin printing ◄───
Eject page now
Generate sample labels
View labels on screen

Use print form {}
Save settings to print

Destination
Control of printer
Output options
Page dimensions

To print the labels select the **Begin printing** option from the **Print** menu. It may be advisable to select the **Generate sample labels** options before printing labels for the entire file. By generating sample labels you will be able to see if the text is aligned correctly on you label stationery without wasting pages of labels.

Either display the labels on the screen or output to the printer if there is a printer available.

11.6   Saving the label specifications

To save the label specifications select the **Save changes and exit** option from the **Exit** menu. Give the file an appropriate name.

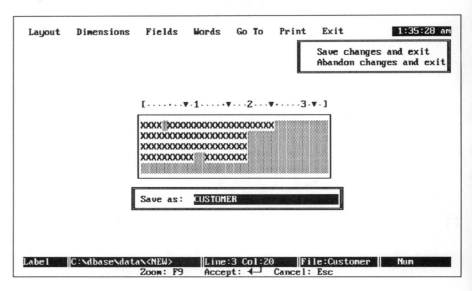

Save the labels as **CUSTOMER**.

12 Data entry forms

You have already seen that you can append and edit data using the dBASE default data entry screen. In some cases this may not be adequate for the following reasons:

- When entering information from a form it is difficult to translate that information to a screen that has a different layout.

- Data may need to be checked before being entered into the database ie *all* character fields may need to be entered in upper-case.

By creating your own customised data entry screen (which can also be used for editing) you are able to decide on an appropriate layout and provide *validation* of data.

The example below shows a customised data entry screen for the PROPERTY database:

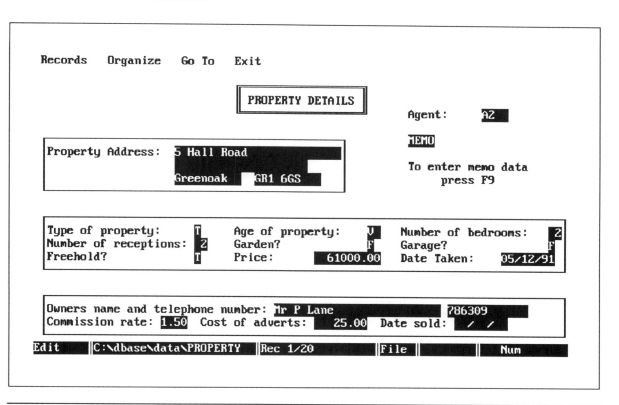

Instead of the data being displayed with the fields in a column, the fields have been grouped and displayed with boxes around them. In this chapter you will look at the methods used for creating a customised data entry form.

12.1　Preparing for this chapter

In order to complete this chapter you need the following files:

File name	File type	Chapter
ESTATE	Catalog	4
PROPERTY	Database	4
STAFF	Database	4
CUSTOMER	Database	5

 If you have not created these files in the previous chapters you will need to refer back to the chapter numbers listed above and create the files.

 If you have purchased the disks that accompany this book you can copy the necessary files from the appropriate floppy disk. To do this, complete the following instructions:

1　Make sure you have created a sub-directory on the hard disk called DBASE\DATA (*see* Setting-up a data directory, page viii).

2　Load dBASE (*see* 3.2 Starting the program, page 9).

3　Follow the instructions for Using the diskettes on page viii. The batch file is called **C12**.

12.2　Printing the structure of a database

Before attempting to design a form it is advisable to print out the structure of the database and use this to sketch the layout. It is much easier to design the form from within dBASE if you already have a layout in mind.

To print the structure, select the appropriate database from the **Data** panel. Access the **Modify structure/order** option. Access the **Layout** menu and select the **Print database structure** option.

```
 Layout   Organize   Append   Go To   Exit                    10:31:59
┌─────────────────────────────────────────────┐
│  Print database structure                    │            Bytes remaining:    38
│  Edit database description        │ Dec │ Index │
│  Save this database file structure            │
│                                   │ ███ │  N │
│   2 │ AREA     │ Character │ 20   │     │  N
│   3 │ TOWN     │ Character │ 10   │     │  N
│   4 │ POSTCODE │ Character │ 10   │     │  N
│   5 │ TYPE     │ Character │ 1    │     │  N
│   6 │ AGE      │ Character │ 2    │     │  N
│   7 │ NO_BEDS  │ Numeric   │ 2    │  0  │  N
```

The usual print options are available. To print the structure select the **Begin printing** option.

 Highlight the **PROPERTY** database in the **Data** panel of the Control Centre. Press ⎡Enter⎤. Select the **Modify structure/order** option. Access the **Layout** menu. Select **Print database structure**. Select **Begin printing**. When finished, access the **Exit** menu and, as you have not made any changes, select the **Abandon changes and exit** option.

12.3   Creating a form

First make sure that the database for which you want to create the form is open. Select the **Create** option from the **Forms** panel in the Control Centre.

If you have forgotten to open the database or have opened the wrong database you can select the **Use different database file** option from the **Layout** menu to specify the database you want to use.

Once the option to create a new form has been issued, a blank form appears and the **Layout** menu displayed. At this point you can select the **Quick layout** option. This will add all the fields, with the field name, to the form in the standard layout (one underneath another). You can then change the field names to more meaningful prompts and move the fields around to produce the required layout.

The other alternative is to bring in the fields one at a time. By doing this you can position the cursor at the point where you want the field to go. When you add the fields on an individual basis, only the field is added, not the field name. You can enter your own prompts and then bring in the field. In this exercise you will use the second method, you will bring in the fields individually. When completing the consolidation exercises you may want to try the *quick layout* method.

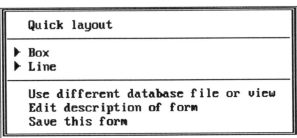

To move from the menus to the form press the ⎡Esc⎤ key. Access the menus in the usual way by pressing ⎡F10⎤ or ⎡Alt⎤ plus the first letter of the menu name.

```
Form      C:\dbase\data\<NEW>                        File:Property    Num
              Position selection bar: ↑↓     Select: ◄┘     Leave menu: Esc
         Arrange all fields in the current view vertically on the layout
```

1 Open the **PROPERTY** database (make sure it is above the line in the **Data** panel). Move across to the **Forms** panel and select the **Create** option.

2 Press Esc to leave the menus.

12.4   Adding text to the form

You can move around the form by using the arrow keys. Titles, prompts and help information can be entered at any point by simply moving the cursor to the required position and typing. Text can be positioned using the **Position** option from the **Word** menu. For example, to add a centred title to a form you would move to the required line, type the title and then access the **Word** menu, select the **Position** option and select **Center**. The text will be centred horizontally.

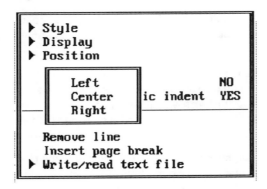

It is always a good idea to leave a few lines at the top of the form otherwise, when the form is used, the dBASE menu, displayed at the top of the screen, will be hidden. In order to allow for the menu at the top and the status bar at the bottom, the form should not be more than 22 rows in length. If you are working with a database comprising a large number of fields, the data entry form can take up more than one screen. When you are creating the form the screen will scroll beyond the 22nd row as you add the fields. When you display the data using the form you can page up and down to see the screens that make up the form.

1 Move to row 3 and type **PROPERTY DETAILS**.

2 Access the **Words** menu and select the **Position** option. Select **Center**.

12.5   Drawing lines and boxes

```
Quick layout

Box        ◄─────────
Line

Use different database file
Edit description of form
Save this form
```

The appearance of a form can be enhanced by the use of lines and boxes. To draw a line or box access the **Layout** menu and select the **Box** or **Line** option.

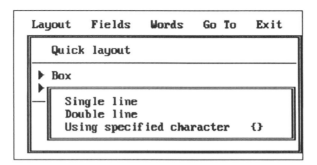

The available options are to draw a single or double line or a line made up of characters of your choice. For example, you may want to underline a title with asterisks (*). Once you have chosen the type of line it is a case of reading the instructions at the bottom of the screen. If drawing a box, you will be prompted to move your cursor to the top left-hand corner of the box and press Enter to confirm.

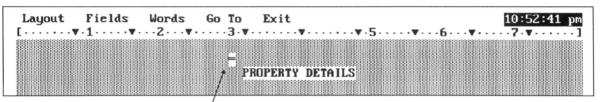

Position cursor at top left of box
Always read the instructions at the bottom of the screen

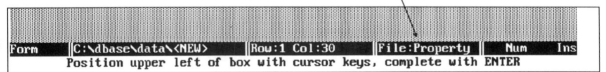

If drawing a line, the prompt will read *Position start of line with cursor keys complete with Enter.* You will then be prompted to stretch the box using the arrow keys. Grow the box to the required size and press Enter to confirm.

If drawing a line the prompt will read *Complete line drawing with Enter.*

Access the **Layout** menu and select the **Box** option. Select **Double line**. Move the cursor to the line above the heading **PROPERTY DETAILS** and two columns to the left. Press Enter to complete. Use the right and down arrows to stretch the box around the title. Press Enter to confirm.

12.6   Adding fields

When adding fields individually only the field itself is added to the form, the field name is excluded. Before (or after) loading the field you need to enter some form of prompt so that the person entering the records knows what to enter!

To add a field, first position the cursor where the field is to be placed. Access the **Fields** menu and select **Add field**. A list of available fields will be displayed. Highlight the required field and press Enter .

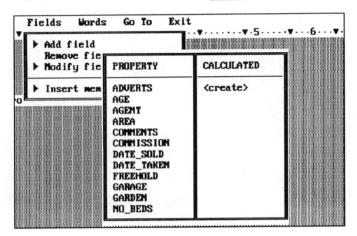

The keyboard shortcut for adding a field is F5 . Position the cursor, press F5 and a list of available fields is displayed.

A menu is displayed which allows you to specify the *display attributes* and *editing options* for the field. These options will be looked at in Chapter 19. For the moment, leave this screen unchanged and exit by pressing Ctrl + End (as indicated at the bottom of the screen).

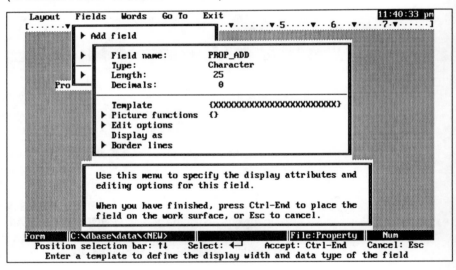

1   Move the cursor to row 7 column 2 and type **Property Address:**.

2   Move the cursor to row 7 column 21. Either press F5 or access the **Fields** menu and select the **Add fields** option. Select the **PROP_ADD** field. Press Ctrl + End to accept the display attributes. The field will appear on the screen as a row of Xs.

3 Move the cursor to row 8 column 21 and repeat the steps to load the **AREA** field. Load the **TOWN** and **POSTCODE** fields as outlined below. Draw a single line box around the address details.

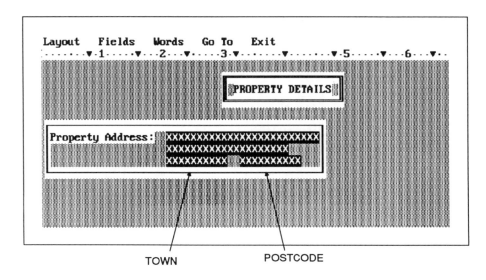

TOWN POSTCODE

12.7   Saving the form

It is always a good idea to save regularly. Then, if anything does go wrong, you can always abandon and re-load the form as it was before. To save the form without exiting, access the **Layout** menu and select the **Save this form** option. Enter a suitable name for the form. If you are only designing one form for the database you can give it the same name as the database. On occasion, you may want to have more than one form for a database. This may be the case if you are working with confidential records. You may want one form to contain all the fields in the database and another which excludes confidential data such as salary details. If you are creating several forms to be used with the database give the forms meaningful names so that they can be easily identified.

1 Save the form as **PROPERTY**.

2 Complete the form as shown in the following example (*see* next page). Re-save the form using the **Save this form** option from the **Layout** menu.

```
······▼·1····▼····2·▼·····3·▼······▼·······▼·5·····▼···6···▼····7·▼·····
```

┌─────────────────────────┐
│ PROPERTY DETAILS   │
└─────────────────────────┘

Property Address: XXXXXXXXXXXXXXXXXXXXXXXXX
                  XXXXXXXXXXXXXXXXXXXX   Agent: XXXX
                  XXXXXXXXXX XXXXXXXXXX

Type of property: X   Age of property: XX   Number of bedrooms: 99
Number of receptions: 99   Garden?   L   Garage?   L
Freehold?   L   Price: 9999999.99   Date Taken: DD/MM/YY

Owners name and telephone number: XXXXXXXXXXXXXXXXXXXXXXXX XXXXXXXXXXX
Commission rate: 9.99 Cost of adverts: 99999.99 Date sold: DD/MM/YY

12.8   Moving a field

You have now added all the fields to the form apart from the COMMENTS field
which is a memo field. At the moment there is not sufficient room to display the
memo prompt. To make room, you will move the AGENT field up.

If you need to move or copy information on the form you must first highlight the
information. To do this, move the cursor to the first character to be moved or copied
and press F6. You will be prompted (at the bottom of the screen) to complete the
selection with Enter. Before doing this, highlight (using the arrow keys) all the
required information and then press Enter.

To move the highlighted information, move the cursor to the required position and
press F7. If, by moving the information to the new position, other information is
going to be overwritten, dBASE will prompt you with the message *Delete covered
text & fields?(Y/N)*. If you had not intended to delete the covered text, type **N** for No
at this point.

To copy the highlighted information to a new position follow the same procedure for
moving but press F8 instead of F7.

1   Move the cursor to the beginning of the Agent prompt. Press F6 and use the
    right arrow (→) to highlight the prompt and the field (to the end of the Xs).
    Press Enter to confirm.

2   Move the cursor to row 2 column 56 and press F7 to move. Press
    Enter to confirm. Move any other fields or prompts that may be incorrectly
    placed.

12.9   Adding memo fields to a form

When adding or editing memo data you press F9 to *zoom* in on the data. Ideally you should include this information on the form.

When using the default append and edit screens, the whole screen opens up when you zoom in on the memo field. When creating a form, you can determine exactly how large the memo window is to be. You can make it as large as the screen or you can make it smaller so that other information on the screen can still be seem.

To add a memo field press F5 in the usual way and select the field from the list. Press Ctrl + End to accept the display attributes. You will then be prompted to position the cursor at the top left-hand corner of the memo window.

```
Form      C:\dbase\data\PROPERTY   Row:4 Col:51    File:Property    Num      Ins
    Position upper left of memo window with cursor keys, complete with ENTER
```

So, if you want the memo window to take up the whole screen you would position the cursor at the top left-hand corner of the screen. Complete with Enter. In exactly the same way as you drew the boxes, you now have to stretch the window to its full size. Again, complete with Enter. You will now be asked to position the *memo marker*.

```
Form      C:\dbase\data\PROPERTY   Row:0 Col:0     File:Property    Num      Ins
       Position memo marker with cursor keys, complete with ENTER
```

The memo marker is simply the word MEMO which will appear on the form. When the cursor is moved to this field and F9 pressed, the window will open up to the defined size so that the memo data can be added or edited. To position the marker, move the cursor to the required position and press Enter.

1. You need to add the **COMMENTS** field to the form. Add the field in the usual way pressing Ctrl + End to accept the display attributes. Do not worry about positioning the field at this stage.

2. Position the cursor at the top left-hand corner of the screen and press Enter. Stretch the window to the bottom right-hand corner of the screen and press Enter again. You will be prompted to position the memo marker. Move the cursor to row 4 column 56 and press Enter. The memo marker will now be displayed.

3. Type the help information as displayed in the following screen (*see* next page).

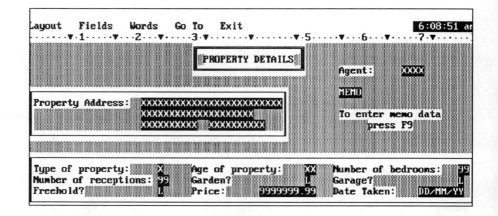

12.10   Saving the form and exiting

To save the form and exit from the form environment, access the **Exit** menu and select the **Save changes and exit** option.

Exit from the form by accessing the **Exit** menu and selecting the **Save changes and exit** option.

12.11   Using the form

Whenever you open the database the form will be opened as well. To see your form whenever you add or edit records, move to the **Forms** panel, and select the required form before adding or editing records.

1   Making sure that the **PROPERTY** database is open, move to the **Forms** panel and press F2 to edit or browse the data using the form. If you access the browse mode press F2 again, to toggle to edit mode. You will now be able to page up and down through your records, displayed with the created form.

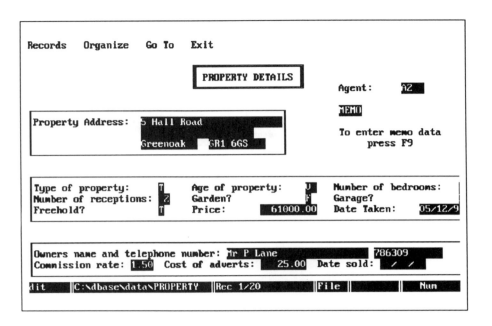

2   Exit from edit mode and close all files.

12.12   Consolidation exercises

 Create a screen form for the **CUSTOMER** database. The example below and on the next page show one possible layout for the form and memo window.

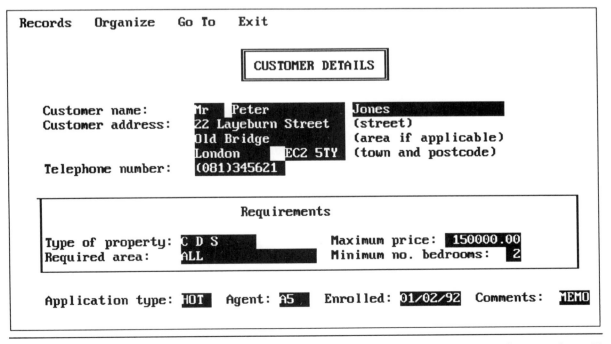

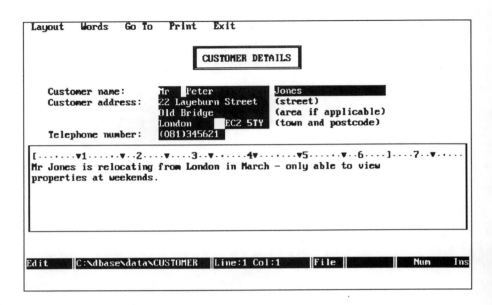

```
  Layout   Words   Go To   Print   Exit

                         ┌─────────────────────┐
                         │   CUSTOMER DETAILS   │
                         └─────────────────────┘

     Customer name:      Mr   Peter          Jones
     Customer address:   22 Layeburn Street   (street)
                         Old Bridge           (area if applicable)
                         London      EC2 5TY  (town and postcode)
     Telephone number:   (081)345621

  [········▼1·····▼··2····▼····3··▼·····4▼······▼5·····▼··6····]····7··▼·····
  Mr Jones is relocating from London in March - only able to view
  properties at weekends.




  Edit    ║C:\dbase\data\CUSTOMER  ║Line:1 Col:1    ║File ║          ║ Num    Ins
```

List the structure of the **STAFF** database to the printer. Use the structure listing to design a screen form. Use the space below to design the screen:

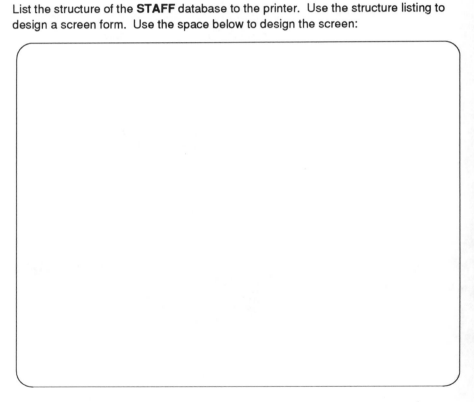

If you require further practice, create a screen form for your personal database.

See Apendix 1, page 250 for solutions.

13 The dBASE Application Generator

The last panel in the Control Centre is the **Applications** panel. The **Applications** panel is designed to enable you to write dBASE programs (*see* Part 3) or use the dBASE Applications Generator to create complete *applications*. An application is usually made up of one or more menus and is designed to *pull together* the files you have created using the other panels.

In this chapter you will create a very simple application which will give access, via a menu, to the PROPERTY database. You will be able to add, edit and delete records and print the report.

13.1 Preparing for this chapter

In order to complete this chapter you need the following files:

File name	File type	Chapter
ESTATE	Catalog	4
PROPERTY	Database	4
PROPERTY	Form	12
CUSTOMER	Database	5
CUSTOMER	Form	12
CUSTOMER	Label	11
PRICE	Index tag	10
ALL	Query	8
ALL	Report	9
COMMENTS	Query	9
COMMENTS	Report	9

 If you have not created these files in the previous chapters you will need to refer back to the chapter numbers listed above and create the files.

 If you have purchased the disks that accompany this book you can copy the necessary files from the appropriate floppy disk. To do this, complete the following instructions:

 1 Make sure you have created a sub-directory on the hard disk called DBASE\DATA (*see* Setting-up a data directory, page viii).

2 Load dBASE (*see* 3.2 Starting the program, page 9).

3 Follow the instructions for Using the diskettes on page viii. The batch file is called **C13**.

Creating an application

To create an application use the same process as for creating any other file. Move the cursor to the **Create** option in the **Applications** panel and press Enter .

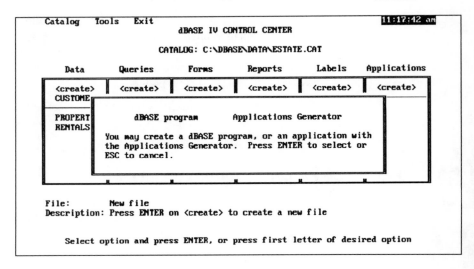

At this stage you can either create a dBASE program or use the Applications Generator.

If you choose to use the Applications Generator, you will be prompted for the following:

- application name and description
- the type of menu (bar, pop_up or batch)
- main menu name (should follow DOS rules for file naming)
- database or view to be used in the application
- the order of the records (the name of the tag to be used)

Once you have filled in the details press Ctrl + End to confirm.

1 Move to the **Applications** panel and select the **Create** option. Select the **Applications Generator** option.

2 Enter the following:

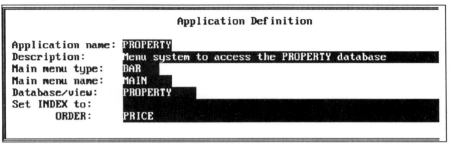

```
                          Application Definition

Application name: PROPERTY
Description:      Menu system to access the PROPERTY database
Main menu type:   BAR
Main menu name:   MAIN
Database/view:    PROPERTY
Set INDEX to:
        ORDER:    PRICE
```

3 Press **Ctrl + End** to confirm.

You are now presented with a sign on banner. The details in this banner will be displayed every time the application is run.

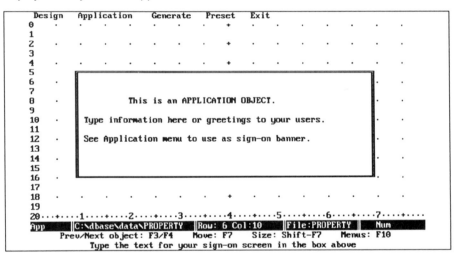

```
 Design    Application    Generate    Preset    Exit
0   .    .     .     .     .     .     +     .     .     .     .     .     .
1   .
2   .    .     .     .     .     .     +     .     .     .     .     .     .
3
4   .    .     .     .     .     .     +     .     .     .     .     .     .
5
6   .    ┌──────────────────────────────────────────────────────┐     .     .
7        │                                                        │
8   .    │            This is an APPLICATION OBJECT.              │     .     .
9        │                                                        │
10  .    │ Type information here or greetings to your users.      │     .     .
11       │                                                        │
12  .    │ See Application menu to use as sign-on banner.         │     .     .
13       │                                                        │
14  .    │                                                        │     .     .
15       │                                                        │
16  .    └──────────────────────────────────────────────────────┘     .     .
17
18  .    .     .     .     .     .     +     .     .     .     .     .     .
19
20...+....1....+....2....+....3....+....4....+....5....+....6....+....7....+....
 App    C:\dbase\data\PROPERTY   Row: 6 Col:10   File:PROPERTY    Num
         Prev/Next object: F3/F4    Move: F7    Size: Shift-F7    Menus: F10
              Type the text for your sign-on screen in the box above
```

To delete the existing text, move the cursor to a line containing text and press **Ctrl + Y**. All the text can be deleted in this way leaving a blank box. You can then enter your own text.

Delete the text in the banner box and enter the text shown in the following illustration:

```
┌──────────────────────────────────────────────┐
│                                                │
│                                                │
│                                                │
│                 PROPERTY DETAILS               │
│                                                │
│               FOR XYZ ESTATE AGENTS            │
│                                                │
│                                                │
│                                                │
└──────────────────────────────────────────────┘
```

Even after defining the banner it will not be displayed when running the application unless you set the **Display sign on banner** option from the **Application** menu to **Yes**.

Access the **Applications** menu and select the **Display sign-on banner** option. Select **Yes**. Press Esc to remove the menu.

13.3   Generating a quick application

You now have the straightforward task of creating a *quick application*.

1 To generate a quick application, access the **Application** menu and select the **Generate quick application** option. Fill in the screen as shown below entering your own name as the application author:

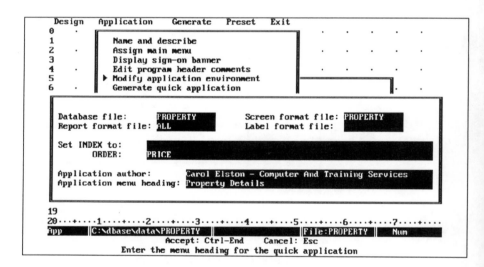

2 Press Ctrl + End to confirm.

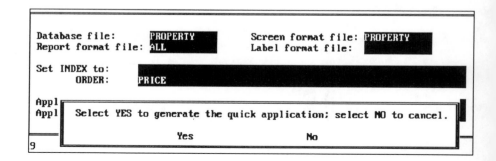

3 Select the **Yes** option to generate. dBASE will generate the required code. When finished, the prompt *Generation is complete. Press any key..* is displayed. Press any key as prompted, generation is now complete.

4 Save the application by accessing the **Exit** menu and select the **Save all changes and exit** option.

13.4   Running an application

To run an application, highlight the application name in the **Application** panel of the Control Centre and press ⌷ **Enter** ⌷. There are two choices; **Run application** or **Modify application**.

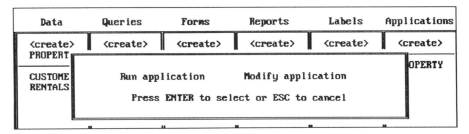

 1 Run the application called **PROPERTY**. When you select the **Run application** option you will be prompted with a message *Are you sure?*, respond with the **Yes** option.

The first time the program is run, dBASE will *compile* the code. By compiling, dBASE changes the code to a form that is quicker to process. When finished, press any key and the sign on banner will appear. The application menu will then be displayed:

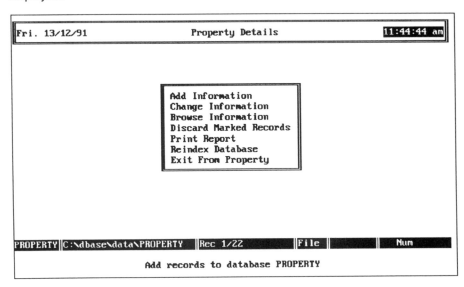

2 Test the application by following the points on the next page:

- Select the **Add** option - you should see a blank template displayed using your screen form - add the following record and then access the **Exit** menu and select the **Exit** option.

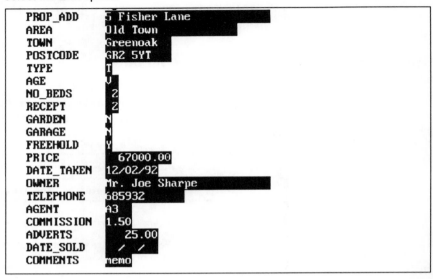

```
PROP_ADD      5 Fisher Lane
AREA          Old Town
TOWN          Greenoak
POSTCODE      GR2 5YT
TYPE          T
AGE           U
NO_BEDS       2
RECEPT        2
GARDEN        N
GARAGE        N
FREEHOLD      Y
PRICE            67000.00
DATE_TAKEN    12/02/92
OWNER         Mr. Joe Sharpe
TELEPHONE     685932
AGENT         A3
COMMISSION    1.50
ADVERTS          25.00
DATE_SOLD      /  /
COMMENTS      memo
```

- Select the **Change** option - again the screen form is used to display the current record - exit

- Select the **Browse** option - move across to the **PRICE** field and notice that the records are ordered by price - mark the last record entered for deletion

- Select **Discard marked records** - this option will pack the database removing any records marked for deletion - when complete, press any key to continue

```
Position by

SEEK Record
GOTO Record
LOCATE Record
Return
```

- Select the **Print report** option - a positioning menu is displayed to allow you to position the record pointer before printing - to print the entire report select the **Return** option - you now have the option to display the report on the screen, as labels or to the printer

- Select the **Reindex database** option - this will re-generate all the index tags associated with the **PROPERTY** database - this can be a useful option if you suspect that the index files may have become corrupted

- Select the **Exit** option to return to the Control Centre

1   Create a simple application for the **CUSTOMER** database. The application will use the following files :

Database   **CUSTOMER**
Index tag   **NAME**
Form   **CUSTOMER**
Report   **COMMENTS**
Label   **CUSTOMER**

2   Test the application.

See Appendix 1, page 252 for solutions.

14   Consolidation

This chapter is designed to include all the topics covered in Part 1. The completion of the tasks is optional as the files created will not be referred to in the later chapters.

The files created in this chapter are not available on disk but a sample solution can be found in Appendix 1.

14.1   The scenario

The estate agents have decided to expand operations and manage properties on a rental basis. They have already started taking properties onto their books and have been running a manual system for the past two months. They have now decided to proceed with this side of the business and computerise the records.

The manual records include the following details:

- property owner's name

- address of the property

- home and work telephone numbers of the owner

- asking rent (monthly)

- type of property - using the same codes as used for the PROPERTY database:

    D - Detached
    C - Cottage
    F - Flat
    T - Terrace
    S - Semi

- number of bedrooms and reception rooms

- whether the property has a garage or garden

- agent dealing with the property (A1 - A6)

- commission rate being charged for renting the property - as a rule of thumb this will be 10% for rents of under £500 per month and 12% for more expensive properties

- date the property is rented

- general comments

Creating the database

 1 Use dBASE to create a database to hold the manual records. Call the database **RENTALS**. The new database should be part of the **ESTATE** catalog. Design the structure below:

Field name	Field type	Field width	Dec

➲ Add the following details to the database (all properties are in Greenoak), including suitable memo information:

1 Mr J Brown has a 2 bed-roomed cottage to rent with 1 reception room and both garage and garden. The address is 10 Hanover Lane, Lumley GR4 7JP. His home phone number is 897532. He can be reached at work on (098) 765231. The asking rent is £400 per month. The property is to be managed by Agent 5 for a commission rate of 10%.

2 Mrs Linda Farrow has a 2 bed-roomed flat to rent with 1 reception room. The property has neither garage nor garden. The address is 156 High Street, Old Town GR2 6YT. Her home phone number is 894321. The asking rent is £375 per month. The property is to be managed by Agent 4 for a commission rate of 12%.

3 Mr Terry Parker has a 4 bed-roomed detached property to rent with 2 reception rooms and both garage and garden. The address is 21 Littlebrook Ave, Farley GR7 8TY. His home phone number is 785431. He can be reached at work on 987432. The asking rent is £670 per month. The property is to be managed by Agent 2 for a commission rate of 10%.

4 Miss Karen Harris has a 2 bed-roomed flat to rent with 1 reception room and garage but no garden. The address is 12a Princes Lane, Lumley GR4 7TF. Her home phone number is 765194. She can be reached at work on 785902. The asking rent is £350 per month. The property is to be managed by Agent 3 for a commission rate of 12%.

5 Mr Brian Douglas has a 1 bed-roomed flat to rent with 1 reception room and neither garage nor garden. The address is 26 High Street, GR1 8YT. His home phone number is 876983. The asking rent is £275 per month. The property is to be managed by Agent 4 for a commission rate of 12%.

6 Mr Henry Jay has a 3 bed-roomed semi to rent with 2 reception rooms and both garage and garden. The address is 32 Greebank Road, Lumley GR4 7YT. His home phone number is 567392. He can be reached at work on 998321. The asking rent is £500 per month. The property is to be managed by Agent 4 for a commission rate of 10%.

7 Mrs Frances Dover has a 1 bed-roomed flat to rent with 1 reception room and garage but no garden. The address is 56b High Street, Old Town GR2 6GH. Her home phone number is 985621. The asking rent is £250 per month. The property is to be managed by Agent 3 for a commission rate of 12%.

8 Mr D Hughes has a 3 bed-roomed detached property to rent with 2 reception rooms and both garage and garden. The address is 21 Jasmin Lane, Farley GR8 2HG. His home phone number is 679342. He can be reached at work on 982341. The asking rent is £600 per month. The property is to be managed by Agent 1 for a commission rate of 12%.

9 Mrs J Clare has a 2 bed-roomed flat to rent with 1 reception room and neither garage nor garden. The address is Flat 2, 9 Buck Lane, Old Town GR2 8JK. Her home phone number is 874563. The asking rent is £300 per month. The property is to be managed by Agent 2 for a commission rate of 12%.

10 Miss Diane Glover has a 3 bed-roomed terrace to rent with 2 reception rooms and neither garage nor garden. The address is 12 The Avenue, GR1 6JK. Her home phone number is 985342. She can be reached at work on 956412. The asking rent is £400 per month. The property is to be managed by Agent 1 for a commission rate of 12%.

See Appendix 1, page 253 for solutions.

14.3   Viewing and changing the database data and structure

1 Open the **RENTALS** database and browse the data.

2 Lock the field(s) containing the owner's name and scroll the remaining fields so that you can see the owner's work telephone number and the rent.

3 Search for the first property in the file managed by Agent 3.

4 Add two more records to the database. They are both flats. Use the ditto key to enter the property type for the second record.

5 Switch to edit mode, page up or down to record 6 and change the home telephone number to 895215.

6 Move to record 8 and change the area of the property to Lumley. Undo this last change.

7 Delete the last record and pack the database.

8 You need to add a new field to the database to hold the date that the property will be available for rent. Change the structure of the database to include this new field and then edit the existing records and add appropriate dates.

See Appendix 1, page 254 for solutions.

14.4   Querying the database

Use the *Query by example* feature to find the following:

1 You have a customer who wants to rent a one bedroom flat. List the owner's name, home telephone number, the area and rent for all such flats.

2 You have a customer wanting to rent a property in Lumley for less than £450 per month. Do you have any on your books?

3 A customer is desperate to rent a property with the only criteria, that there must be a garage.

4 A customer needs to rent a property immediately. Do you have any properties that are available now?

5 A customer is looking for a flat or terrace property in Farley. Do you have any at the moment?

6   A customer has been told about a property you have for rent in Jasmin Lane but they are not sure of the number. Can you find the details? (use the $ operator).

7   Create a query for each type of property on our books displaying a sub-set of fields. Save the queries as **COTTAGE**, **DETACHED**, **FLAT**, **TERRACE** and **SEMI**. Access one of the queries from the Control Centre.

See Appendix 1, page 255 for solutions.

14.5   **Indexing, reports and labels**

1   Produce an index tag for the **RENTALS** database so that the records appear in order with lowest rent to highest rent.

2   Making sure that the **RENTALS** database is open with the new index, create a report. List the address, type, number of bedrooms and rent.

[Tip: Either create a query containing these fields and then produce the report on the query (using the **Quick layout** option), or use the entire database as a basis for the report and bring the fields into the report one by one.]

3   Produce name and address labels for all the property owners.

See Appendix 1, page 257 for solutions.

14.6   **Forms and applications**

1   Produce a data entry form for the **RENTALS** database. Print the structure of the database and design the layout for the form on paper before using dBASE to create the form.

2   Produce a simple application to access the **RENTALS** database.

See Appendix 1, page 259 for solutions.

Part 2

Dot Prompt

15 Objectives

The objective of this Part is two-fold:

- To learn the syntax of the dBASE language by initially repeating the operations carried out in Part 1 while entering the commands at the dot prompt. You will then look at additional dBASE commands that cannot be accessed via the Control Centre.

- To look at some more advanced features that can be used at the dot prompt or incorporated in the files created from within the Control Centre. This will involve producing more complex reports, queries and screen forms.

15.1 Preparing for this Part

If you have completed Part 1 you will have generated all the files necessary to begin this part. If you are starting from this point, you will need to either copy the files from the Part 2 diskette or return to the relevant chapters in Part 1 to create the files.

 If working through this part without the accompanying disks, you will need to create the following files. You can either create them all now, or create them as they are needed. You will find individual lists of the required files at the beginning of each chapter.

File name	File type	Chapter
ESTATE	Catalog	4
PROPERTY	Database	4
CUSTOMER	Database	5
STAFF	Database	4
CUSTOMER	Form	12
PROPERTY	Form	12
ALL	Query	8
ALL	Report	9

If you have purchased the disks that accompany this book you can copy the necessary files from the appropriate floppy disk. To do this, complete the following instructions (*see* next page):

1 Make sure that you have created a sub-directory on the hard disk called
   DBASE\DATA (*see* Setting-up a data directory, page viii).

2 Load dBASE (*see* 3.2 Starting the program, page 9).

3 Follow the instructions for Using the diskettes on page viii. The batch file is
   called **C15**.

16   Commands at the Dot Prompt

Part 1 explained how to create and modify dBASE files from within the Control Centre. When issuing any instruction from within the Control Centre dBASE generates a standard command using the dBASE language and syntax rules. In this chapter you will go briefly through the topics covered in Part 1, looking at how the instructions could be issued directly in the dBASE language. The majority of the commands covered in this chapter have been discussed in detail in Part 1. If you are unsure of any aspect, refer to the background information in the appropriate chapter.

16.1   Preparing for this chapter

In order to complete this chapter you need the following files:

File name	File type	Chapter
ESTATE	Catalog	4
PROPERTY	Database	4
CUSTOMER	Database	5
CUSTOMER	Form	12
PROPERTY	Form	12

 If you have not created these files in the previous chapters you will need to refer back to to the chapter number listed above and create the files.

 If you have purchased the disks that accompany this book you can copy the necessary files from the appropriate floppy disk. Refer to 15.1 Preparing for this Part, page 114. Use the batch file **C15**.

16.2   Moving between environments

> Exit to dot prompt
> Quit to DOS

To issue a dBASE command you need to access the Dot Prompt environment. To access the Dot Prompt from the Control Centre press $\boxed{\text{Alt + E}}$ to access the **Exit** menu and select the **Exit to dot prompt** option.

> Are you sure you want
> to abandon operation?
>
> Yes   No

The keyboard shortcut for exiting to the Dot Prompt is the $\boxed{\text{Esc}}$ key. You will be prompted to respond **Yes** or **No** to this request.

To return to the Control Centre *either* press $\boxed{\text{F2}}$ *or* type **ASSIST** and press $\boxed{\text{Enter}}$ whilst at the Dot Prompt.

1 Move from the Control Centre to the Dot Prompt using the **Exit** menu.

2 Use the Esc key to move back to the Dot Prompt.

Status bar

As you will probably have noticed, the Dot Prompt environment is not particularly user friendly. The only helpful information is on the *status bar* situated at the bottom of the screen.

`Command`   `NumCaps Ins`

 If your system is not displaying the status bar it is because your copy of dBASE has been configured with the status bar turned off. To display the status bar type **SET STATUS ON** and press the Enter key.

The status bar displays the name of the active database (if there is a database in use), the current record and whether the Insert , Caps Lock and Num Lock keys are on.

Help

```
Syntax error

SET CATALOG ESTATE

Cancel  Edit  Help
```

Help can be accessed by pressing F1 at any time. As within the Control Centre the help given is context sensitive. If accessing a command the help will be applicable to that command. If you enter a command that is incorrect dBASE will automatically offer you three options, to **Cancel** the command, **Edit** the command or obtain **Help**.

If you choose the help option, dBASE will give help on the appropriate command.

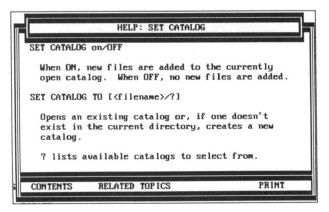

History

One of the biggest drawbacks to entering commands at the Dot Prompt is that you have to type! If you are a two finger typist prone to spelling mistakes the **History** feature will certainly be a help. dBASE History allows you to scroll through the last 20 commands issued and either re-issue the command or edit the command if you have made a typing mistake. You will use this facility throughout Part 2.

Another handy tip, all dBASE commands can be abbreviated to the first four characters. Database names and field names must always be entered in full.

16.4   Using a database and modifying the data

Set catalog to

The first step when opening a database is to access the appropriate catalog. To do this type either of the following commands where <filename> is the name of the catalog:

SET CATALOG TO ?
SET CATALOG TO <filename>

By using the ? , dBASE provides a list of available catalogs.

1   Type the following command at the dot prompt:

     SET CATALOG TO ESTATE

2   Press **Enter** to complete the command.

Use

To open a database which is part of the current catalog type **USE ?**.

A list of available database files will be given. Alternatively you can include the name of the database. For example, **USE PROPERTY**. This will open the specified database directly. This second approach can also be used to add a database to the current catalog. If a catalog is open and you open a database that is not currently in that catalog the database will be added to the catalog.

1   Open the **CUSTOMER** database by typing **USE CUSTOMER**. Note the change to the status bar.

| Command | C:\dbase\data\CUSTOMER | Rec 1/10 | File | | Num |

2   Open the **PROPERTY** database by typing **USE ?** and selecting the appropriate database.

Close

The **Close** command can be used with a file name or the command **All**. **CLOSE DATABASES** will close the database(s) currently in use. **CLOSE ALL** will close all databases and associated files eg screen formats, reports etc.

 Type **CLOSE DATABASES**. The status bar will be cleared showing that the current database is no longer in use.

16.5   Adding records

To add records to a database you must first open the database using the **Use** command.

Append

Once opened the **Append** command will add a blank record to the end of the database and display the default data entry template.

 1   Add a record to the **PROPERTY** database.

USE PROPERTY
APPEND

Notice that when a field is full (for example, the **DATE_TAKEN** field) a bell sounds and the cursor automatically moves to the next field.

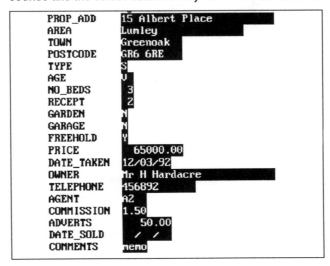

2   Add the following comment to the memo field; **This Victorian semi has been on the market with another agent for over a year. With this more realistic price it should sell quickly.**

Set format to

If you have created a customised data entry form you can open it from the dot prompt by either typing **SET FORMAT TO <filename>**, where filename is the name of the format file, or **SET FORMAT TO ?** and then choose from the list.

Set bell off

By default the bell is **On** as you witnessed when you appended the last record. The bell is designed to warn you that the field is full and that the cursor will automatically move to the next field. If you are a speed typist you may find that you have pressed the **Enter** key to move to the next field before realising that dBASE has moved for you!

Set confirm on

As well as turning the bell off you can also turn confirm on. Although usually set **Off**, by setting confirm **On** you are telling dBASE not to automatically move to the next field. When confirm is set to **On** you will need to press the **Enter** key to move to the next field even if the current field is full.

1   Type the following at the dot prompt to demonstrate a range of commands:

    CLOSE ALL
    CLEAR
    SET BELL OFF
    SET CONFIRM ON
    USE PROPERTY
    SET FORMAT TO PROPERTY
    APPEND

2   Add another record. You should find that the bell no longer sounds and that you need to press the **Enter** key at the end of every field. Exit to the dot prompt.

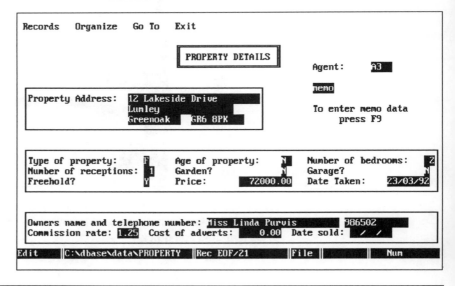

3 Press ⬆ seven times. The **Close all** command should be displayed.

4 Press **Enter** to activate the command. Press ⬆ to the **Clear** command and activate the command. This is known as *using history*.

16.6 Moving around the database

The following commands can be used to move around the database:

Go The **Go** command can be used to move to a particular record. For example, **Go 5** will move the record pointer to record number 5. The command **Go** can, in fact, be excluded. Typing **5** at the dot prompt will have the same effect.

Go top The **Go top** command will move the record pointer to the first record in the database. This will be record 1 in a non-indexed database.

Go bottom The **Go bottom** command will move the record pointer to the last record in the database.

Skip The **Skip** command will move the record pointer to the next record in the database. **Skip** can be followed by a positive or negative number depending on the number of records to be skipped. For example, **Skip 10** will move the record pointer on 10 records. **Skip -10** will move the record pointer back 10 records

16.7 Browsing and editing

Browse

The **Browse** command will display the database in a tabular format. Once browsing the data you can display a single record by pressing **F2**.

Records Organize Fields Go To Exit				
SURNAME	FIRSTNAME	TITLE	STREET	AREA
Jones	Peter	Mr	22 Layeburn Street	Old Bridge
Kemp	Mary	Miss	38 Fairfield Lane	Lumley
Jones	Fred	Mr	12 Portland Rd	Chapelforth
Samuals	Deborah	Ms	32 Lemming Lane	Lumley
Hughes	Linda	Miss	12 The Avenue	Farley
Smith	John	Mr	45 Hargarth Street	
Price	Jill	Mrs	32 Wayside Ave	Old Town
Kelly	P	Mr	6 Levin Way	Lumley
Hill	David	Mr	12 Young Street	Lumley
Summers	Kevin	Mr	45 Lowham Road	Kingley

Edit

The **Edit** command will access the current record and display the fields using the default data entry form or a customised screen form if open.

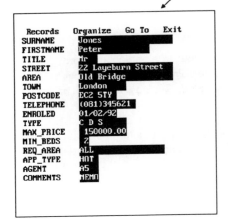

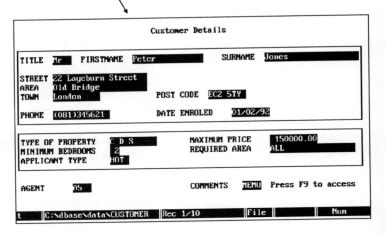

Once in edit mode, the F2 key will toggle to browse mode. By pressing F2 again you will return to edit mode.

To edit a particular record follow the **Edit** command with the record number, eg **Edit 6** will edit record number 6 in the current database.

Using the edit and browse modes is covered in detail in Chapter 5. The editing facilities are covered in Chapter 6.

1　Open the **CUSTOMER** database. Type **BROWSE** to view the records in browse mode. Press Escape to exit without saving.

2　Type **SET FORMAT TO CUSTOMER** to open the screen form. Type **EDIT** to view the current record in edit mode. Exit without saving. Close the database and clear the screen.

16.8　Deleting, recalling and packing records

Delete

The **Delete** command will mark the current record for deletion. The following show some examples of this command.

Delete record　　The **Delete record 10** option will mark record 10 for deletion.

Delete all	**Delete all** will mark all the records in the current database for deletion.
Delete next	The **Delete next 10** option will mark the next 10 records for deletion (including the current record).

Recall

The **Recall** command will unmark the current record for deletion.

Recall record	**Recall record** followed by a number will recall the specified record if it is currently marked for deletion.
Recall all	The **Recall all** option will recall all records which are currently marked for deletion.
Recall next	The **Recall next 5** option will recall the next 5 records if they are marked for deletion.

Pack

Until the **Pack** command is issued any record marked for deletion can be recalled. By packing the database, the records marked for deletion are removed. When a database is packed all associated index tags are re-generated.

1   Open the **PROPERTY** database and delete records **5, 10** and **12**.

2   Recall record **5**.

3   Delete the next five records. Access browse mode, the DEL indicator will be displayed at the bottom of the screen for all deleted records.

4   Exit to the dot prompt. Recall all records.

5   Delete the last record added to the **PROPERTY** database earlier in this chapter.

6   Pack the database.

16.9   Creating, opening and modifying files

You have already seen how to open a database file. Listed below are the commands to create, open and modify the different file types already looked at in Part 1. Each command should be followed by the file name. (These are just examples and are not intended to be entered at this stage.)

Create	creates a new database file. For example, **CREATE STAFF** will create a new database file called staff.

Modify structure	allows you to change the structure of the current database.
Index on..tag..	creates a new index tag for the current database. For example: **INDEX ON PRICE TAG PRICE** **INDEX ON SURNAME+FIRSTNAME TAG FULLNAME**
Set order to tag	makes the specified tag the master. The tag can also be set at the time of opening the database. The following examples produce the same result: **USE PROPERTY ORDER TAG PRICE** **USE PROPERTY** **SET ORDER TO TAG PRICE**
Create view	creates a new **Query** file.
Set view to	opens a **Query by example** (QBE) file.
Modify view	modifies the specified **Query** file.
Set format to	opens the specified screen form. The database must be open first.
Create screen	creates a new screen form for the current database.
Modify screen	modifies the specified screen form.
Report form	displays the specified report to the screen. The report is printed if the option **To print** is added to the command. Conditions can also be included within the command. For example: **REPORT FORM PROPERTY TO PRINT** **REPORT FORM PROPERTY FOR TYPE="F"**
Create report	creates a new report for the current database.
Modify report	modifies the specified report.
Label form	works in the same way as the **Report form** command. Labels are created using the **Create label** command and modified by the **Modify label** command.

Consolidation exercise

This consolidation exercise is designed to reinforce topics covered in Part 1 and introduce the use of a range of commands at the dot prompt. If you are starting the book at this point, it is strongly recommended that you complete this exercise before continuing. If you incur any problems, initially refer to the appropriate Chapter in Part 1. If you require further help, a detailed solution can be found in Appendix 2.

Complete the following tasks by entering commands at the dot prompt.

1　Open the **ESTATE** catalog and open the **PROPERTY** database and **PROPERTY** screen form.

2　Go to record number **5** and change the **DATE_TAKEN** field to **17/02/92**. Save the change.

3　Add a new record to the database. Save the record.

4　Delete the record you have just added and pack the database.

5　Create a Query file for the **CUSTOMER** database, call it **GRCUSTS**. Include the following fields in the query; **TITLE, SURNAME, STREET, AREA, TOWN, POSTCODE**.

6　Restrict the records included in the query to customers who live in Greenoak. Save the query.

7　Create a report called **GRCUSTS** using the **GRCUSTS** query file. This report will be in the form of a letter.

8　Select the **Quick layout**, **Mailmerge layout** options from the **Layout** menu.

9　Select the **Modify ruler** option from the **Words** menu. Move across to the seven inch marker and type a closing square bracket, ⊡ , to set the right margin.

10　Access the **Bands** menu and make sure that the **Word wrap band** is set to **Yes**.

11　Add the following fields and text to the details band:

TITLE SURNAME
STREET
AREA
TOWN POSTCODE

today's date

Dear TITLE SURNAME

12 Complete the letter in the following way:

As outlined in our recent newsletter, an advertisement feature will appear in next week's edition of the Greenoak Times. The feature will include all properties currently on offer for both sale and rent.

I have enclosed a voucher which can be exchanged for a free copy of the paper at Dalton's newsagents in the High Street.

Yours sincerely,

Your name
Advertising Director

13 Display the report to screen from the dot prompt.

14 Restrict the report further by adding a condition to the command issued in 7. Only send the letter to customers living in Lumley. Print the letters.

See Appendix 2, page 262 for solutions.

17   Querying at the dot prompt

In Chapter 8 you learnt how to produce Query by example files (*see* Chapter 18 for more advanced querying using the Query by example facility). This chapter will consider the commands available from the dot prompt which allow you to display and query data.

17.1   Preparing for this chapter

In order to complete this chapter you need the following files:

File name	File type	Chapter
ESTATE	Catalog	4
PROPERTY	Database	4
CUSTOMER	Database	5

 If you have not created these files in the previous chapters you will need to refer back to to the chapter number listed above and create the files.

 If you have purchased the disks that accompany this book you can copy the necessary files from the appropriate floppy disk. To do this, complete the following instructions:

1. Make sure that you have created a sub-directory on the hard disk called DBASE\DATA (*see* Setting-up a data directory, page viii).

2. Load dBASE (*see* 3.2 Starting the program, page 9).

3. Follow the instructions for Using the diskettes on page viii. The batch file is called **C17**.

17.2   List and display

The **List** command lists all the records in the current database to the screen. Used in this form, the **List** command is only suitable for displaying the contents of a database with a limited number of fields and records. If the database has a total field width exceeding 80 characters, the data will wrap round onto the next line. If there are more than 22 records the data will scroll past and only the last 22 records will be in view. The **List** command is usually used to list records to the printer. To do this type **LIST TO PRINT**.

The **Display** command displays the current record. The **Display all** command has the same effect as the **List** command except that the display pauses after a screenful of records so that the data can be read. The prompt "Press any key to continue" is displayed.

Both the **Display** and **List** commands can include the **Off** option to turn off the record numbers.

Field headings can be turned off by including the **Set heading off** command before issuing the **Display** or **List** command.

17.3 Limiting fields

With large databases you will need to limit the fields that are displayed with the **List** or **Display** commands. You can do this by listing the required fields separated by commas (,).

 1 Type the following at the dot prompt:

USE PROPERTY
DISPLAY ALL PROP_ADD, AREA, TYPE, AGE, PRICE

```
Record#  prop_add                area            type age        price
      1  5 Hall Road                             T    U       61000.00
      2  89 Cliff Road           Lumley          F    N       51000.00
      3  6 Brook Road            Farley          T    U       55000.00
      4  4 Hever Court           Old Town        D    M      150000.00
      5  6 Elm Road              Lumley          T    E       89000.00
      6  90 Pimly Rise           Lumley          C    O       92000.00
      7  43 Trewitt Ave          Farley          D    PR     125000.00
      8  23 Yew Bank Drive       Lumley          D    PO     167000.00
      9  32 Leder Road           Old Town        C    U       80000.00
     10  8 Oak Lane              Farley          S    PO      99000.00
     11  76 Ruin Grove           Old Town        T    U       63000.00
     12  9 Bookers Avenue        Lumley          S    PR      65000.00
     13  56 Rainforest Way       Farley          D    N      340000.00
     14  7 Kelly Park Drive      Lumley          S    M       83000.00
     15  6 Kirk Way                              F    M       48000.00
     16  90 Otway Road           Farley          D    E      450000.00
     17  4 Garden Terrace        Old Town        T    U       67000.00
     18  12 Lewis Mount          Lumley          S    M       81000.00
     19  6 Taper Ave             Old Town        F    U       67000.00
     20  13 May Lane             Lumley          C    O      105000.00
Press any key to continue...
```

2 Press ↑ to access the last command and add **OFF** to the end to turn off the record numbers.

DISPLAY ALL PROP_ADD, AREA, TYPE, AGE, PRICE OFF

3 Turn the headings off:

SET HEADING OFF
DISPLAY ALL PROP_ADD, AREA, TYPE, AGE, PRICE OFF
SET HEADING ON

4   If you have a printer attached, type the following:

USE CUSTOMER
LIST FIRSTNAME, SURNAME, TELEPHONE, AGENT TO PRINT

17.4   Limiting records

The following examples use the **Display** command, the syntax for the **List** command is identical.

The records displayed can be limited by specifying a condition. The general syntax is as follows:

DISPLAY <fields> FOR <condition>

Where <fields> is the list of fields to be included and <condition> a valid dBASE statement. If a condition is included the **All** option can be excluded from the **Display** command. The following examples will make this clearer. Type the command line at the dot prompt.

Type the following at the dot prompt:

1   You need to display all the properties in Lumley which you can do by including the condition, **AREA = "Lumley"**. Character text must be included in quotes or square brackets. Be careful with case, if you typed **AREA = "LUMLEY"** (all in capitals) dBASE would not find any matches.

USE PROPERTY
DISP PROP_ADD, TYPE, AGE, AREA FOR AREA = "Lumley"

2   The following command will display all properties which are priced at less than £90,000 (*refer* to page 54, 8.10 *Including criteria numeric fields*, for a full list of numeric operators).

DISP PROP_ADD, TYPE, AGE, PRICE FOR PRICE <90000

3   The following command will display all properties taken onto the books before 1 January 1992.

DISP OWNER, TELEPHONE, DATE_TAKEN FOR DATE_TAKEN <{1/1/92}

4   The following command will display all properties with a garage, ie the **GARAGE** field is set to **True**.

DISP PROP_ADD, PRICE, GARAGE FOR GARAGE

5   The logical **Not** command can be used to exclude records meeting a condition. In this case all properties will be displayed where the **GARDEN** field is **False**.

DISP PROP_ADD, PRICE, GARDEN FOR .NOT. GARDEN

6   The following command uses the logical **And** command. The price must be more than £60,000 and less than £90,000.

DISP PROP_ADD, PRICE FOR PRICE >60000 .AND. PRICE <90000

7   The property must be priced at less than £90,000 and located in the Lumley area.

DISP PROP_ADD, AREA, PRICE FOR PRICE<90000 .AND. AREA="Lumley"

8   The condition can get more complex (up to 240 characters in length). Type the whole command on the one line:

DISP PROP_ADD FOR PRICE<90000 .AND. AREA="Lumley" .AND. NO_BEDS>2

To check that the command is correct, issue the command again but include the **PRICE, AREA** and **NO_BEDS** fields.

9   This command uses the logical **Or** command and will display all properties in Farley OR Lumley.

DISP PROP_ADD, AREA, PRICE FOR AREA="Lumley" .OR. AREA="Farley"

10 Be careful when using the logical **And** and **Or** in the same command. Try entering the next two commands which produce quite different results (type the whole command on the same line):

DISP PROP_ADD, AREA, PRICE FOR AREA="Lumley" .OR. AREA="Farley" .AND. PRICE<90000

```
. disp prop_add,area,price for area ="Farley".or. area="Lumley" .and. price<9000
0
Record#  prop_add                 area                      price
      2  89 Cliff Road            Lumley                 51000.00
      3  6 Brook Road             Farley                 55000.00
      5  6 Elm Road               Lumley                 89000.00
      7  43 Trewitt Ave           Farley                125000.00
     10  8 Oak Lane               Farley                 99000.00
     12  9 Bookers Avenue         Lumley                 65000.00
     13  56 Rainforest Way        Farley                340000.00
     14  7 Kelly Park Drive       Lumley                 83000.00
```

DISP PROP_ADD, AREA, PRICE FOR (AREA="Lumley" .OR. AREA="Farley") .AND. PRICE<90000

```
. disp prop_add,area,price for (area ="Farley".or. area="Lumley") .and. price<90
000
Record#  prop_add                 area                      price
      2  89 Cliff Road            Lumley                 51000.00
      3  6 Brook Road             Farley                 55000.00
      5  6 Elm Road               Lumley                 89000.00
     12  9 Bookers Avenue         Lumley                 65000.00
     14  7 Kelly Park Drive       Lumley                 83000.00
     18  12 Lewis Mount           Lumley                 81000.00
```

In the first example the price criterion is only applied to the **AREA="Farley"** condition. By putting brackets around the area conditions the price criterion applies to both.

11 On occasion you may want to specify a criterion that searches for data held within a field. For example, with the **CUSTOMER** database you have a field called **TYPE**. This field contains the codes for the types of property the customer is interested in. If they would consider purchasing a detached, semi or terraced house the **TYPE** field would be entered as a combination of the codes **D S T**. If you needed to find all customers interested in buying a semi you would need to search for the code **S** within the **TYPE** field. You can do this using the **$** operator (*refer* to page 59, 8.17 *Searching for part of a string*, for further details).

USE CUSTOMER
DISP ALL FIRSTNAME, SURNAME, TELEPHONE, TYPE FOR "S" $ TYPE

```
. display all firstname, surname, telephone, type for "S" $ type
Record#  firstname      surname              telephone    type
     1   Peter          Jones                (081)345621  C D S
     3   Fred           Jones                (0532)33921  T S C
     4   Deborah        Samuels              567432       D S
     7   Jill           Price                456365       F T S
     9   Dennis         Howard               986300       S T
    11   Mary           King                 872190       S T
    12   Joseph         Glover               780254       S D
.
```
```
Command  C:\dbase\data\CUSTOMER    Rec EOF/14        File            Num
```

12 Customers with no particular preference as to the type of the property may have been entered as **ANY**. To display these customers as well you will need to change the command (type the whole command on the same line):

DISP ALL FIRSTNAME, SURNAME, TELEPHONE, TYPE FOR "S" $ TYPE .OR. TYPE="ANY"

13 If there are no records with the **TYPE** field entered as **ANY**, append a record with **TYPE** as **ANY** and repeat the query.

17.5 Finding records (Locate and Seek)

Specific records can be found by specifying a search criterion. There are two methods available, referred to as **Locate** and **Seek**.

The **Locate** command can be used on a non-indexed file. dBASE carries out what is termed a sequential search. It starts at the beginning of the database and searches every record *either* until the record is found *or* the end of the database is reached. If a match is found the **Continue** command can be used to find the next match.

1 Type the following at the dot prompt:

USE PROPERTY
LOCATE FOR TYPE="F"
EDIT

dBASE will point to the first record where the type of property is entered as **F** (Flat). If no match is found, dBASE displays the message "End of locate scope".

2 Press $\boxed{\textbf{Escape}}$ to leave edit mode without saving any changes.

3 The **Continue** command will look for the next record matching the criterion specified in the last **Locate** command. Type **CONTINUE** to locate the next record meeting the criterion. Use **History** to repeat this command until the last match is found.

The **Seek** command is used on a indexed file and is usually quicker than the **Locate** command. The field does not need to be specified as dBASE automatically searches on the index field. The **Seek** command has the added advantage that all matches will be consecutively placed in the indexed file. This alleviates the need for a **Continue** command as the records matching the criterion can be easily viewed in browse mode.

1 Type the following at the dot prompt to create an index tag for the **CUSTOMER** database based on the **SURNAME** field.

USE CUSTOMER
INDEX ON SURNAME TAG SURNAME

2 Once an index is in place, the index tag can be set as the master index at the same time as the database is opened. Type the following:

CLOSE ALL
USE CUSTOMER ORDER TAG SURNAME
SEEK "Smith"
BROWSE

At the end of the search the record pointer will either be pointing to the first record where the surname is Smith or, if there is no match, to the end of file.

3 Press $\boxed{\textbf{Escape}}$ to leave browse mode without saving any changes.

17.6 Using criteria to change data (Replace)

The **Replace** command is one of the most powerful dBASE commands. Although the command can be used to replace the contents of a field in the current record, **Replace** is usually used for global replacing. For example, if you were dealing with personnel records you may want to calculate a 10% pay rise. You could do this by replacing the contents of the salary field with 1.1*salary.

1 You may decide that the property market is in a slump and you need to reduce the price of all properties by a fixed amount. If you decided on a £500 decrease the syntax of the command is as follows:

USE PROPERTY
REPLACE ALL PRICE WITH PRICE-500

2 To cancel this price decrease, repeat the command but change the **- 500** to **+ 500**.

3 You may want to make more selective price cuts. You may decide to reduce the properties by **5%** for those priced over £100,000 and by **3%** if £100,000 or less.

REPLACE ALL PRICE WITH PRICE*.95 FOR PRICE>100000
REPLACE ALL PRICE WITH PRICE*.97 FOR PRICE <=100000

17.7 Consolidation exercises

1 Using the **CUSTOMER** database, list the structure to the printer by typing:

USE CUSTOMER
LIST STRUCTURE TO PRINT

Use this structure listing to help you complete the following:

2 Display all the records only showing the **FIRSTNAME**, **SURNAME** and **TELEPHONE** fields.

3 Display the name and telephone number of the customer and the agent code for all "HOT" customers.

4 Display all customers interested in properties in the £100,000 plus price bracket.

5 Display all customers requiring a property in the town centre - the post code is GR1 (stored as 1 in the **REQ_AREA** field). You will need to use the **$** command. Don't forget that some customers have not specified a preference for area and have been entered as ALL in the **REQ_AREA** field.

6 Display all customers requiring a terrace property with a maximum price limit of £60,000 or more (you will need to use the logical **And** command)

7 Display all customers requiring a semi with a minimum of 3 bedrooms.

8 Display all customers who enrolled in the first quarter of 1992.

9 Display all customers who might be interested in a property in Farley (post code 7,8 or 9) with two bedrooms. Narrow it down further by adding the fact that it is a semi.

10 Open the **PROPERTY** database and print the structure.

11 Use the **Locate** command to find the record numbers of all properties priced at more than £100,000.

12 Index the **PROPERTY** database on the **OWNER** field. Call the index tag **OWNER**. Use the **Seek** command to find the record for the property owned by Mr D Swan.

13 All properties managed by Agent 1 have had an advertisement placed in the local paper. You need to add £25 to each of their advertising bills. Use the **Replace** command.

See Appendix 2, page 264 for solutions.

18   Further querying by example

It is recommended that you revise Chapter 8, before looking at these further examples of using the dBASE Query by example facility.

18.1   Preparing for this chapter

In order to complete this chapter you need the following files:

File name	File type	Chapter
ESTATE	Catalog	4
PROPERTY	Database	4
CUSTOMER	Database	5
STAFF	Database	4
CUSTOMER	Form	12
PROPERTY	Form	12

 If you have not created these files in the previous chapters you will need to refer back to to the chapter number listed above and create the files.

 If you have purchased the disks that accompany this book you can copy the necessary files from the appropriate floppy disk. To do this, complete the following instructions:

1 Make sure that you have created a sub-directory on the hard disk called DBASE\DATA (*see* Setting-up a data directory, page viii).

2 Load dBASE (*see* 3.2 Starting the program, page 9).

3 Follow the instructions for Using the diskettes on page viii. The batch file is called **C18**.

18.2   Sorting the query file

Records included in a query can be sorted on any field by moving the cursor to the field in the database skeleton and selecting the **Sort on this field** option from the **Fields** menu.

Property			GARDEN	GARAGE	FREEHOLD	↓PRICE	DAT

```
        Add field to view
        Remove field from view

        Edit field name
        Create calculate         Ascending   ASCII      (0..9,A..Za..z)
                                  Descending  ASCII      (z..aZ..A,9..0)
        Sort on this fie
        Include indexes          Ascending   Dictionary (0..9,Aa..Zz)
                                  Descending  Dictionary (zZ..aA,9..0)
```

View <NEW>	Property-> PROP_ADD	Property-> AREA	Property-> PRICE

Query   C:\dbase\data\<NEW>   Field 12/20   Num

Upper case letters sort before lower case letters

The options are **ASCII** or **Dictionary** with the choice of **Ascending** or **Descending**. The difference between the two options is best shown by example. If you sort the CUSTOMER database by the SURNAME field, the **ASCII** option will sort records as Adams to Zachs followed by adams to zachs. Names entered in lower case will be listed after the names as proper nouns (first character upper case) or in upper case. With the **Dictionary** option, case is ignored. Depending on which option is chosen the following codes are entered; ASC, DSC, ASCDIST, DSCDICT. The code will be followed by a number; 1 for the primary sort field; 2 for the secondary field and so on.

Alternatively, the codes can be typed directly into the database skeleton.

1   Open the **PROPERTY** database at the dot prompt and type **CREATE VIEW**. Type **PROPSORT** as the query filename.

2   Remove all fields from the view and then add the **PROP_ADD** and **PRICE** fields to the view.

3   Type **ASC1** in the **PRICE** column of the database skeleton and activate the query. The properties should be listed, lowest price through to highest price.

Property.dbf	AGE	NO_BEDS	RECEPT	GARDEN	GARAGE	FREEHOLD	↓PRICE	DAT
							ASC1	

View PROPSORT	Property-> PROP_ADD	Property-> PRICE

4   Return to query design by accessing the **Exit** menu.

To include a secondary sort field, type the relevant code into the field column followed by the digit 2. Alternatively, you could use the **Sort on this field** option from the **Fields** menu.

5   Remove **PRICE** from the view and add **AREA** and **TYPE**. Delete the sort code from the **PRICE** field and insert the code **ASC1** for the **AREA** field and **DSC2** for the **TYPE** field. Activate the query.

Property.dbf	↓PROP_ADD	↓AREA	TOWN	POSTCODE	↓TYPE	AGE	NO_BEDS	RECEPT
		ASC1			DSC2			

View ─			
<NEW>	Property-> PROP_ADD	Property-> AREA	Property-> TYPE

6   Return to query design.

18.3   Calculated fields

Calculated fields can be included in a query by selecting the **Create calculated field** option from the **Field** menu. A calculated field can be defined as a valid dBASE expression and is usually made up of a number of fields. For example, knowing the price of properties on the books and knowing the commission rate being charged, you can calculate the amount of commission due by using the expression PRICE*COMMISSION/100.

1   Add the **PROP_ADD**, **PRICE**, **COMMISSION** and **AGENT** fields to the view skeleton.

2   Select the **Create calculated field** option from the **Fields** menu. You can either type the expression or use **Shift + F1** to access the **Pick** menu.

3   Select the fields and operators that make up the expression. Enter the expression as **PRICE*COMMISSION/100**

Calc'd Flds	┌CONVALUE=────────────────┐ │↓COMMISSION * PRICE/100 │

4 Add the calculated field to the skeleton by pressing F5 . Name the field
   COMVALUE.

5 Activate the query and return to query design.

PROP_ADD	PRICE	COMMISSION	AGENT	COMVALUE
5 Hall Road	59170.00	1.50	A2	887.55
89 Cliff Road	49470.00	1.50	A2	742.05
6 Brook Road	53350.00	1.50	A3	800.25
4 Hever Court	142500.00	1.25	A1	1781.25
6 Elm Road	86330.00	1.25	A2	1079.13
90 Primly Rise	89240.00	1.50	A3	1338.60
43 Trewitt Ave	118750.00	1.50	A5	1781.25
23 Yew Bank Drive	158650.00	1.50	A3	2379.75
32 Leder Road	77600.00	1.25	A1	970.00
8 Oak Lane	96030.00	1.50	A3	1440.45
76 Ruin Grove	61110.00	1.25	A3	763.88
9 Bookers Avenue	63050.00	1.50	A3	945.75
56 Rainforest Way	323000.00	1.50	A1	4845.00
7 Kelly Park Drive	80510.00	1.50	A5	1207.65
6 Kirk Way	46560.00	1.50	A6	698.40
90 Otway Road	427500.00	1.50	A1	6412.50
4 Garden Terrace	64990.00	1.25	A2	812.38

18.4 Using a condition box

Instead of entering criteria into several fields in the database skeleton you can enter
the whole condition as a dBASE expression into a *Condition box*. To use a
condition box, select the **Add condition box** option from the **Condition** menu. A
box appears to the right of the screen.

Press F9 to enlarge the box so that it covers the entire screen. By pressing
 F9 again the box will shrink back to the original size. The expression can be
entered using the usual dBASE syntax.

1 Add a condition box by selecting the Add condition box from the Condition
   menu. Press F9 to expand the box and type the following expression:

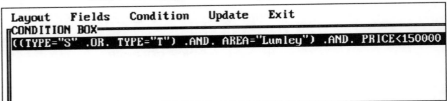

```
Layout    Fields    Condition    Update    Exit
┌CONDITION BOX────────────────────────────────────────
│((TYPE="S" .OR. TYPE="T") .AND. AREA="Lumley") .AND. PRICE<150000
│
│
│
```

2 Press F9 to shrink the box back to the original size. Press F3 to move back
   to the database skeleton.

3 Add the fields included in the expression to the view. Activate the query and
   return to query design.

4   Remove the condition box by selecting the **Delete condition box** option from the **Condition** menu.

5   Exit from query design without saving the query.

18.5 Using numeric operators and groups

The following numeric operators can be used in a query:

SUM
AVG
MIN
MAX
CNT

The operators are entered into the database skeleton under the appropriate field. The field must be added to the view. For example, if you wanted to find the average price of properties in the PROPERTY database you would need to add the PRICE field to the view skeleton and type AVG in the PRICE column of the database skeleton.

Property.dbf	RECEPT	GARDEN	GARAGE	FREEHOLD	↓PRICE	DATE_TAKEN	OWNER
					AVG		▄▄▄▄

To take this a stage further you could find the average price of all flats:

Property.dbf	↓TYPE	AGE	NO_BED	RECEPT	GARDEN	GARAGE	FREEHOLD	↓PRICE
	"F"							AVG

To find the average price of all the different types of properties you can use the **Group by** operator. By placing this operator in the TYPE column of the database skeleton the records would be grouped by type and the average price calculated for each group.

Property.dbf	↓TYPE	AGE	NO_BED	RECEPT	GARDEN	GARAG	FREEHOLD	↓PRICE
	GROUP BY							AVG

1   Create a query for the **PROPERTY** database called **PROPCALC**.

2   To find the average price of properties in Lumley, add the **PRICE** field to the view skeleton and type the **AVG** command in the **PRICE** column of the database skeleton.

3 Type the condition **"Lumley"** in the **AREA** column of the database skeleton (remember to include the quotes and make them proper nouns).

4 Activate the query and return to query design.

5 Use the **Group by** operator to find the average price of properties in each area of Greenoak. Add **PRICE** and **TYPE** to the view. Type **AVG** in the **PRICE** column and **GROUP BY** in the **AREA** column of the database skeleton. Activate the query and return to query design.

6 Find the lowest priced property on the books and the highest priced property. Remove all the operators from the database skeleton and fields from the view skeleton. Add **PRICE** to the view and type **MIN** as the operator in the **PRICE** column. Activate the query and return to query design.

7 Use the same procedure to find the property with the highest price. Use the **MAX** operator. Exit from query design without saving the query.

<table>
<tr><td>**18.6**</td><td>**Queries from multiple databases**</td></tr>
</table>

On occasion you may want to perform a query that requires information from more than one database. For example, you may want to list all properties and the name of the agent responsible for selling the property. To do this you need information from two databases, PROPERTY and STAFF. As these two databases have a common field you can use the **Link** feature to combine the databases. The common field is the AGENT field in PROPERTY and AGENT in STAFF (your field may have a different name if you created the STAFF file as part of the consolidation exercise for Chapter 4). Both fields contain the codes A1, A2, A3 etc. The following example will show the steps involved.

1 Create a query for the **PROPERTY** database called **PROPAG**. Clear all fields from the view skeleton.

2 Access the **Layout** menu and select the **Add file to query** option.

3 Select the **STAFF** database.

4 You now need to link the two databases on the common field. To do this, cursor to the **AGENT** field (or the appropriate field if named differently) in the **STAFF** database skeleton and access the **Layout** menu.

5 Select the **Create link by pointing** option. The code **LINK1** is displayed.

6 Press F3 to move to the **PROPERTY** skeleton. Move across to the **AGENT** field and press Enter . The code **LINK1** appears.

Property.dbf	FREEHOLD	PRICE	DATE_TAKEN	OWNER	TELEPHONE	AGENT	COMMI
						LINK1	

Staff.dbf	AGENT	SURNAME	FNAME	TITLE	STREET	AREA	TOWN	POSTCODE
	LINK1							

6   Add the **PROP_ADD** field from the **PROPERTY** database to the view.

7   Press ☐F4☐ to move to the **STAFF** database skeleton. Add the **FNAME** and **SURNAME** fields from the **STAFF** database to the view (remember, your field names may be different). Activate the query in the usual way. Exit from query design without saving the query.

PROP_ADD	FNAME	SURNAME
5 Hall Road	Clare	Jones
89 Cliff Road	Clare	Jones
6 Brook Road	Barry	Brown
4 Hever Court	David	Smith
6 Elm Road	Clare	Jones
90 Pimly Rise	Barry	Brown
43 Trewitt Ave	Alex	Greeves
23 Yew Bank Drive	Barry	Brown
32 Leder Road	David	Smith
8 Oak Lane	Barry	Brown
76 Ruin Grove	Barry	Brown
9 Bookers Avenue	Barry	Brown
56 Rainforest Way	David	Smith
7 Kelly Park Drive	Alex	Greeves
6 Kirk Way	Linda	Levin
90 Otway Road	David	Smith
4 Garden Terrace	Clare	Jones

19   Validation with a screen form

In Chapter 12 you created screen forms for the database files. The intention there was to customise the layout so that it was easier for the person entering or editing the records. In this chapter you will modify the forms to include the dBASE validation commands.

To validate the data simply means to check the information being entered into the database. A well known computing phrase is "garbage in, garbage out". If you do not check that the information being entered is correct, you cannot expect to get any meaningful reports or listings from the data.

Data can be checked on a character by character basis or as a complete entry. For example, with a character field, you could check that the data has been entered in upper case, or that the first letter is upper case. You could also check that only letters have been entered. With a numeric field, you may want to impose a range. For example, you may disallow values above or below given values. You could also specify a range for a date field. If entering records for the current year only, you could specify that dates outside this range not be allowed.

By including validation in the forms already created, a wide range of the available techniques will be covered. When creating future forms, the validation can be included when the form is created.

19.1   Preparing for this chapter

In order to complete this chapter you need the following files:

File name	File type	Chapter
ESTATE	Catalog	4
PROPERTY	Database	4
CUSTOMER	Database	5
STAFF	Database	4 (optional)
CUSTOMER	Form	12
PROPERTY	Form	12
STAFF	Form	12 (optional)

 If you have not created these files in the previous chapters you will need to refer back to to the chapter number listed above and create the files.

 If you have purchased the disks that accompany this book you can copy the necessary files from the appropriate floppy disk. To do this, complete the following instructions:

1 Make sure that you have created a sub-directory on the hard disk called DBASE\DATA (*see* Setting-up a data directory, page viii).

2 Load dBASE (*see* 3.2 Starting the program, page 9)

3 Follow the instructions for Using the diskettes on page viii. The batch file is called **C19**.

19.2 Modifying the screen form

To modify an existing screen form *either*:

- Open the appropriate database. Move the cursor to the **Forms** panel of the Control Centre, highlight the form name and press Enter . Select the **Modify layout** option *or*:

- Type the commands at the dot prompt, for example:

  USE <database name>
  MODIFY SCREEN <form name>

  USE PROPERTY
  MODIFY SCREEN PROPERTY

Modify the screen form for the **PROPERTY** database. The form name is **PROPERTY**.

19.3 Validating a field

When you created the form for PROPERTY you used F5 as a keyboard shortcut for adding the fields to the form. Once the fields have been added, F5 can be used to edit the display attributes of the field. Simply move the cursor to the field on the form (not the field name or prompt) and press F5 . The **Display attributes** menu will appear.

1 Move the cursor to the **AGENT** field so that the cursor is positioned on the Xs that make up the field. Details on the field are displayed at the bottom of the screen.

```
Form     ║C:\dbase\data\PROPERTY ║Row:4 Col:67   ║File:Property ║   Num     Ins
            Add field:F5   Select:F6   Move:F7   Copy:F8   Size:Shift-F7
          PROPERTY->AGENT     Type: Character    Width:    4   Decimal:  0
```

2   Press ⌑F5⌑ to edit the display attributes of the **AGENT** field. The following
    menu is displayed:

```
┌─────────────────────────────────────────────────┐
│  Field name:        AGENT                         │
│  Type:              Character                     │
│  Length:            4                             │
│  Decimals:          0                             │
│  ─────────────────────────────────────────────   │
│  Template           {XXXX}                        │
│ ▶ Picture functions {}                            │
│ ▶ Edit options                                    │
│   Display as                                      │
│ ▶ Border lines                                    │
└─────────────────────────────────────────────────┘
```

Three options are available referred to as the **Template**, **Picture functions** and
Edit options. Each option will be discussed in turn.

19.4   Template

The **Template**, often referred to as the **Picture template**, can be defined to validate
each character or digit making up the field.

To change the template, modify the field, highlight the **Template** option in the menu
and press ⌑Enter⌑.

Character fields

If validating a character field the following choices are displayed:

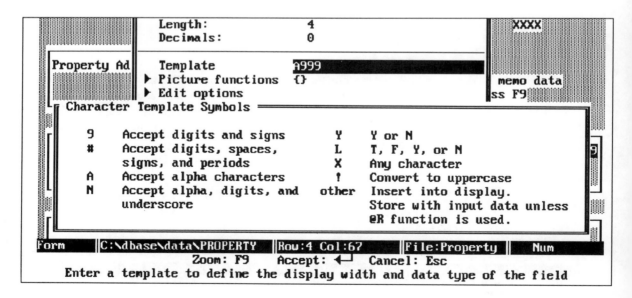

See over for explanations of the template symbols.

| 9 | A **9** indicates that only a digit 0 through 9 or a plus or minus sign can be entered at this position in the field. |

9   A **9** indicates that only a digit 0 through 9 or a plus or minus sign can be entered at this position in the field.

The **#** symbol indicates that numbers, blanks and signs (+ , -) can be entered at this position. This could be used for a telephone number, if the template is set as #s instead of 9s, the user would still be forced to enter digits (characters would not be allowed) but a space could be left between the STD code and the number.

A   The **A** indicates that only alpha characters can be entered at this position in the field. Only the letters A-Z (upper or lower case) can be included, spaces and punctuation characters are not allowed.

N   The **N** indicates that only letters (A-Z), digits (0-9) and the underscore character can be included.

Y   Used to validate logical fields, the **Y** indicates that only **Y** for Yes or **N** for No can be entered at this position.

L   Used to validate logical fields. You can only enter **T** for True, **F** for False, **Y** for Yes and **N** for No.

X   The **X** will allow any character to be entered.

!   The **!** symbol will convert any character to upper case (the **!** symbol does not force the user to enter a character).

Other   Any other characters entered into the template (apart from those listed above) will be skipped over when data is entered but will be stored in the database as part of the field. For example, in the PROPERTY database all the properties are located in Greenoak and all post codes begin with the characters **GR**. You could include these characters in the template so that the user does not have to enter them each time. The template could be GR9X9AA. The user would just need to fill in the third, fifth, sixth and seventh characters.

On occasion you may want to include characters in the template but not save them as part of the field, for example, brackets around the STD code in a telephone number. You can do this by using the **R** function as you will see later.

Numeric fields

When validating a numeric field some of the above template codes are applicable. In addition, the codes, explained over, can be used:

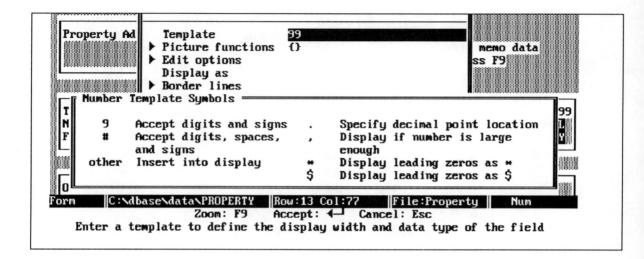

. The period (.) can be used to specify the decimal point location eg 999.99

, The comma (,) can be used as a separator for large numbers eg 99,999.99

* The asterix (*) can be used to display leading zeros. For example if the template ***.99 was used, the number 7.25 would display as 007.25.

$ The dollar sign ($) can be used if you want leading zeros to be displayed as $s.

Logical fields

When validating a logical field only the following templates are available:

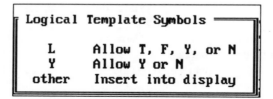

1 The **AGENT** field in the **PROPERTY** database is defined as character with a width of four. The field will always contain the letter A followed by up to three digits, so the template can be set to A999. Change the template from **XXXX** to **A999**. Press Enter to confirm the changes.

```
┌─────────────────────────────────────────────────────┐
│    Field name:        AGENT                           │
│    Type:              Character                       │
│    Length:            4                               │
│    Decimals:          0                               │
│   ┌───────────────────────────────────────────────── │
│    Template           [A999]                          │
│  ► Picture functions  {}                              │
│  ► Edit options                                       │
└─────────────────────────────────────────────────────┘
```

19.5 Picture functions

Rather than validating on a character by character basis, the **Picture functions** option can be used to define the way the whole field looks.

To define a function, modify the field, move the cursor to the **Picture functions** option and press ⌈ **Enter** ⌋.

Character fields

When modifying the **Picture functions** of a characater field the following options are displayed:

```
┌───────────────────────────────────────────┐
│  Alphabetic characters only    A    OFF    │
│  Upper-case conversion         !    OFF    │
│  Literals not part of data     R    OFF    │
│  Scroll within display width   S    OFF    │
│  Multiple choice               M    OFF    │
│ ┌─────────────────────────────────────────│
│  Trim                          T    OFF    │
│  Right align                   J    OFF    │      Not available
│  Center align                  I    OFF    │
│  Horizontal stretch            H    OFF    │
│  Vertical stretch              U    OFF    │
│  Wrap semicolons               ;    OFF    │
└───────────────────────────────────────────┘
```

A
By setting the function to **A**, the user can only enter alpha characters (A to Z). It should be noted that spaces are not allowed and so this function could not be used for fields where more than one word might be entered. For example, the AREA field could contain the text "Lumley", "Farley" or "Old Town". If you set the function to A you would not be able to enter the space character between Old and Town.

!
The ! function can be used to force all alpha characters to uppercase.

R
The **R** function is known as the **Literals not part of data** function and is used when the template contains characters that should not be saved as part of the field. For example, if the template is set as (####)-###### the brackets and dash would be saved as part of the field. By setting the function to **R**, only the data replacing the # character would be saved as part of the field.

S	The **Scroll** function (S) can be useful when you have a database comprising a large number of fields. You may find that when creating the screen form the layout looks a little cramped. One solution is to continue the form onto a second screen. Alternatively you can define a smaller display width for some of the fields and use the **Scroll** function to scroll within the field.
M	The **Multiple choice** function (M) is one of the most useful validation tools. By specifying a number of possible choices, the user is only able to select from those choices - they cannot enter any other values.
	When the **M** function is chosen, dBASE displays an empty box. The possible choices should be entered separated by a comma (,). The first choice in the list will be displayed in the empty data entry form. The user can then press the ⌷ **Spacebar** ⌷ to scroll through the possible choices.

The options displayed in the bottom half of the menu are not available for use with the form. These options are designed for the **Label** and **Report** generators.

Numeric fields

The following functions are available when validating numeric fields; by default all options are set to **Off**. Again, the options in the bottom half of the menu are not available for use with the form. In addition, the first three options are not available with the form.

```
┌─────────────────────────────────────────────────┐
│ Positive credits followed by CR  C    OFF        │   ⟩ Not available
│ Negative debits followed by DB   X    OFF        │
│ Use () around negative numbers   (    OFF        │
│ Show leading zeroes              L    OFF        │
│ Blanks for zero values           Z    OFF        │
│ Financial format                 $    OFF        │
│ Exponential format               ^    OFF        │
├─────────────────────────────────────────────────┤
│ Trim                             T    OFF        │   Not available
│ Left align                       B    OFF        │
│ Center align                     I    OFF        │
│ Horizontal stretch               H    OFF        │
│ Vertical stretch                 V    OFF        │
└─────────────────────────────────────────────────┘
```

L	If set to **On**, this function will show any leading zeros.
Z	If set to **On** this function will display blanks for zero values. This can be useful if you want a numeric field to be displayed as blank before a value is entered.

$ If set to **On** this option will display a numeric value in financial format, preceded by a £ sign and to 2 decimal places.

^   If set to **On** this option will display the data in exponential format.

1   Continuing with the validation of the **AGENT** field, select the **Function** option.

2   Set the **Upper-case conversion** option (!) to **On** by highlighting the option and pressing $\boxed{\textsf{Enter}}$.

3   Press $\boxed{\textsf{Ctrl + End}}$ to save the change.

19.6   Editing options

The **Editing** options are designed to give you control over the way the data is added or edited. The following options are available:

```
Editing allowed          YES
Permit edit if           {}
Message                  {}
Carry Forward            NO
Default value            {}
Smallest allowed value   {}
Largest allowed value    {}
Accept value when        {}
Unaccepted message       {}
```

Editing allowed

If set to **No**, the user can see the value in the field but cannot change it. This is a useful feature if you have a number of different screen forms for the same database. You may want to have one form which allows both read and write access to all the fields; the user can see and change all the data, and a second form that only allows read access to some fields.

Permit editing if

This option is known as the **Conditional editing** option. The field can only be edited if a condition is met. For example, you may decide to include a logical field in the database called SOLD. As soon as the property is sold this field is changed to **Yes**. You may also have a D_SOLD field to record the date the property was sold and a field to record the purchaser's name. You could use this function to specify that the date sold and purchaser name fields could only be edited if the date sold field is set to **Yes**.

Message

The Message option can be used to display a message at the bottom of the screen when the field is being added or edited. This option is particularly useful when using the **Multiple choice** function, to outline the choices and tell the user to press the **Spacebar** to toggle through the choices.

Carry forward

This option can be used to automatically carry forward the value from the same field in the previous record. This feature can be useful if entering batches of records. For example, if you had a number of new properties to add to the PROPERTY database, you may decide to sort them by area and enter all the properties in Lumley followed by the properties in Farley and so on. If this was the case you could use the **Carry forward** option for the AREA field. The AREA field for the first record would be entered as Lumley. This would then be carried forward to the consecutive fields. Once you had entered all the Lumley properties you would need to overwrite the AREA field with Farley. This value would then be carried forward until changed again.

Default value

If a field has the same value for the majority of the records in the database, you may want to set up a default value for that field. By doing this the value will automatically be entered into the field for each record. The value can then be changed if necessary. For example, the TOWN field is usually Greenoak. You could, therefore, set up the TOWN field with a default value of Greenoak.

Smallest and Largest allowed value

The **Smallest** and **Largest allowed value** options can be used for numeric or date fields to specify the smallest and largest number or date that can be entered. If a number or date is entered outside the specified range a message appears at the bottom of the screen prompting the user to press the **Spacebar** to re-enter the value. The accepted range of values is displayed to help the user.

Accept value when

This option can be used to enter a valid dBASE expression which is used to test the value entered. The expression can be a simple range check, eg PRICE >500 .AND. PRICE <1000 (this could also be defined using the **Smallest** and **Largest allowed value** options), or a complex expression including ANDs, ORs and parentheses.

Unaccepted message

This option is used with the **Accept value when** option to display an error message if the value entered is unacceptable.

 1 Continuing with the validation of the **AGENT** field, select the **Edit** options and use the **Message** option to include the message **Enter agent code, e.g. A1, A2, A3 etc.**

---

2 Press Ctrl + End to save the changes.

3 Press Ctrl + End again to preserve the changes and return to the form. The **AGENT** field is now displayed as **A999** on the form.

Completing the validation

Continuing with the validation of the screen form for the **PROPERTY** database, include the following **Templates**, **Functions** and **Edit** options:

PROP_ADD

Addresses are difficult fields to validate, they can contain house numbers and usually contain several words. In this case you will just include a message.

1 Move the cursor to the **PROP_ADD** field and press F5.

2 Select the **Edit** option from the menu, highlight the **Message** option and press Enter. Type the message; **Enter the house/flat number and street**.

AREA

The **AREA** field can be validated using the **Multiple choice** function.

1 Modify the **AREA** field, select the **Picture functions** option and select the **Multiple choice** option.

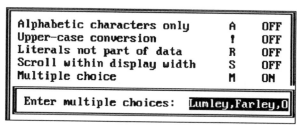

```
Alphabetic characters only      A    OFF
Upper-case conversion           !    OFF
Literals not part of data       R    OFF
Scroll within display width     S    OFF
Multiple choice                 M    ON

Enter multiple choices:   Lumley,Farley,0
```

2 Type the choices as **Lumley,Farley,Old Town,** Each choice should be separated by a comma with a comma at the end to give the option of leaving the field blank (for properties in the centre of town).

3 Press Enter to save and Ctrl + End to save the changes to the function.

4 Use the **Edit** options to include a message, **Press SPACEBAR for choices**.

5 Press Ctrl + End twice to exit back to the form.

TOWN

To date, all the properties on the books have been located in Greenoak. You can use the **Default edit** option to make Greenoak the default entry for the **TOWN** field.

1 Modify the **TOWN** field and select the **Edit** options.

2 Select the **Default** option and type **"Greenoak"** (the quotes are needed). Press $\boxed{\text{Enter}}$ to confirm.

3 Include a suitable message and press $\boxed{\text{Ctrl + End}}$ to save the changes. Exit back to the form.

POSTCODE

As all the properties are in Greenoak all post codes begin with the letters GR. You can include these as literals in the template.

1 Modify the **POSTCODE** field and select the **Template** option. Change the template to **GR9X9AA**.

```
Field name:        POSTCODE
Type:              Character
Length:            10
Decimals:          0

Template           {GR9X9AAXXX}
▶ Picture functions {!}
▶ Edit options
  Display as
▶ Border lines
```

2 Press $\boxed{\text{Enter}}$ to confirm. Change the function so that the ! function is set to **On**. Add a suitable message and exit back to the form.

TYPE

The TYPE field can be validated as a **Multiple choice** field.

1 Set the choices as **T,F,D,C,S**.

```
Enter multiple choices:   T,F,D,C,S
```

2 Include a message that reads; **<T>errace, <F>lat, <D>etached, <C>ottage, <S>emi - Press SPACEBAR to choose.**

AGE

The AGE field can also be set as **Multiple choice**.

1 Set the choices as; **O,V,E,PR,PO,M,N.**

2 Include a message that reads **Old, Victorian, Edwardian, Pre war, Post war, Modern, New - press SPACEBAR to choose.**

NO_BEDS

Use the **Smallest** and **Largest allowed values** options from the **Edit** options to set the minimum number of bedrooms to **0** and the maximum to **8**.

```
Editing allowed          YES
Permit edit if           {}
Message                  {Enter number of bedrooms}
Carry Forward            NO
Default value            {}
Smallest allowed value   {0}
Largest allowed value    {8}
Accept value when        {}
Unaccepted message       {}
```

RECEPT

Use the **Smallest and Largest values** options to set the minimum number of reception rooms to **0** and the maximum to **5**.

GARDEN

1   Change the template so that the **GARDEN** field is displayed as **Y** or **N**.

```
Field name:         GARDEN
Type:               Logical
Length:             1
Decimals:           0

Template            Y
▶ Picture functions {}
▶ Edit options
Display as
▶ Border lines
```

2   Repeat the process for the **GARAGE** and **FREEHOLD** fields.

PRICE

1   Change the template to include a comma (,) to separate the thousands and hundreds and include two decimal places.

2   Change the function so that the **Financial format** option is set to **On**.

3   Set the minimum price to **£30,000** and the maximum price to **£900,000**.

```
┌─────────────────────────────────────────────────┐
│  Field name:      PRICE                           │
│  Type:            Numeric                          │
│  Length:          10                               │
│  Decimals:        2                                │
│  ──────────────────────────────────────────────── │
│  Template         {99999,999}                      │
│ ▶ Picture functions  {$}                           │
│ ▶ Edit options                                     │
│  Display as                                        │
│ ▶ Border lines                                     │
└─────────────────────────────────────────────────┘
```

TELEPHONE

⊃ Change the template to # characters.

ADVERTS

⊃ Change the function so that **Financial format** option is **On** and the **Blanks for zeros** option is **On**.

⊃ 1 It is not necessary to include any validation for the **DATE_TAKEN**, **DATE_SOLD**, **OWNER** and **COMMISSION** fields.

   2 Save the form and append two records. Notice the validation.

19.8　　　　Consolidation exercises

⊃ Include similar validation for the **CUSTOMER** database. The screen form is called **CUSTOMER**.

⊃ If you have created a screen form for the **STAFF** database, modify the form and include suitable validation. If the **STAFF** database does not have a customised screen form (this file is not included on the disk) create one called **STAFF** and include the validation as you add each field.

⊃ If you need further practice use your **PERSONAL** database (created in Chapter 4 as an optional exercise, not included on the disk). Create a screen form, if you don't already have one, and include suitable validation.

See Appendix 2, page 265 for solutions.

dBASE functions

The dBASE function library contains a selection of in-built commands designed to help when using dBASE in all of the three environments. In this chapter you will look at ways in which you might use functions at the dot prompt. This will be followed by examples using functions in query files. Many of these functions will be used again in Parts 3 and 4 to develop a series of programs.

Functions begin with the function name followed by parenthesis (). Most functions require information (parameters) within the brackets:

FUNCTION(P1,P2,P3....)

There are far too many functions to look at them all, but the following selection will give you a good understanding of the types of functions available, the syntax and their uses.

20.1 Preparing for this chapter

In order to complete this chapter you need the following files:

File name	File type	Chapter
ESTATE	Catalog	4
PROPERTY	Database	4
CUSTOMER	Database	5
ALL	Query	8
ALL	Report	9

 If you have not created these files in the previous chapters you will need to refer back to to the chapter number listed above and create the files.

 If you have purchased the disks that accompany this book you can copy the necessary files from the appropriate floppy disk. To do this, complete the following instructions:

1 Make sure that you have created a sub-directory on the hard disk called DBASE\DATA (*see* Setting-up a data directory, page viii).

2 Load dBASE (*see* 3.2 Starting the program, page 9).

3 Follow the instructions for Using the diskettes on page viii. The batch file is called **C20**.

STR() function

The **STR()** (string) function is designed to convert numeric data to character format so that an operation can be performed. The actual data is not changed. The first parameter is the data to be converted, usually a file name, the second parameter the length of data and the third parameter the number of decimal places to be displayed.

The following example shows how the **STR()** function can be used to create a joint index on a character and numeric field for the PROPERTY database. You have already seen in Chapter 10 that you can create secondary and tertiary indexes by concatenating the required fields. It was mentioned there, that problems occur when the fields are not of the same type. The string function can be used convert the numeric field to a character field to create the index. It is important to remember that the actual data is not changed.

 Type the following at the dot prompt:

USE PROPERTY
INDEX ON TYPE + STR(PRICE,10,2) TAG TY_PR
BROWSE

Records	Organize	Fields	Go To	Exit					
POSTCODE	TYPE	AGE	NO_BEDS	RECEPT	GARDEN	GARAGE	FREEHOLD	PRICE	DATE_TAKE
GR3 9YU	C	U	2	1	T	F	T	77600.00	08/01/91
GR4 3ER	C	O	2	1	T	T	T	89240.00	12/01/92
GR6 5TB	C	O	3	2	T	T	T	96757.50	24/03/92
GR9 6TY	D	PR	3	2	T	T	T	118750.00	21/10/91
GR3 6SA	D	M	4	3	T	T	T	142500.00	11/11/91
GR5 4RW	D	PO	4	2	T	T	T	158650.00	01/03/92
GR8 5RQ	D	N	5	3	T	T	T	323000.00	19/03/91
GR7 4RT	D	E	5	3	T	T	T	427500.00	21/03/92
GR1 8UX	F	M	1	1	F	F	T	46560.00	13/01/92
GR6 5TA	F	N	2	1	F	F	F	49470.00	05/01/92
GR2 4TC	F	U	1	1	T	T	F	64990.00	02/03/92
GR4 9IU	S	PR	3	2	T	F	T	63050.00	17/11/91
GR6 6RE	S	U	3	2	N	N	Y	63050.00	12/03/92
GR4 5RW	S	M	3	2	T	T	T	78570.00	12/12/91
GR7 5TB	S	M	3	2	T	F	T	80510.00	05/10/91
GR9 5TR	S	PO	3	2	T	T	T	96030.00	21/01/91
GR7 6EW	T	U	4	2	F	F	T	53350.00	10/01/92

Browse	C:\dbase\data\PROPERTY	Rec 9/21		File		Num

The data is ordered by TYPE ie cottages followed by detached properties etc. Within TYPE, the properties are ordered by PRICE; lowest to highest.

UPPER() and LOWER() functions

The **UPPER()** and **LOWER()** functions have one parameter, the data to be converted to upper or lower case. This can be useful if data has been entered into the database without validation. You can use the **Replace** command to replace all the contents of a field with the upper or lower case equivalent.

 1   Type the following at the dot prompt:

   USE CUSTOMER
   EDIT

2   Change some of the property type codes to lower case for the first few records in the database. For example:

```
   Records    Organize    Go To    Exit
   SURNAME     Jones
   FIRSTNAME   Peter
   TITLE       Mr
   STREET      22 Layeburn Street
   AREA        Old Bridge
   TOWN        London
   POSTCODE    EC2 5TY
   TELEPHONE   (081)345621
   ENROLED     01/02/92
   TYPE        C d s
   AGE         0 V E
   MAX_PRICE    150000.00
   MIN_BEDS    2
   REQ_AREA    ALL
   APP_TYPE    HOT
   AGENT       A5
   COMMENTS    MEMO
```

3   Exit from edit mode, saving the changes and type the following at the dot prompt:

   REPLACE ALL TYPE WITH UPPER(TYPE)
   GO TOP
   BROWSE

The TYPE field data should all appear in upper case.

TRIM() function

The **TRIM()** function is used to trim trailing blanks from a character field. This can be useful when concatenating fields (adding them together) for display purposes.

1 Try the following examples:

USE CUSTOMER
DISPLAY ALL TITLE+FIRSTNAME+SURNAME
DISPLAY ALL TRIM(TITLE)+TRIM(FIRSTNAME)+SURNAME

2 If you trim off all the spaces you will need to add a space character between the fields.

DISPLAY ALL TRIM(TITLE)+" "+TRIM(FIRSTNAME)+" "+SURNAME

20.3   Date functions

Date functions are used to change the way a date is displayed.

The **DATE()** function is used to return the system date. It does not require any parameters.

The **DTOC()** function (date to character) converts date type data to a character format. This can be useful when concatenating fields.

The **CMONTH()** function (character month) takes the month part of a date and displays it in character format, eg April.

The **YEAR()** function can be used to return the year part of a date.

The **DTOS()** function (date to string) can be used for indexing purposes. If you need to produce a joint index on a character field and a date field the date to string function can be used to convert the date to a string so that it can be concatenated with the string in order to create the index. It is converted as YYYYMMDD. For example, 12/3/92 would be converted to 19920312. As with the string function, this does not affect the data.

Type the following examples at the dot prompt:

USE CUSTOMER
LIST TRIM(TITLE)+" "+TRIM(SURNAME)+" enrolled on "+DTOC(ENROLED)

```
. list trim(title)+" "+trim(surname)+" enrolled on "+dtoc(enroled)
Record#  trim(title)+" "+trim(surname)+" enrolled on "+dtoc(enroled)
      1  Mr Jones enrolled on 01/02/92
      2  Miss Kemp enrolled on 01/01/92
      3  Mr Jones enrolled on 12/09/91
      4  Ms Samuels enrolled on 01/01/92
      5  Miss Hughes enrolled on 03/12/91
      6  Mr Smith enrolled on 05/01/92
      7  Mrs Price enrolled on 15/12/91
      8  Mr Kelly enrolled on 17/11/91
      9  Mr Howard enrolled on 21/12/91
     10  Mrs Sumton enrolled on 23/02/92
     11  Ms King enrolled on 07/03/92
     12  Mr Glover enrolled on 12/04/92
     13  Miss Morris enrolled on 12/03/92
     14  Mr Philips enrolled on 12/03/92
```

USE PROPERTY
DISPLAY ALL OWNER, TELEPHONE, CMONTH(DATE_TAKEN)
DISPLAY ALL OWNER, CMONTH(DATE_TAKEN), YEAR(DATE_TAKEN)

USE PROPERTY
INDEX ON AGENT+DTOS(DATE_TAKEN) TAG AGENT
BROWSE

Records	Organize	Fields	Go To	Exit				
FREEHOLD	PRICE	DATE_TAKEN	OWNER		TELEPHONE	AGENT	COMMISSION	ADV
T	77600.00	08/01/91	Miss L Price		987321	A1	1.25	
T	323000.00	19/03/91	Mr D Swan		651803	A1	1.50	
T	142500.00	11/11/91	Karen Bright		456821	A1	1.25	1
T	427500.00	21/03/92	Mr Young		567349	A1	1.50	
T	59170.00	05/12/91	Mr P Lane		786309	A2	1.50	
F	49470.00	05/01/92	Gerald Tims		654219	A2	1.50	
T	86330.00	15/02/92	Fred Collins		456298	A2	1.25	
T	64990.00	19/02/92	Keith Perry		(072)459231	A2	1.25	
Y	63050.00	12/03/92	Mr H Hardacre		456892	A2	1.50	
T	96030.00	21/01/91	Mr T Hill		768451	A3	1.50	
T	63050.00	17/11/91	Helen Smith		453981	A3	1.50	
T	61110.00	02/12/91	John Franks		546987	A3	1.25	
T	78570.00	12/12/91	Miss Davis		762543	A3	1.25	
T	53350.00	10/01/92	Mr H Jones		753216	A3	1.50	
T	89240.00	12/01/92	Ms H Green		324786	A3	1.50	
T	158650.00	01/03/92	Mr H Lewis		834652	A3	1.50	
F	64990.00	02/03/92	Miss J Tailor		(081)876402	A4	1.50	

Browse	C:\dbase\data\PROPERTY	Rec 9/21	File	Num

20.4   Conditional functions

The **IIF(P1.P2,P3)** function (immediate if) needs three parameters. The first parameter is a condition. The second parameter tells dBASE what to do if the condition is true and the third parameter tells dBASE what to do if the condition is false.

1   Type the following at the dot prompt:

USE PROPERTY
DISPLAY OWNER, TELEPHONE, IIF(DATE_SOLD={ / / },"Not Sold","Sold")

2   Edit a couple of records and enter a date in the **DATE_SOLD** field. Run the command again.

20.5   Using functions in queries

Functions can be used in the design of both queries and reports. In the following examples you will create two queries using a range of dBASE functions. You will then use one of those queries as a basis for a mail merge report.

---

1 Create a query for the **PROPERTY** database called **PROPDET**.

2 Add the **PROP_ADD** field to the view.

3 Create a calculated field and enter the expression as
   "Priced at: £"+ STR(PRICE,10,2). This expression concatenates the string
   Priced at: £ and the **PRICE** field. As the **PRICE** field is numeric, you need to
   use the **STR()** function.

4 Add this calculated field to the view giving it an appropriate name.

Property.dbf	↓PROP_ADD	AREA	TOWN	POSTCODE	TYPE	AGE	NO_BEDS	RECEPT

	PROP_PRICE=
Calc'd Flds	↓"Priced at: £"+TRIM(STR(PRICE,10,2))

5 Activate the query and return to query design.

6 Now display the type of property in full. For example, instead of displaying F, for
   flat, display the whole word. You can do this by using nested IIF() functions.
   Create another calculated field. Enter the following expression all on the same
   line:

   **IIF(TYPE="T","Terrace",IIF(TYPE="S","Semi",IIF(TYPE="D","Detached",
   IIF(TYPE="C","Cottage","Flat"))))**

7 Add the field to the view and give it a suitable name.

8 Activate the query and return to query design.

PROP_ADD	PROP_PRICE	FULLTYPE
5 Hall Road	Priced at: £ 61000.00	Terrace
89 Cliff Road	Priced at: £ 51000.00	Flat
6 Brook Road	Priced at: £ 55000.00	Terrace
4 Hever Court	Priced at: £ 150000.00	Detached
6 Elm Road	Priced at: £ 89000.00	Terrace
90 Pimly Rise	Priced at: £ 92000.00	Cottage
43 Trewitt Ave	Priced at: £ 125000.00	Detached
23 Yew Bank Drive	Priced at: £ 167000.00	Detached
32 Leder Road	Priced at: £ 80000.00	Cottage
8 Oak Lane	Priced at: £ 99000.00	Semi
76 Ruin Grove	Priced at: £ 63000.00	Terrace
9 Bookers Avenue	Priced at: £ 65000.00	Semi
56 Rainforest Way	Priced at: £ 340000.00	Detached
7 Kelly Park Drive	Priced at: £ 83000.00	Semi
6 Kirk Way	Priced at: £ 48000.00	Flat
90 Otway Road	Priced at: £ 450000.00	Detached
4 Garden Terrace	Priced at: £ 67000.00	Terrace

9 Save the query and return to the Control Centre.

In the next example you will create a query that can be used to produce a letter to
be sent to all customers.

1 Create a query for the **CUSTOMER** database called **LETTER**.

2 Remove all fields from the view skeleton.

3 Add a calculated field and enter the expression as

TRIM(TITLE)+" " + TRIM(FIRSTNAME)+" "+SURNAME.

Customer.dbf	SURNAME	FIRSTNAME	TITLE	STREET	AREA	TOWN	POSTCODE	T

Calc'd Flds	FULLNAME= ↓TRIM(TITLE)+" "+TRIM(FIRSTNAME)+" "+SURNAME

4 Add the field to the view and name it **FULLNAME**.

5 Add another calculated field and enter the expression; **TOWN+POSTCODE**. Add the field to the view and name it **ADDRESS**.

6 Add a third calculated field to be used as the letter salutation. Enter the expression as **"Dear "+TRIM(TITLE)+" "+SURNAME**.

Customer.dbf	SURNAME	FIRSTNAME	TITLE	STREET	AREA	TOWN	POSTCODE	T

Calc'd Flds	ADDRESS= ↓TOWN + POSTCODE	"Dear"+" "+TRIM(TITLE)+" "+TRIM(SURNAME)

7 Add the field to the view and name it **SALUTATION**.

8 Add the **STREET** and **AREA** fields to the view. Activate the query and return to query design.

FULLNAME	ADDRESS		SALUTATION
Mr Peter Jones	London	EC2 5TY	Dear Mr Jones
Miss Mary Kemp	Greenoak	GR5 6RW	Dear Miss Kemp
Mr Fred Jones	Leeds	LS4 5TO	Dear Mr Jones
Ms Deborah Samuals	Greenoak	GR4 6TD	Dear Ms Samuals
Miss Linda Hughes	Greeoak	GR8 5RT	Dear Miss Hughes
Mr John Smith	Bradford	BD4 546	Dear Mr Smith
Mrs Jill Price	Greenoak	GR3 6UP	Dear Mrs Price
Mr P Kelly	Greenoak	GR5 6TY	Dear Mr Kelly
Mr David Hill	Greenoak	GR4 5SD	Dear Mr Hill
Mr Kevin Summers	Lowston	LO4 5YT	Dear Mr Summers

9   Save the query and return to the Control Centre.

20.6   Using functions in reports

You will now use this query to create a letter.

1   Make sure that the **LETTER** query is open. Create a report called **LETTER**.

2   Select the **Quick layout** option from the **Layout** menu. Select the **Mailmerge layout** option.

3   Use F5 to add the fields in the order indicated below to act as the address block for the letter:

   FULLNAME
   STREET
   AREA
   ADDRESS

You will notice that the box containing the available fields includes the option to calculate fields. You could have calculated the fields for this report from within the report generator rather than producing a query file.

LETTER	CALCULATED	PREDEFINED	SUMMARY
ADDRESS AREA FULLNAME SALUTATION STREET	<create>	Date Time Recno Pageno	Average Count Max Min Sum Std Var

4   To add the system date, press F5 and select the **Date** option from the **Predefined** section of the box. Leave a blank line and add the **SALUTATION** field.

5   Type the letter content as shown on the following page:

```
Page      Header  Band────────────────────────────────────────────────────
Report    Intro   Band────────────────────────────────────────────────────
Detail            Band────────────────────────────────────────────────────


XXXXXXXXXXXXXXXXXXXXXXXXXXXXXXXXX
XXXXXXXXXXXXXXXXXXXXX
XXXXXXXXXXXXXXXXXXXXX
XXXXXXXXXXXXXXXXXX

DD/MM/YY

XXXXXXXXXXXXX

Please find enclosed a copy of our latest magazine detailing all
the properties currently available.

If you are interested in viewing any of the properties please
contact any of our agents on 784329.

Yours sincerely
Report  ║C:\dbase\data\LETTER    ║Line:16 Col:15  ║View:LETTER   ║  Num    Ins
          Add field:F5   Select:F6   Move:F7   Copy:F8   Size:Shift-F7
```

6 Save the report.

7 To produce the letter for all customers who enrolled in 1992, type the following at the dot prompt:

REPORT FORM LETTER FOR ENROLED>={1/1/92}

If you want to print the letters, add **TO PRINT** to the end of the command.

In this next example you will amend the report called ALL created in Part 1.

1 Open the query called **ALL** and then modify the report called **ALL**.

2 At the moment the **AREA** column is blank for properties in the centre of town (see Chapter 9, page 71). You can change this so that it reads Centre instead.

3 Move to the **AREA** field in the detail band and press Delete . Press F5 to add a new field and select the **Create** option in the **Calculated** column.

4 Name the new calculated field as **FULLAREA**. The expression for this field involves the use of the **Immediate if** function; if the area field is blank, display the word **Centre**, otherwise display the content of the **AREA** field.

```
   Name                      {FULLAREA}
   Description               {Area of Greenoak}
   Expression                {IIF(AREA="","Centre",AREA)}

   Template                  {XXXXXXXXXXXXXXXXXXXX}
 ▶ Picture functions         {T}
   Suppress repeated values  NO
   Hidden                    NO
```

5   Make sure the Template is 20 characters in length, the length of the **AREA** field. Press ⌐Ctrl + End⌐ to save change.

6   Print the report and exit, saving all changes.

21 Setting the environment and file management

This chapter will look at changing the working environment in readiness for programming. It also looks at ways in which you can manage files, covering the copying and deleting commands.

21.1 Preparing for this chapter

In order to complete this chapter you need the following files:

File name	File type	Chapter
ESTATE	Catalog	4
PROPERTY	Database	4
CUSTOMER	Database	5
STAFF	Database	4
CUSTOMER	Form	12
PROPERTY	Form	12

 If you have not created these files in the previous chapters you will need to refer back to to the chapter number listed above and create the files.

If you have purchased the disks that accompany this book you can copy the necessary files from the appropriate floppy disk. To do this, complete the following instructions:

1   Make sure that you have created a sub-directory on the hard disk called DBASE\DATA (*see* Setting-up a data directory, page viii).

2   Load dBASE (*see* 3.2 Starting the program, page 9).

3   Follow the instructions for Using the diskettes on page viii. The batch file is called **C21**.

21.2 Set commands

The environment can be changed by using the **Set** commands, some of which you have already used. You used the **Set bell off** and **Set confirm on** commands when you were appending and editing.   The syntax for the **Set** command can take two forms:

SET <name> ON/OFF
SET <name> TO <value>

Set commands can be chosen from a menu by typing **SET**. The following menus appear:

```
 Options    Display    Keys    Disk    Files
 ┌──────────────────────────────────────┐
 │   Alternate        OFF                │
 │   Autosave         OFF                │
 │   Bell             OFF                │
 │   Carry            OFF                │
 │   Catalog                             │
 │   Century          OFF                │
 │   Confirm          ON                 │
 │   Currency sign    LEFT               │
 │   Cursor           ON                 │
 │   Date order       DMY                │
 │   Date separator   /                  │
 │   Decimal places   {2}                │
 │   Deleted          OFF                │
 │   Delimiters       OFF                │
 │   Development      ON                 │
 │   Device           SCREEN             │
 │   Encryption       ON                 │
 │   Escape           ON                 │
 │   Exact            OFF                │
 └──────────────────────────────────────┘
```

Options menu

The **Options** menu allows you to change **Set** commands from **On** to **Off** (or vice versa) or change the value of the command.

Display menu

The **Display** menu gives the option to change the colours of the normal display text, the enhanced text and the screen border. The colours can be chosen from a chart.

```
 ┌──────────────────────────────────┐
 │   Display mode      EGA25         │
 ├──────────────────────────────────┤
 │ ▶ Standard - All                 │
 │   ▶ Normal text                  │
 │   ▶ Messages                     │
 │   ▶ Titles                       │
 │ ▶ Enhanced - All                 │
 │   ▶ Highlight                    │
 │   ▶ Boxes                        │
 │   ▶ Information                  │
 │   ▶ Fields                       │
 ├──────────────────────────────────┤
 │ ▶ Perimeter of screen            │
 └──────────────────────────────────┘
```

Colours can also be changed by using the **Set color to** command. For example:

SET COLOR TO W/B, R+/N, G

The first pair of characters represent the foreground and background colours for the normal display text. The second pair represent the enhanced display text (e.g. status bar, field entry in edit and append), and the last character defines the colour of the screen border. The colour codes are as follows:

G - Green   N - Black
R - Red   GR - Yellow
B - Blue   RB - Magenta
W - White   BG - Cyan

If the ⊞ character follows the colour code the text will be brighter. If the ⊡ character follows the code the text will flash on and off.

1   If you have a colour monitor type the following at the dot prompt:

SET COLOR TO R/N, B/W, GR
CLEAR

2   To turn colour off, type:

SET COLOR TO

3   To turn the colour back to the default, type:

SET COLOR TO W+/B, B/W, N

Keys menu

The **Keys** menu allows the function keys to be re-assigned. The only key that cannot be changed is F1 , the **Help** key.

```
F2          assist;
F3          list;
F4          dir;
F5          display structure;
F6          display status;
F7          display memory;
F8          display;
F9          append;
F10         edit;
CTRL-F1
CTRL-F2
CTRL-F3
CTRL-F4
CTRL-F5
CTRL-F6
CTRL-F7
CTRL-F8
CTRL-F9
CTRL-F10
```

The function keys can also be changed by using the **Set function** command.

The semi-colon (;) is used within a function key definition to represent a press of the
| Enter | key.

1 Type the following at the dot prompt:

**SET FUNCTION F5 TO "USE PROPERTY;SET FORMAT TO PROPERTY;
APPEND;"**

2 Press | F5 | to call up the command and then press | Esc | to abandon.

Disk menu

The **Disk** menu will allow you to change the default drive and path. This can also
be set using the **Set default** command. For example:

SET DEFAULT TO A

Files menu

The **Files** menu will allow you to define the output device and open the screen form
and index files.

21.3   CONFIG.DB

If you find that there are several **Set** commands that you need to change on a
regular basis you may decide to store these commands in a file called CONFIG.DB.
This file is accessed by dBASE every time you load dBASE. dBASE first looks for
the file in the current sub-directory. If it is not there, it looks in the C:\DBASE
sub-directory. It then carries out all the commands in the CONFIG file. In this case,
dBASE will look in the C:\DBASE\DATA sub-directory first. It will then look in the
C:\DBASE sub-directory for the default CONFIG file which comes with dBASE.

You can look at the default CONFIG.DB file by typing:

TYPE C:\DBASE\CONFIG.DB

You can edit this file by using the dBASE editor (*see* 23.4 dBASE editor, page 179).
If you are considering modifying or creating a CONFIG file, read the appropriate
instructions before continuing. Modify the default CONFIG by typing:

MODIFY COMMAND C:\DBASE\CONFIG.DB

You can then make changes to the file and save using the **Exit** menu.

If you want to create your own CONFIG.DB file in the data sub-directory, type:

MODIFY COMMAND CONFIG.DB

As this file does not exist you will be presented with an empty file. You can then
type your commands. The following is an example of a personalised CONFIG file.

```
BELL = OFF
CONFIRM = ON
STATUS = ON
COLOR = W/B,W/R,N
PROMPT = DBASE>
F5 = "USE PROPERTY;SET FORMAT TO PROPERTY,APPEND,"
```

The **Prompt** command is used to changed the prompt to something more user friendly than the dot!

To test the file, leave dBASE by typing **QUIT** at the dot prompt. Then re-load dBASE.

The **Tedit** command can be used within the CONFIG file to change the editor accessed by the **Modify command** command. The **WP** command can be used to access a different editor or word processor for accessing memo fields.

If this is an area of interest, it is suggested that you read the appropriate sections referring to the CONFIG.DB in the dBASE product manuals.

21.4   File management

You can either manage your files using dBASE commands or you can access most DOS commands from within dBASE. If you are using the diskettes that accompany this book, you have already seen that DOS can be accessed from within the Control Centre. To use a DOS command at the dot prompt, simply prefix the command with an expanation mark (!). For example, typing **!DIR/W** will display a wide directory.

The following dBASE commands can be used to manage files:

Erase command

The **Erase** command will erase the named file. The **Delete file** command has the same effect. You cannot use wild card characters as you can with DOS. For example if you wanted to erase all the program files from a disk you could use the DOS command **!DEL *.PRG**. If you used the dBASE **Erase** or **Delete file** command you would have to erase each file individually.

Copy to command

The **Copy to** command will make a copy of the current database. It is advisable to use the dBASE **Copy** command in preference to the DOS **Copy** command because the dBASE command will copy all the files making up the database file. For example, if you type the commands below, dBASE will copy the PROPERTY.DBF file and the PROPERTY.DBT file.

For example, the commands:

USE PROPERTY
COPY TO A:PROPERTY

will make a copy of the PROPERTY database on a floppy disk.

COPY TO PROPOLD FOR DATE_SOLD>{01/01/91}
DELETE FOR DATE_SOLD>{01/01/91}

will make a of copy all properties which have been sold to a new database. The records that have been copied are then deleted from the PROPERTY database.

The **Copy** command can also be used to copy the records in a database to another product. For example, to copy the PROPERTY database to Lotus 1-2-3 you would type:

USE PROPERTY
COPY TO PROP WKS

This would create a Lotus 1-2-3 file called PROP. You can copy data to a number of different applications by including the relevant file type at the end of the command. These are listed in the dBASE Reference Manual under the **Copy** command.

Copy structure command

The **Copy structure** command makes a copy of the structure of the database but does not copy the records. This can be useful if you want to create a new database that has a similar structure to an existing database. You can then use the **Modify structure** command to make any changes. For example, you may want to create a new database to hold details on customers who want to rent properties. You could copy the structure of the existing customer database.

USE CUSTOMER
COPY STRUCTURE TO CUSTRENT

If required you can specify a field list (the entire command should be typed on the one line):

COPY STRUCTURE TO CUSTRENT FIELDS TITLE, FIRSTNAME, SURNAME, TELEPHONE

This would make a copy of the structure of the CUSTOMER database only including the fields specified.

Part 3

Programming

22 Scenario and objectives

22.1 Scenario

This Part will concentrate on the third working environment of dBASE by introducing the programming language. You have already seen, in the last Part, that dBASE commands can be given directly by using the dBASE language. By issuing these commands at the dot prompt, dBASE immediately acts upon those commands. dBASE interprets the command, and, assuming the syntax is correct, carries out the instruction.

At a basic level, a dBASE program is simply a number of dBASE commands (as issued at the dot prompt) stored together in a program file. When the program is run, dBASE carries out all the instructions in the program one after another. In addition to the commands used at the dot prompt, dBASE also has a number of commands that can only be used in programs. For example, you may want to carry out a number of commands a set number of times; the dBASE programming language contains special commands which instruct the program to loop round and repeat instructions.

In this Part you will begin by creating simple programs made up of a number of commands already used at the dot prompt. You will then be introduced to the new commands that can only be used when writing programs.

22.2 Objectives

The initial objective of this part is to build a simple menu-driven system using four database files that can be related to form a complete database system. In order to give some variety, you will be using a different system to the one used in Parts 1 and 2. The system is designed for a company providing training courses on standard PC applications. The system comprises four files; ORDERS, CLIENTS, COURSES and TRAINERS. You will use the CLIENTS file for examples and the COURSES file for optional consolidation exercises.

This Part will involve producing a menu driven system for the CLIENTS database file. This system will comprise four modules:

- Module 1 - A module for adding records to the database using a customised screen and validation techniques (see 23.6 Creating the addition module, page 181).

- Module 2 - A module for making changes to existing data. This will involve writing a simple edit routine (*see* 24.7 Creating the edit module, page 193).

- Module 3 - A module for record deletion. This module will form the basis of an exercise to consolidate the commands covered in the earlier modules (*see* 25.6 Consolidation exercises, page 200).

- Module 4 - A module for producing a monthly summary report to show the account number and the total invoice value for each client that has placed an order during the current month (*see* 26.3 Programming the report, page 204).

These four modules will then be 'pulled together' into a menu structure (*see* 27.3 Creating the menu program, page 209).

22.3   Preparing for Parts 3 and 4

 If working through Parts 3 and 4 without the accompanying disks, you will need to create the following files. You can either create them all now, or create them as they are needed. You will find individual lists of the required files at the beginning of each chapter.

File name	File type	Chapter
TRAINING	Catalog	22
ORDERS	Database	22
CLIENTS	Database	22
COURSES	Database	22
TRAINERS	Database	22
CLIENTS	Form	22
COURSES	Form	22

 If you have purchased the disks that accompany this book you can copy the necessary files from the appropriate floppy disk. The following instructions will copy the database and form files listed above. The program files can be copied from disk as the Part progresses. This is to give you the option of creating the files yourself.

 1   Make sure that you have created a sub-directory on the hard disk called DBASE\DATA (*see* Setting-up a data directory, page viii).

2   Load dBASE (*see* Starting the program, Chapter 3, page 9).

3   Insert the diskette for Parts 3 and 4 in drive A and type the following DOS command at the dot prompt:

!A:\C22.

If you intend to work through Parts 3 and 4 without the diskettes it is recommended that you create the following files at this stage.

1   Create a new catalog called **TRAINING**.

2   Create a new database called **ORDERS** with the following structure. The account number (**ACNO**) will be the master index tag. Specify this at the time of defining the structure.

Field	Field Name	Type	Width	Dec	Index
1	ORDNO	Character	4		N
2	ACNO	Character	5		Y
3	ODATE	Date	8		N
4	C_CODE	Character	6		N
5	C_DATE	Date	8		N
6	NUMBER	Numeric	2		N
7	TOT_COST	Numeric	9	2	N
*** Total ***			43		

3   Create an index tag based on the **ORDNO** field. If you want this index to be in numeric order rather than character order you will need to use the **VAL()** function. The value function works in the opposite way to the string function (**STR()**) used in Part 2. It converts a string to a value (numeric) in order to carry out an operation. The actual data is not affected.

INDEX ON VAL(ORDNO) TAG ORDNO

4   Add the following records:

```
. LIST
Record#  ORDNO ACNO  ODATE     C_CODE C_DATE   NUMBER   TOT_COST
      1  1     SMI02 24/01/92 LOTADV 20/02/92      1     150.00
      2  2     WES01 24/01/92 PARINT 04/03/92      2     500.00
      3  3     WES01 26/01/92 DOSINT 28/02/92      3     375.00
      4  4     WES01 26/01/92 WORINT 07/03/92      1     250.00
      5  5     YEL01 26/01/92 LOTADV 20/02/92      2     300.00
      6  6     YEL01 26/01/92 DBAINT 02/03/92      2     500.00
      7  7     FRE01 26/01/92 DBAADV 26/02/92      1     300.00
      8  8     BRO01 26/01/92 LOTINT 22/02/92      3     750.00
      9  9     KIN01 26/01/92 DBAINT 02/03/92      2     500.00
     10  10    SMI01 28/01/92 DBAINT 12/03/92      1     250.00
     11  11    BRO01 28/01/92 VENINT 08/03/92      2     640.00
     12  12    FRE01 28/01/92 VENINT 08/03/92      1     320.00
     13  13    SMI01 28/01/92 EXCINT 26/02/92      2     500.00
     14  14    BRO01 28/01/92 HARINT 07/03/92      4    1000.00
     15  15    FRE01 28/01/92 EXCINT 26/02/92      2     500.00
```

5 Create a database called **CLIENTS** with the following structure (include index tags on the **ACNO** and **SURNAME** fields):

Field	Field Name	Type	Width	Dec	Index
1	ACNO	Character	5		Y
2	COMPANY	Character	25		N
3	SURNAME	Character	12		Y
4	FIRST	Character	12		N
5	ADD1	Character	20		N
6	ADD2	Character	15		N
7	PCODE	Character	9		N
*** Total ***			99		

6 Add the following records:

```
SMI01 Peter Smith, Smith & Sons, 23  High Road, Greenoak GR1 4RF
BRO01 Mary Brown, Coopers & Brown Ltd, 45 Main Street, Greenoak GR2 8UT
WES01 Bruce West, Computer Supplies Ltd, 7 Sunny Street, Greenoak GR2 3WS
YEL01 Susie Yelland, The Royal Infirmary, 3 West Street, Greenoak GR1 6LM
FRE01 Jack French, Clear Insurance, 6 Green Street, Greenoak GR1 4RC
KIN01 Elizabeth King, The Gold Centre, 5 Jewel Road, Greenoak GR6 4NC
PET01 Kylie Peters, Goodwin Cars Ltd, 34 East Road, Greenoak GR3 9TA
DAV01 Bette Davies, Dept of Social Admin, 6 New Road, Greenoak GR1 5RD
FRY01 George Fry, Real Assurance, 9 The Avenue, Greenoak GR1 5KU
TAY01 Sue Taylor, Fry Street College, 56 Fry Street, Greenoak GR2 5IN
DOU01 Wesley Douglas, Challenge Bank, 5 Blue Road, Greenoak GR1 8AA
SMI02 Ken Smith, Carters Building plc, 89 Eastside Rd, Greenoak GR1 3BA
PET02 June Peterson, Freeman Tull & Reeves, 53 Cook Street, Greenoak GR6 8DQ
SMI03 David Smitters, A1 Confectionary Ltd, 91 Long Street, Greenoak GR1 6MC
GRE01 Carol Greeves, All Sports Ltd, 21 Camp Road, Greenoak GR1 7JS
BRO02 Lyn Broom, Lyn Broom & Co. Ltd, 3 Tower Close, Greenoak GR2 9HD
```

7 Create a suitable screen form to include any appropriate validation. Call the form **CLIENTS**. The following is just an example:

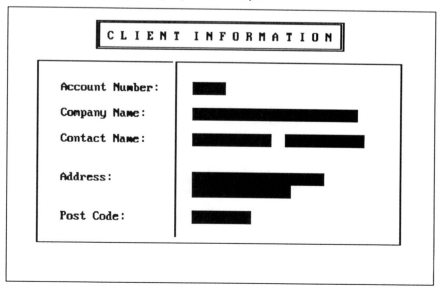

8 Create a database called **COURSES** with **C_CODE** as an index tag:

Field	Field Name	Type	Width	Dec	Index
1	C_CODE	Character	6		Y
2	COURSE	Character	25		N
3	LEVEL	Character	15		N
4	DAYS	Numeric	2		N
5	PRICE	Numeric	6	2	N
6	PLACES	Numeric	3		N
7	TR_CODE	Character	5		N
*** Total ***			63		

9 Add the following records:

C_CODE	COURSE	LEVEL	DAYS	PRICE	PLACES	TR_CODE
LOTADV	Lotus 1-2-3	Advanced	1	150.00	6	BRO01
LOTINT	Lotus 1-2-3	Introductory	2	125.00	7	BRO01
DBAINT	dBASE IV	Introductory	2	125.00	7	BRO01
DBAADV	dBASE IV	Advanced	2	150.00	4	BRO01
VENINT	Ventura Publisher	Introductory	2	160.00	5	HAR01
VENADV	Ventura Publisher	Advanced	1	170.00	4	HAR01
HARINT	Harvard Graphics	Introductory	2	125.00	7	JON01
WORINT	WordPerfect	Introductory	2	125.00	7	HAR01
WORADV	WordPerfect	Advanced	2	150.00	6	HAR01
EXCINT	Excel	Introductory	2	125.00	7	GRE01
EXCADV	Excel	Advanced	1	150.00	6	GRE01
DOSINT	DOS	Introductory	1	125.00	7	JON01
DOSADV	DOS	Advanced	1	150.00	6	JON01
PARINT	Paradox	Introductory	2	125.00	7	GRE01

10 Create a suitable screen form to include validation. Call the form **COURSES**.

11 Create a database called **TRAINERS** with **T_CODE** as an index tag:

Field	Field Name	Type	Width	Dec	Index
1	T_CODE	Character	5		Y
2	SNAME	Character	15		N
3	FNAME	Character	10		N
4	PHONE	Character	10		N
*** Total ***			41		

Record#	T_CODE	SNAME	FNAME	PHONE
1	BRO01	Brown	Jane	783 456
2	HAR01	Harvey	John	456 723
3	JON01	Jones	Mary	782 413
4	GRE01	Green	Robert	325 176

23 Programming with dBASE

As soon as an application requires automation, dBASE at the dot prompt level becomes inefficient. This is the time to start looking at the programming language and programming techniques.

23.1 Preparing for this chapter

In order to complete this chapter you need the following files:

File name	File type	Chapter
TRAINING	Catalog	22
CLIENTS	Database	22
COURSES	Database	22 (optional)
CLIENTS	Form	22
COURSES	Form	22 (optional)

 If you have not created these files in the Chapter 22 you should do so before continuing.

 If you have purchased the disks that accompany this book you can copy the necessary files from the appropriate floppy disk. Refer to the instructions for Preparing for this Part in Chapter 22.

23.2 Check-list for programming

Before launching into the vast array of commands and functions it is advisable to consider the following guidelines for writing programs:

❶ Establish the overall objectives of the system and make sure that the people using the system agree with these objectives.

❷ Define the information that needs to be entered into the system (the *inputs*), and the information that needs to be taken out of the system in the form of reports and queries (the *outputs*) and the operations that are needed to turn the inputs into outputs.

❸ Break the system into modules and code each module individually.

❹ Document each module as the code is produced.

⑤ Structure the code, include indents and be consistent with case; if you decide to enter the code in upper case, do not change to lower case partway through.

⑥ Include validation and helpful prompts.

⑦ Test each module thoroughly.

⑧ Create a menu structure to pull together all the modules.

⑨ Test your system thoroughly.

⑩ Don't re-invent the wheel! If someone in the organisation has written a similar system or has used similar routines, incorporating their code may save a great deal of time.

There are two ways to program with dBASE IV. As you have already seen, you can use the applications generator provided with dBASE IV. You can also create your own programs using the dBASE editor, or your own favourite editor (see 21.3 CONFIG.DB, page 168).

You may find that the applications generator produces systems that meet all your requirements, although any application generator, however sophisticated, will have short falls. That being the case, you will need to have a working knowledge of the programming language to enable you to enhance the generated system.

dBASE IV gives you the best of both worlds. You can generate sophisticated menus and screen layouts using the applications generator and then either choose to let the generator produce the code for the routines or gain greater flexibility and write the routines yourself. On occasion, for totally customised systems, you may need to create the whole system yourself.

Whichever method you choose to develop your systems, you will need to acquire a thorough understanding of the dBASE programming language. With any programming language it is a case of not trying to run before you can walk. You need to build a foundation before considering the more sophisticated features of the dBASE programming language.

23.3   Program files

dBASE refers to program files as command files; a file containing a number of commands. Command files are saved with an extension of PRG and should be named using the usual DOS conventions. Command files can be created from within the **Applications** panel of the Control Centre or from the dot prompt. To create a command file at the dot prompt type:

MODIFY COMMAND name

The dBASE editor searches the disk for a file called "name.PRG". If it cannot find one, it assumes that you want to create the file and displays an empty editing screen. Once you have entered the dBASE editor you can type the dBASE commands that make up your program.

The dBASE editor resembles a basic word processing package and is adequate for most editing tasks. You may wish to specify an editor of your own choice (*see* page 168). However, the dBASE editor is resident in memory, which makes it easier and faster to use than an external editor. It will edit files of unlimited size with command lines of up to 1024 characters.

The editor includes the same range of editing keys used to create reports or screen formats; [F6] to select, [F7] to move and [F8] to copy. The menus are accessed by [F10] or by pressing [Alt + letter], where letter is the first letter in the menu name, eg [Alt + W] to access the **Word** menu.

There are several other shortcut key combinations that can be used to speed up your editing:

[Ctrl + T]	to delete the current word
[Ctrl + Bck Space]	to delete the previous word
[Ctrl + N]	to insert a line
[Ctrl + Y]	to delete a line

In addition to the usual cursor movement keys, the following key combinations can be used to move around the file:

[Ctrl + PgUp]	to move to the first line in the file
[Ctrl + PgDn]	to move to the last line in the file
[Ctrl + →]	to move to the next word
[Ctrl + ←]	to move to the previous word

The command file can be saved or abandoned in the usual ways by accessing the **Exit** menu or you can use the shortcuts:

[Ctrl + End]	to save the command file and return to the dBASE dot prompt
[ESC]	to abandon the command file and return to the dBASE dot prompt

The available menu options are similar to those used in previous activities. As the need arises, you will look at the options in more detail.

When producing a program file of any size or complexity it is important to include full documentation. This documentation will be of invaluable help to anyone else who needs to work with your programs and will also help you when you return to look at programs. When you are working with a program, the code may seem self explanatory but if you return to that program in six months time the purpose of the code may be far from clear.

Comments can be included anywhere within a program and are identified by an asterisk (*) or the word **NOTE** at the beginning of the line or by two ampersands (**&&**) before the comment. dBASE will ignore any text following two [&] symbols or any lines beginning with the [*] symbol or word **NOTE**. The following example shows the different ways of commenting:

* This is a comment
NOTE this is a comment
Report form CLIENTS to print   && this is a comment

It is advisable to include comments throughout a program outlining exactly what each routine is designed to do. Comments should stand out from the program statements and should not interfere with the user's ability to read and understand the code. One popular method for achieving this is to box the comment in asterisks.

As well as including comments within the program you may want to include a program specification at the beginning of each program. This could include the name of the program file, the purpose, the date created and last edited and the author. For consistency it may be useful to create a program file that contains a template for documentation purposes. This template can then be incorporated at the beginning of each program file and filled in with relevant information. The following is an example of a heading template using the [*] character to denote a comment.

```
 Layout   Words   Go To   Print   Exit
[·······▼1·····▼··2····▼····3··▼·····4▼······▼5·····▼··6····▼·
*************************************************************************
*                                                                      *
* Name of file: MENU.PRG           Author: CAROL ELSTON               *
*                                                                      *
*                                                                      *
* Creation Date: 1/5/92            Date of last update: 10/5          *
*                                                                      *
* Comments: Menu program to access the Add, Edit, Delete and          *
*           Report routines for the CLIENTS database                  *
*                                                                      *
*************************************************************************
```

If using the disk, you can copy the program to be used as a heading template. Type the following at the dot prompt:

!COPY A:\C23\HEADING.PRG

1 At the dot prompt type:

   MODIFY COMMAND HEADING

2 Produce a blank template similar to the following example:

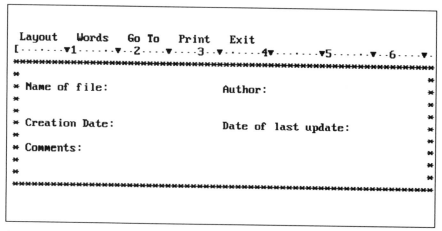

3 Save the file by either selecting the **Save** option from the **Exit** menu or by pressing Ctrl + End , the keyboard shortcut.

23.6   Creating the addition module

In this example you will create a very simple program file to add records to the CLIENTS database. Adding records to a database file could not be easier, it is simply a case of issuing the **Append** command, a blank template is produced and the record details entered. However for the sake of database integrity (keeping the data input consistent with the standards set) it is recommended that screen forms are used for data input and editing.

The screen form gives the database designer firm control over how the user changes information and also what information can be changed. By giving the user access to the inbuilt full screen commands **Append, Browse** and **Edit** the designer has very little control over data consistency. In addition, different screen formats can be designed for different user needs. The following are just some of the advantages of using a customised screen form:

- Prompts can be expanded and elaborated upon

- The order of data entry can be changed to conform with the sequence on the paper document from which the data is being transferred

- Fields can be omitted completely from the input/edit screen or displayed only, preventing editing

- Data can be validated to produce tighter control over the type of data entered

The creation of screen forms was covered in some detail in Chapter 12, with validation being introduced in Chapter 19. The following notes serve as a reminder.

A screen format can either be created by using the **Create screen** command, by writing a dBASE program using the file extension FMT or by incorporating code into a dBASE program file. At this level the **Create screen** command provides an adequate screen format, however for more advanced applications it may be necessary to either adapt or write the format file.

To use a customised screen it is necessary to open a database file and its associated screen format file. The **Append** and **Edit** commands will then access the customised screen.

 1 At the dot prompt type the following:

USE CLIENTS
SET FORMAT TO CLIENTS
EDIT

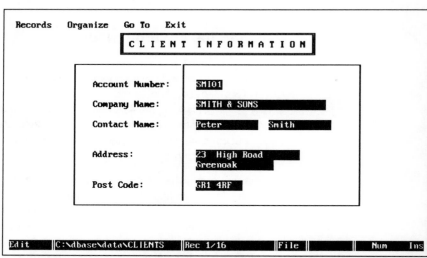

2 The customised screen should be in view. Press ⎡**Esc**⎤ to exit and abandon.

Later in this Part you will include an addition routine to a menu driven system. In preparation for this you will create a small program file using **Modify command.** This command allows both the creation and modification of a program file.

1   If working with the disk you can copy the program to add a record to the
          CLIENTS database by typing the following at the dot prompt:

          !COPY A:\C23\CLIADD.PRG

      2   Type **MODI COMM CLIADD** to edit the program. Fill in your details in the
          heading (*see* 3 below) and study the code. Access the **Exit** menu to return to
          the dot prompt.

 1   At the dot prompt type:

          MODI COMM CLIADD

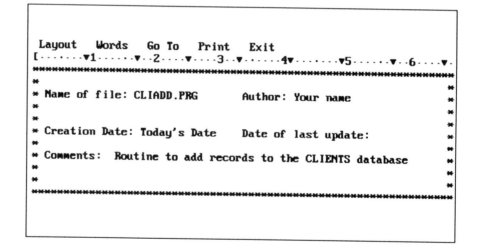

      2   Before you enter the commands you can read in the template heading file you
          created earlier. Access the **Word** menu and select the option **Write/read text
          file**. Select the **Read file** option and type **HEADING.PRG** as the file name (you
          need to include the file extension otherwise dBASE will assume a file type of
          TXT, a text file).

      3   Fill in the relevant details as shown below:

      4   Type in the following commands:

          SET BELL OFF
          SET CONFIRM ON

          USE CLIENTS
          SET FORMAT TO CLIENTS
          APPEND
          CLOSE FORMAT

```
CLOSE ALL
CLEAR
SET BELL ON
SET CONFIRM OFF
RETURN
```

Although the **Return** command is not strictly necessary in a program called from the dot prompt, you will need to include this command when you call the routine from a menu program. The **Return** command tells dBASE to return to the point of call. The same is true for the **Close format** command. It is superfluous if followed by **Close all**. You will however, remove the **Close all** command when you add the program to the menu.

23.7 Running a dBASE program

Command files can be run from the **Applications** panel of the Control Centre, from the dot prompt or from within another program. To run a program from the dot prompt type the command **Do** followed by the program name. For example to run the program CLIADD, you would type **DO CLIADD**.

```
Compilation error

DO CLIADD

Cancel  Edit  Help
```

The first time you run a new program, dBASE will convert the program to a form that is more easily used by the dBASE interpreter. This new file has the same name as the program file but has the extension DBO, which stands for *dBASE object code*.

If your program contains an error, a help screen will be displayed. You have the choice to **Cancel** out of the program, **Edit** the program or get **Help**.

1 Run the program by typing **DO CLIADD** at the dot prompt. If the program has an error select the **Cancel** option from the **Error** menu and modify the command file.

23.8 Consolidation exercise

1 Write a program to append records to the **COURSES** database. The screen format file is called **COURSES**. Call the program **COURSADD**.

2 Include the heading template and fill in the appropriate details.

3 Run and test the program.

See Appendix 3, page 267 for solutions.

24 Program interaction

There is little point in writing a program that can only be used once. By definition, a computer program is a collection of instructions that need to be repeated on a regular basis. In practice this means that the program needs to contain a certain amount of variable data. For example, if you were to write a program to edit the records in the CLIENTS database you would need to position the record pointer at the appropriate record before accessing the program. Alternatively, you could halt the program and ask the user to provide information which could be used to pin-point the required record. For example, you could ask them to enter the client surname and then search for that surname.

When developing systems for users with little or no experience of dBASE, it is important to include all interaction within the program. To expect a novice user to set up the environment before running the program is asking for disaster!

24.1 Preparing for this chapter

In order to complete this chapter you need the following files:

File name	File type	Chapter
TRAINING	Catalog	22
CLIENTS	Database	22
COURSES	Database	22 (optional)
CLIENTS	Form	22
COURSES	Form	22 (optional)
HEADING	Program	23

 If you have not created these files in the previous chapters you will need to refer back to the chapter number listed above and create the files.

 If you have purchased the disks that accompany this book you can copy the necessary files from the appropriate floppy disk. To do this, complete the following instructions:

1   Copy the database and form files by following the instructions for Preparing for Parts 3 and 4 on page 173.

2   Copy the program file by typing **!COPY A:\C23\HEADING.PRG** at the dot prompt.

24.2   Displaying messages

If the program is going to interact with the user you are going to need a method of communicating. You can do this by displaying messages and providing prompts for user input. The easiest method of displaying information on the screen or printer is to use the dBASE **Query** command (?). Any text or field preceded by a ⟨ **?** ⟩ will be echoed back to the current output device. This a very useful tool that can be used either at the dot prompt or within a program.

Type the following examples at the dot prompt to give some indication of the possible uses:

1   The **?** can be used to echo character strings - the message must be enclosed in single or double quotes or by square brackets [].

   ?"Turn the printer on"

2   The **?** can be used the perform the operations of a simple calculator.

   ?22/7

3   The **?** can be used to display the content of a field.

   USE CLIENTS
   ?SURNAME

4   The **?** can be used to combine text and field data - this is called concatenation.

   ?"His name is "+SURNAME

24.3   Memory variables

Memory variables can best be described as temporary fields. A memory variable is defined in a similar way to a field with both the type and length being stated. Whereas a field is a permanent storage location a memory variable is designed to only hold information during the running of a program. It is very much a temporary storage location.

Memory variables have many uses; holding the results of calculations, the response to questions, values to search for, are just a few examples. The data type of a memory variable is determined by its initial value. It can hold **Character**, **Numeric**, **Date** or **Logical** details (not **Memo**). Many conventions exist for the naming of memory variables, the one adopted in this book is to start the memory variable name with the letter M. It is important that memory variables can be easily distinguished from field and file names.

The following examples show how these different types of memory variables can be initialised. Type the following examples at the dot prompt:

1   Both the following commands create a memory variable called **MNUM** and set its value to **6**. **MNUM** will automatically be defined as **Numeric**. Initialising using an equals sign can be adopted when initialising all types of memory variable but tends to only be used for **Numeric** types.

STORE 6 TO MNUM
MNUM = 6

2   The following example creates a **Character** memory variable called **MANS** with a width of **3** and an initial value of **Yes**. The text must be enclosed in single or double quotes or square brackets.

STORE 'Yes' TO MANS

3   This example creates a **Character** memory variable called **MNAME** with a width of **10**. The **SPACE()** function is used to initialise **MNAME** as blank.

STORE SPACE(10) TO MNAME

4   This example creates a **Logical** memory variable called **MLOGIC** which has been initialised to **True**.

STORE .T. TO MLOGIC

5   Both the following commands create a **Date** memory variable called **MDATE**. The second example, which is simpler, can only be used with dBASE IV. The first example (used with dBASE III) uses the **CTOD()** function (character to date), to translate the character string "25/12/92" to a date.

STORE CTOD("25/12/92") TO MDATE
STORE {25/12/92} TO MDATE

6   Type **DISPLAY MEMORY** to check that the memory variables have been defined.

24.4 Prompting for user input

If you prompt a user for information from within a program, you need to store that information so that you can gauge the response. You do this by storing the response in a memory variable. There are a number of methods available, their suitability depending on the situation.

Accept

The **Accept** command should be used to allow the entry of a single value. The value entered will be stored in a character type memory variable even if it is a digit.

1   Type the following example at the dot prompt:

ACCEPT "Edit another record? Y/N: " to MREPLY

As soon as you press the | **Enter** | key, the command will run and the following prompt displayed on the screen:

Edit another record? Y/N:

2   Type **Y** or **N** in response to the prompt and press the | **Enter** | key. Your response is stored in the **MREPLY** memory variable.

Input

The **Input** command is usually used to prompt for numeric data although character data can be input if enclosed in quotes or square brackets.

1   Type the following example at the dot prompt:

INPUT "Enter the price: " to MPRICE

As soon as you press the | **Enter** | key, the command will run.

2   Type **52.50** in response to the prompt. The value will be stored in the **Numeric** memory variable called **MPRICE**.

Wait

The **Wait** command halts a program until a key is pressed. Used on its own, the **Wait** command displays the prompt "Press any key to continue..". If required, the prompt can be customised and the response (a single key press) held in a memory variable.

1   Type **WAIT** at the dot prompt. The prompt "Press any key to continue... " will be displayed. The key press is not captured.

2   Change the command to include a message:

WAIT "Press C to Continue, S to Stop: " TO MWAIT

The customised prompt is displayed and the response is stored in the **MWAIT** memory variable.

@ command

The @ command can be used to draw lines and boxes on the screen. The @ character is followed by screen co-ordinates. For example @3,10 represents row 3 column 10. The screen comprises 80 characters across, (0-79) and 24 lines down (0-23). The command @R,C TO R,C, where R is the row co-ordinate and C the column co-ordinate draws a line or box between the co-ordinates. If the two row co-ordinates, or the 2 column co-ordinates have the same value then a line is drawn, otherwise a box is drawn.

Type the following commands at the dot prompt:

1   Draw a horizontal line across the top of the screen.

   CLEAR
   @2,5 TO 2,75

2   Draw a double lined box.

   @10,5 TO 15,75 DOUBLE

If you are working with a colour monitor you can fill areas of the screen with different colours by specifying the co-ordinates.

3   Fill the area specified by the co-ordinates with a red background.

   CLEAR
   @5,5 FILL TO 18,75 COLOR W/R

For further information on colour, *refer* to 21.2 Set commands, page 165.

Say and Get commands

The **Say** and **Get** commands are used together to display information on the screen and capture user input. If used independently, each command is preceded by an @ character and two numbers which represent the screen co-ordinate.

The **Get** command, which is usually accompanied by a **Say** command, displays the contents of a field or memory variable allowing the contents to be changed. A **Get** command, or number of **Get** commands, must always be accompanied by a **Read** command. Until dBASE reaches the **Read** command the contents of the fields or memory variables cannot be changed.

Type the following examples at the dot prompt:

1   These two commands clear the screen and display the message 'Printing..' at row 10 column 10.

```
CLEAR
@10,10 SAY 'Printing..'
```

2   Display 'Please wait' at row 15 column 40.

```
@15,40 SAY 'Please wait'
```

3   Clear the screen, open the **CLIENTS** database and position the cursor at row 10 column 10. Display the contents of the **SURNAME** field of the current record.

```
CLEAR
USE CLIENTS
@10,10 SAY SURNAME
```

4   Position the cursor at row 10 column 10 and allow the contents of the **SURNAME** field to be edited. Change the surname to **Cooper**.

```
CLEAR
@10,10 GET SURNAME
READ
```

5   Display the content of the **SURNAME** field which has been changed to Cooper.

```
?SURNAME
```

6   Change the surname back to **Smith**.

```
CLEAR
@10,10 SAY 'Please change the surname: ' GET SURNAME
READ
```

7   If using the **Get** command to capture a response as a memory variable, the memory variable must be defined before the **Get** command. This example defines a character memory variable called **MQUEST** with a length of **3**. The memory variable is initially blank and is used to hold the response to the **Say, Get** command.

```
STORE SPACE(3) TO MQUEST
CLEAR
@10,15 SAY "Continue? YES/NO: " GET MQUEST
READ
```

24.5   Validating user input

In Chapter 19, you discovered the advantages of including validation in screen forms. You included **Picture functions** to validate the whole field and **Templates** to validate on a character by character basis. You can include exactly the same validation when accepting user input to a program. You do this by including the **Function** command (works in the same way as the **Picture function**) and the **Picture** command (works in the same way as the **Template**). The following examples will act as a reminder of the validation clauses available. For further details, *refer* to Chapter 19, Validation with a screen form.

Type the following examples at the dot prompt:

[Note: The ; (semi-colon) is a line continuation character, used in dBASE programs to aid clarity. At the dot prompt type the whole command on the one line, leaving out the semi-colon.]

1   In this example, the **Function** command will convert all characters to upper case. The **Picture** command stipulates that the first three characters must be letters and the last two digits.

```
STORE SPACE(5) to MACNO
CLEAR
@10,10 SAY "Enter the Account Number: " GET MACNO;
    FUNCTION "!" PICTURE "AAA99"
READ
```

Type three letters in lower case followed by two numbers. Type **?MACNO**, the memory variable should contain three upper case letters followed by two numbers. Use the history facility to repeat the above commands and try entering an account number made up of two numbers followed by three letters.

2   In the next example, the **M function** defines a multiple choice field, the two choices being **Yes** and **No**.

```
STORE 'YES' TO MANS
CLEAR
@10,10 SAY "Edit another record? " GET MANS;
    FUNCTION "M YES,NO"
READ
```

3   In the following example, the **Picture** specifies that the price should be displayed to **2** decimal places. The **Range** specifies that the price entered must be in the range **50** to **999**.

```
STORE 100 TO MPRICE
CLEAR
@10,10 SAY "Enter price: " GET MPRICE PICTURE "999.99";
    RANGE 50,999
READ
```

You will find that some dBASE programmers combine the **Function** and **Picture** commands. The following commands produce exactly the same result. It is simply a matter of preference as to which is used.

```
FUNCTION "!" PICTURE "AAA99"
PICTURE "@! AAA99"
```

24.6   dBASE generated code

When files are created, from within the Control Centre or the dot prompt, dBASE actually produces program files. Some of these files can be looked at and some cannot.

One of the files generated when a screen form is created comprises a number of **Say, Get** commands. You may be interested, at this stage, to look at the code.

 Type the following at the dot prompt:

    CLOSE ALL
    MODIFY COMMAND CLIENTS.FMT

You need to include the file extension as this is not a dBASE program file (PRG).

The code at the top and bottom of the program sets up the environment. Some of the commands should look familiar. The code that actually generates the screen is shown below. It looks very similar to the examples used in this chapter (press **PgDn** to scroll through the code):

```
@1,21 TO 3,58 DOUBLE
@ 2,23 SAY "C L I E N T   I N F O R M A T I O N"
@ 4,12 TO 18,67
@ 4,33 SAY ""
@ 5,33 SAY ""
@ 6,16 SAY "Account Number:"
@ 6,33 SAY " "
@ 6,36 GET Acno PICTURE "@! AAA99" ;
   MESSAGE "The Account Number should be the 1st 3;
      letters of client surname plus 2 digits"
@ 7,33 SAY ""
@ 8,16 SAY "Company Name: "
@ 8,33 SAY " "

@ 8,36 GET Company PICTURE "@! XXXXXXXXXXXXXXXXXXXXXXXXX";
   MESSAGE "Enter the Company Name"
@ 9,33 SAY ""
@ 10,16 SAY "Contact Name: "
@ 10,33 SAY " "
@ 10,36 GET First PICTURE "!XXXXXXXXXX" ;
   MESSAGE "Enter the firstname of the client"
@ 10,48 SAY " "
@ 10,50 GET Surname PICTURE "!XXXXXXXXXX" ;
   MESSAGE "Enter the surname of the client"
@ 11,33 SAY ""
@ 12,33 SAY ""
@ 13,16 SAY "Address:     "
@ 13,33 SAY " "
@ 13,36 GET Add1 PICTURE "XXXXXXXXXXXXXXXXXXXX" ;
```

```
     MESSAGE "Enter Address"
@ 14,33 SAY ""
@ 14,36 GET Add2 PICTURE "XXXXXXXXXXXXXXX"
@ 15,33 SAY ""
@ 16,16 SAY "Post Code:"
@ 16,33 SAY ""
@ 16,36 GET Pcode PICTURE "XXXXXXXXX" ;
    MESSAGE "Enter the postcode"
@ 17,33 SAY ""
```

24.7 Creating the edit module

In this section you will use the commands covered in this chapter to create a new program file called **CLIEDIT**. Although simplistic, this program will allow the user to edit a record within the **CLIENTS** database.

1 If working with the disk you can copy the program to edit records in the **CLIENTS** database by typing the following at the dot prompt:

   !COPY A:\C24\CLIEDIT.PRG

2 Type **MODI COMM CLIEDIT** to edit the program. Fill in your details in the heading (*see* 2 below) and study the code. Access the **Exit** menu to return to the dot prompt. Run the program (*see* 4 and 5 below).

1 Type the following at the dot prompt:

   MODI COMM CLIEDIT

2 Access the **Word** menu and select the **Write/read a file** option. Read the file called **HEADING.PRG**. Fill in the details as shown below.

```
***********************************************************************
*                                                                   *
* Name of file: CLIEDIT.PRG       Author: Your name                 *
*                                                                   *
*                                                                   *
* Creation Date: Today's date     Date of last update:              *
*                                                                   *
* Comments: Routine to edit a record in the CLIENTS database        *
*                                                                   *
***********************************************************************
```

3 Type the code for the edit routine:

   SET TALK OFF
   SET BELL OFF
   SET CONFIRM ON

   USE CLIENTS ORDER TAG ACNO

```
STORE SPACE(5) TO MACNO
CLEAR
@3,0 TO 19,79
@10,10 SAY "Please enter the Account Number: ";
     GET MACNO PICTURE "@! AAA99"
READ

SEEK MACNO
CLEAR
SET FORMAT TO CLIENTS
EDIT
CLOSE FORMAT

CLOSE ALL
CLEAR
SET BELL ON
SET CONFIRM OFF
SET TALK ON

RETURN
```

4   Save and run the program.

5   Type **SMI02** as the account number. If you have an error, edit the program, correct the mistakes and re-run.

Checklist

❶ **SET TALK OFF/ON** - At the dot prompt, dBASE "talks" back, telling us what is happening. This is well illustrated by the **Skip** command. If you type **SKIP** at the dot prompt dBASE responds with the database name and the number of the record skipped to. Usually this type of information is not required when running a program and it is usual practice to turn **Talk Off** at the beginning of a program and **On** again at the end.

❷ Continuation Character (;) - On the **@SAY** line of the program, the semi-colon has been used to split the line. The second half of the command has been indented by pressing the ⌷Tab⌷ key. In order to position the next line back at the margin, press ⌷Shift + Tab⌷ before typing.

❸ **SEEK** - The **Seek** command is used to find a record in an indexed database, (*see* 17.5 Finding records, page 131).

24.8	**Consolidation exercise**

1   Write an edit routine for the **COURSES** database. Call the program **COUREDIT**. Search on the **C_CODE** field. Test the program thoroughly.

See Appendix 3, page 267 for solutions.

25 Testing user response and using program loops

The edit routine produced in the Chapter 24 is very basic but is a good starting point for developing a more sophisticated routine. In general, an editing routine should include the following attributes:

- a prompt to allow the user to specify the record they want to edit

- validation of the data entered by the user

- a search routine to find the selected record

- a message if the record does not exist

- full screen editing using a customised format screen

- the option to edit another record

At the moment, the edit routine assumes that the record exists, and it does not give the user the option to edit more than one record at a time. In order to include these new features it is necessary to consider the dBASE facilities for looping back to the start of a program, to repeat a series of commands. You have already seen how to temporarily save a user response. You now need to look at how you can test that response.

25.1 Preparing for this chapter

In order to complete this chapter you need the following files:

File name	File type	Chapter
TRAINING	Catalog	22
CLIENTS	Database	22
COURSES	Database	22 (optional)
CLIENTS	Form	22
COURSES	Form	22 (optional)
HEADING	Program	23
CLIEDIT	Program	24
COUREDIT	Program	24 (optional)

If you have not created these files in the previous chapters you will need to refer back to to the chapter number listed on the previous page and create the files.

 If you have purchased the disks that accompany this book you can copy the necessary files from the appropriate floppy disk. To do this, complete the following instructions:

1   Copy the database and form files by following the instructions for Preparing for Parts 3 and 4 on page 173.

2   Copy the program files by typing **!COPY A:\CN\PROGRAM.PRG** at the dot prompt, where N is the chapter number and PROGRAM the program name. For example, to copy **HEADING.PRG**, type **!COPY A:\C23\HEADING.PRG**.

25.2   Do while... enddo command

This *looping* command is designed to allow the user to repeat a number of instructions. The **Do while** command can only be used within a program; not at dot prompt level. There are four main ways in which the command is used in dBASE. The objective is the same in each case, namely to repeat a command or set of commands a required number of times.

The main pitfall to avoid is to inadvertently set up an *eternal loop* from which there is no escape. In order to avoid this always make sure that **Escape** is set **On** during program testing. You can then always *escape* out of your program if it doesn't do what you expected. The following examples show the four different ways in which the command can be used:

The following example sets up an eternal loop from which an 'escape hatch' must be specified, for example the RETURN command to return to dBASE command level.

```
DO WHILE .T.
  <commands>
ENDDO
```

The second example is an alternative form of the above code, using a memory variable as an escape from the loop. For example if a particular condition is met the memory variable controlling the loop is set to false

```
STORE .T.  TO MLOOP
DO WHILE MLOOP
   <commands>
    STORE  .F.  TO MLOOP
ENDDO
```

The following code will repeat a command or routine until the end of the file is reached. The **EOF()** function (end of file) returns a **True** or **False** response depending on whether the record pointer is at the end of file. The **Skip** command moves the record pointer to the next record (*see* page 121).

```
DO WHILE .NOT. EOF()
  <commands>
    SKIP
ENDDO
```

This final example repeats a command or routine five times (until the counter reaches a value of 6).

```
STORE 1 TO MCOUNT
DO WHILE MCOUNT < 6
  <commands>
    STORE MCOUNT+1 TO MCOUNT
ENDDO
```

If the **Loop** command is included within the **Do while... enddo** command, the program will *loop* back to the first instruction following the **Do while** command.

As you develop further programs you will see the different uses of this powerful programming structure.

25.3 If...else... endif command

In the most basic form the **If** command can be used to evaluate a single condition. In this case no **Else** clause is required. When two alternative actions can take place depending upon a condition, each can be placed as the result of either the **If** or the **Else** clause

When more than two courses of action are required a series of **If** commands can be used. This is referred to as *nesting* and can become very complicated. In some cases it may be preferable to use the **Do case** command which will be considered later.

The following example shows the basic, single option; if the condition is met, carry out the command.

```
IF <condition>
  <command>
ENDIF
```

This second example shows the double option; if the condition is met carry out command 1 else carry out command 2.

```
IF <condition>
  <command 1>
ELSE
  <command 2>
ENDIF
```

And thirdly, the nested command. The practice of indenting the nested commands makes it easier to understand and also easier to check the structure.

```
IF <condition 1>
   <command 1>
ELSE
   IF <condition 2>
      < command 2>
   ELSE
      <command 3>
   ENDIF
ENDIF
```

You have already looked at several methods for capturing user response. The next stage is to test that response and, depending upon the outcome, perform some function. For example, you could ask the user if they want to edit another record. If the response is yes, you could loop back to the beginning of the program. If the response is no, you could exit from the program.

In the case of the edit program the **If** command could be constructed in the following way (the example is written as logical statements and not in the dBASE language):

IF the user response is Yes
   Loop back to the beginning of the program
ELSE
   exit from the program
ENDIF

Using the edit command in a program

In your first attempt at writing an edit routine you opened the screen form and used the **Edit** command to allow changes to the current record. You could have used **Browse** as an alternative. If you are writing a system for a novice user you may decide to restrict their access to the database. If this is the case, you would certainly not want to use the **Browse** command; it is too easy to make mass changes to the data.

The **Edit** command will just show the current record but the user can always page up and down through the records. If searching on a non-unique field, this may be exactly want you want. For example, if the program is searching on the SURNAME field, there could easily be a number of records with the same surname. The **Seek** command would find the first match and the user could then page down through the remaining matches.

If searching on a unique field, you may want to restrict the user to the selected record. You can do this by using the **Edit record** command. The following examples will show the differences between the commands.

Type the following at the dot prompt:

1   The following commands will give access to record number 6 in the active database. Other records in the file can be accessed by using the PgUp and PgDn keys. Press Esc to exit and abandon any changes made.

```
USE CLIENTS
EDIT 6
```

2   The following command will edit record 6 but other records in the file can not be
    accessed. If you try paging up or down you will be returned to the dot prompt.

```
EDIT RECORD 6
```

3   When using the **Edit record** command in a program you will not know the
    record number. This problem can be solved by using the **RECNO()** function, to
    return the current record number. To show how this function works, type the
    following at the dot prompt:

```
GO TOP
?RECNO()
SKIP 3
?RECNO()
```

25.5   Modifying the edit routine

In this section you will modify the **CLIEDIT** program to include the new commands
covered in this chapter.

1   If working with the disk you can copy the modified version of **CLIEDIT** by typing
    the following at the dot prompt:

```
!COPY A:\C25\CLIEDIT.PRG
```

2   Add appropriate comments to the code. When complete, save and run the
    program.

Modify the **CLIEDIT** program so that it resembles the following.   Add appropriate
comments to the code. When complete, save and run the program.

```
SET TALK OFF
SET BELL OFF
SET CONFIRM ON

USE CLIENTS ORDER TAG ACNO

DO WHILE .T.

    STORE SPACE(5) TO MACNO
    CLEAR
    @3,0 TO 19,79
    @10,10 SAY "Please enter the Account Number: " ;
        GET MACNO PICTURE "@! AAA99"
    READ
```

```
        SEEK MACNO
        CLEAR

        IF .NOT. EOF()
            SET FORMAT TO CLIENTS
            EDIT RECORD RECNO()
            CLOSE FORMAT
        ELSE
            STORE "Y" TO MANS
            @3,0 TO 19,79
            @10,10 SAY "Account Number does not exist re-enter? Y/N ";
            GET MANS FUNCTION "M Y,N"
            READ
            IF MANS = "Y"
                    LOOP    &&loops back to the command following DO WHILE.T.
            ENDIF
        ENDIF

        CLEAR
        STORE "Y" TO MANS
        @3,0 TO 19,79
        @10,10 SAY "Edit another record? Y/N ";
        GET MANS FUNCTION "M Y,N"
        READ
        IF MANS = "Y"
            LOOP
        ENDIF

        CLOSE ALL
        CLEAR
        SET BELL ON
        SET CONFIRM OFF
        SET TALK ON

        RETURN
    ENDDO
```

25.6 Consolidation exercises

 Look carefully at the changes made to the **CLIEDIT** program and make similar changes to the **COUREDIT** program.

 1 Write a deletion routine for the **CLIENTS** database. Call the routine **CLIDEL**. Search on the **ACNO** field. Document each stage of the routine. Test the routine thoroughly.

2   Modify the deletion routine to include an option to pack the database. This option should be included after the user has finished deleting records.

3   Improve the routine by displaying the client name and company name before deleting a record - prompt the user as to whether the record is to be deleted or not - if yes delete, otherwise continue.

4   Improve the pack routine so that the user is only asked if they want to pack when a record has been marked for deletion. (Hint: use the **DELETED()** function; this function returns a **True** or **False** result.)

It is suggested that you attempt this exercise even if working with the diskettes, as with all consolidation exercises help can be found in the appropriate Appendix. If you do not have the time to write the **CLIDEL** program, copy it from disk by typing **!COPY A:\C25\CLIDEL.PRG** as it will be referred to in later chapters.

Write a deletion routine for the **COURSES** database. Call it **COURDEL**.

See Appendix 3, page 268 for solutions.

26   Programming a report

The dBASE Report Generator is sophisticated enough to generate the majority of reports that you are likely to require. However, in order to practice your programming skills, this chapter will look at the steps involved in producing a simple report.

This report will list all clients that have placed orders, totalling the invoice value for those orders. For example, if the client with the account number SMI02, has placed three orders in the current month, you need to total the amount owing. You can do this using the **Total** command.

26.1   Preparing for this chapter

In order to complete this chapter you need the following files:

File name	File type	Chapter
TRAINING	Catalog	22
CLIENTS	Database	22
COURSES	Database	22 (optional)
ORDERS	Database	22
HEADING	Program	23

If you have not created these files in the previous chapters you will need to refer back to to the chapter number listed above and create the files.

IIf you have purchased the disks that accompany this book you can copy the necessary files from the appropriate floppy disk. To do this, complete the following instructions:

1   Copy the database and form files by following the instructions for Preparing for Parts 3 and 4 on page 173.

2   Copy the program file by typing **!COPY A:\C23\HEADING.PRG** at the dot prompt.

26.2   Total command

The **Total** command can be used to total all the numeric fields in a database for a particular field. For example, if you totalled on the ACNO field in the ORDERS database, the numeric fields NUMBER and TOT_COST would be totalled for each account number.

To use the **Total** command, the database must be indexed on the field to be totalled on. With the example above, the ORDERS database would need to be indexed on the ACNO field.

The **Total** command produces a new database file which contains one totalled record for each data value of the index field. In this example, the new database will contain one record for each account number.

To show how the **Total** command works, type the following commands at the dot prompt:

1   Open the database and index tag:

USE ORDERS ORDER TAG ACNO
DISPLAY ALL

```
. use orders order tag acno
Master index: ACNO
. disp all
Record#  ORDNO ACNO  ODATE    C_CODE C_DATE  NUMBER  TOT_COST
     8     8    BRO01 26/01/92 LOTINT 22/02/92      3   750.00
    11    11    BRO01 28/01/92 VENINT 08/03/92      2   640.00
    14    14    BRO01 28/01/92 HARINT 07/03/92      4  1000.00
     7     7    FRE01 26/01/92 DBAADV 26/02/92      1   300.00
    12    12    FRE01 28/01/92 VENINT 08/03/92      1   320.00
    15    15    FRE01 28/01/92 EXCINT 26/02/92      2   500.00
     9     9    KIN01 26/01/92 DBAINT 02/03/92      2   500.00
    10    10    SMI01 28/01/92 DBAINT 12/03/92      1   250.00
    13    13    SMI01 28/01/92 EXCINT 26/02/92      2   500.00
     1     1    SMI02 24/01/92 LOTADV 20/02/92      1   150.00
     2     2    WES01 24/01/92 PARINT 04/03/92      2   500.00
     3     3    WES01 26/01/92 DOSINT 28/02/92      3   375.00
     4     4    WES01 26/01/92 WORINT 07/03/92      1   250.00
     5     5    YEL01 26/01/92 LOTADV 20/02/92      2   300.00
     6     6    YEL01 26/01/92 DBAINT 02/03/92      2   500.00
```

You can see that several orders have been placed by some of the clients.

2   Produce a file with one record for the primary field, totalling numeric fields:

TOTAL ON ACNO TO ORDCLIEN

3   Open the totalled file:

USE ORDCLIEN

4   Display the records in the totalled file. You will see that only the totalled field and some of the numeric fields are relevant.

DISPLAY ALL

```
. total on acno to ordclien
     15 records totaled
      7 records generated
. use ordclien
. disp all
Record#  ORDNO ACNO  ODATE    C_CODE C_DATE   NUMBER   TOT_COST
      1   8    BRO01 26/01/92 LOTINT 22/02/92      9    2390.00
      2   7    FRE01 26/01/92 DBAADU 26/02/92      4    1120.00
      3   9    KIN01 26/01/92 DBAINT 02/03/92      2     500.00
      4  10    SMI01 28/01/92 DBAINT 12/03/92      3     750.00
      5   1    SMI02 24/01/92 LOTADU 20/02/92      1     150.00
      6   2    WES01 24/01/92 PARINT 04/03/92      6    1125.00
      7   5    YEL01 26/01/92 LOTADU 20/02/92      4     800.00
.
Command  C:\dbase\data\ORDCLIEN    Rec EOF/7      File            N
```

26.3   Programming the report

By utilising a range of functions (*see* Chapter 20) and the programming commands covered so far, the program can now be coded. If unsure of any of the code used in this program refer back to the appropriate chapters to refresh your knowledge. The new commands are listed at the end of the program; along with an explanation.

1   If working with the disk you can copy the report by typing the following at the dot prompt:

!COPY A:\C26\CLIREP.PRG

2   Add appropriate comments to the code. When complete, save and run the program.

Create a new program called **CLIREP**. Remember to include the heading. Type the code as shown in the following illustration:

SET TALK OFF
SET SAFETY OFF

USE ORDERS ORDER TAG ACNO

* The order file needs to be summarised to produce one record for
* each customer, totalling the TOT_COST field.

TOTAL ON ACNO TO ORDCLIEN

* Creates a new database containing one record per customer

USE ORDCLIEN

CLEAR

```
STORE 'N' TO MANS
@3,0 TO 19,79
@10,10 SAY 'Do you want to print the report? Y/N....';
  GET MANS FUNCTION "M Y,N"
READ

IF MANS = "Y"
  SET PRINT ON
ENDIF

  *Print a page heading including the date.
  ?'              Computer And Training Services'
  ?
  ?'          Invoice details for the month of '+CMONTH(ODATE)
  ?

  DO WHILE .NOT. EOF()
    ?'Customer Number: '+ACNO

   ?? '   Monthly Invoice Total: '+STR(TOT_COST,6,2)
    ?
    SKIP
  ENDDO

IF MANS = "Y"

  EJECT
  SET PRINT OFF
ELSE
  WAIT
ENDIF

CLOSE ALL
CLEAR

SET SAFETY ON
SET TALK ON

RETURN
```

Checklist

❶ **SET PRINT ON/OFF** - as soon as the program reaches the **Set print on**
command, output will be sent to the printer. When the **Set print off** command is
reached, dBASE will stop sending the output to the printer.

❷ **EJECT** - the **Eject** command sends a form feed to the printer.

❸ **??** - You have already seen that the **Query** command (?) displays information
on the next line. The **Double query** command (??) displays the information at
the next available position on the same line, a line throw is not given.

❹ SET SAFETY ON/OFF - Each time you run the program, the ORDCLIEN database is generated. As a file called ORDCLIEN already exists, dBASE will prompt the user with a message asking whether or not to overwrite the existing file. By turning **Safety Off**, dBASE will automatically overwrite the file without asking. Be sure to always turn **Safety On** again before leaving the program.

26.4   Consolidation exercise

1   Produce a free format report for the **COURSES** database file called **COURREP**. The report should resemble the following example.

Advanced Excel - 1 day(s) @ £150 per day

Introductory Excel - 2 day(s) @ £125 per day

Introductory Harvard Graphics - 2 day(s) @ £125 per day

and so on ......

To achieve this layout you will need to use the **TRIM()** and **STR()** functions. *Refer* to Chapter 20 if necessary.

2   Remember to include comments and test the program thoroughly.

See Appendix 3, page 271 for solutions.

The menu system

The system now comprises of four separate modules which have been thoroughly tested. The next stage is to pull those modules together so that they can be accessed from a menu. The menu program should include the following:

- commands to set up the environment (**Set** commands)

- declaration of memory variables

- commands to display the menu on the screen

- a prompt for the user to select from the menu

- a routine to determine the users choice

- a command to call up one of the modules depending on that choice

The illustration below shows a menu system for the modules. The only new command included in this program that generates the menu, is the **Do case** command.

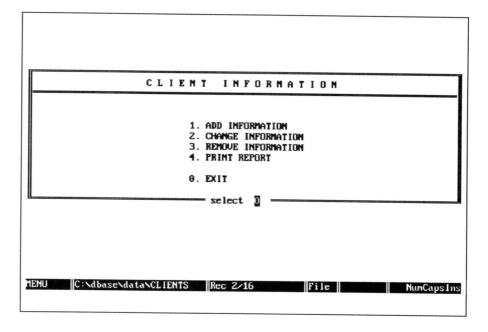

27.1   Preparing for this chapter

In order to complete this chapter you need the following files:

File name	File type	Chapter
TRAINING	Catalog	22
CLIENTS	Database	22
COURSES	Database	22 (optional)
ORDERS	Database	22
CLIENTS	Form	22
COURSES	Form	22 (optional)
HEADING	Program	23
CLIADD	Program	23
CLIEDIT	Program	25 (modified version)
CLIDEL	Program	25
CLIREP	Program	26
COURSADD	Program	23 (optional)
COUREDIT	Program	25 (optional)
COURDEL	Program	25 (optional)
COUSREP	Program	26 (optional)

 If you have not created these files in the previous chapters you will need to refer back to the chapter number listed above and create the files.

 If you have purchased the disks that accompany this book you can copy the necessary files from the appropriate floppy disk. To do this, complete the following instructions:

1 Copy the database and form files by following the instructions for Preparing for Parts 3 and 4 on page 173.

2 Copy the program files by typing **!COPY A:\CN\PROGRAM.PRG** at the dot prompt, where N is the chapter number and PROGRAM the program name. For example, to copy **HEADING.PRG**, type **!COPY A:\C23\HEADING.PRG**.

27.2   Do case... endcase command

The **Do case endcase** command is ideal for menu systems where more than two options are required without the complexity of nested **If** commands.

The following example shows a hypothetical menu from which four branches are possible. The program will do the following:

● pause to allow the user to make a choice

● test to see what choice has been made

- branch in accordance with that choice
- return to the menu

```
DO WHILE .T.
  CLEAR

  <commands to display the menu>

  @18,20 SAY "Select 1, 2, 3 or 4 ...." GET MCHOICE
  READ
  DO CASE MCHOICE
    CASE MCHOICE = '1'
      <commands>
    CASE MCHOICE = '2'
      <commands>
    CASE MCHOICE = '3'
      <commands>
    CASE MCHOICE = '4'
      RETURN
    OTHERWISE
      WAIT 'Please type 1, 2, 3 or 4 when next asked'
  ENDCASE
ENDDO
```

The **Otherwise** command is optional in the **Do case** command but can be very useful in a menu system where a non-valid selection can be made. For example, in the above case, there is no validation on the the MCHOICE field and therefore the user could easily enter a value outside of the range 1 to 4.

Displaying the menu on the screen is simply a case of issuing a number of **@Say** commands including the required screen co-ordinates. If a more elaborate menu display is required, time may be saved by using the **Create screen** command. The forms generator can be used to design the menu layout. The code from the generated .FMT file can then be read into the menu program.

27.3   Creating the menu program

The following menu program will pull together the modules created in the earlier chapters.

1   If working with the disk you can copy the menu program and the modified modules by typing the following at the dot prompt:

   !COPY A:\C27\CLI*.PRG

2   Copy the RESET program by typing the following at the dot prompt:

!COPY A:\C27\RESET.PRG

3   Read the rest of this section and then test the system.

1   Create a program called **CLIMENU**. Read in the heading and type the following
code. Save the program but do not run it at this stage.

```
CLEAR
CLOSE ALL
SET BELL OFF
*SET ESCAPE OFF              &&comment out until tested
SET CONFIRM ON
SET SAFETY OFF
SET TALK OFF

USE CLIENTS ORDER TAG ACNO


DO WHILE .T.

    * ---Display menu options, centred on the screen.
    *    draw menu border and print heading
    CLEAR
    @ 2, 0 TO 14,79 DOUBLE
    @ 3,22 SAY 'C L I E N T   I N F O R M A T I O N'
    @ 4,1 TO 4,78 DOUBLE

    * ---display detail lines

    @ 7,30 SAY '1. ADD INFORMATION'
    @ 8,30 SAY '2. CHANGE INFORMATION'
    @ 9,30 SAY '3. REMOVE INFORMATION '
    @ 10,30 SAY '4. PRINT REPORT      '
    @ 12,30 SAY '0. EXIT'

    STORE 0 TO MCHOICE
    @ 14,33 SAY " select    "
    @ 14,42 GET MCHOICE PICTURE "9" RANGE 0,4
    READ

    DO CASE
      CASE MCHOICE = 0
       * reset options and close files
       DO RESET
       RETURN
```

```
CASE MCHOICE = 1
* add information
DO CLIADD

CASE MCHOICE = 2
* change information
DO CLIEDIT

CASE MCHOICE = 3
* remove information
DO CLIDEL

CASE MCHOICE = 4
* print report
DO CLIREP

ENDCASE

ENDDO
```

Before running the menu program consider the following points:

❶ The exit option calls up a program called **RESET**. It is always a good idea to create a small program that resets the environment. You can then use this when exiting from a program or when you have an error in your program and you use the **Cancel** command at a point before the environment has been reset.

❷ At the beginning and end of each module there are commands to set up the environment. As the modules are now going to be accessed from the menu program, these commands can be included in the menu and can be removed from the individual modules.

❸ Each module contains a command to open and close the CLIENTS database. These can be removed from the three modules using this database as they are now included in the menu program. The report module uses the ORDCLIEN database; you must therefore re-open the CLIENTS database before returning to the menu program.

 1 Create the following program called **RESET**:

```
SET TALK ON
SET CONFIRM OFF
SET BELL ON
SET ESCAPE ON
SET SAFETY ON

CLOSE ALL
CLEAR
RETURN
```

2   Remove the **Set** commands from the top and bottom of all four modules.

3   Remove the **Use clients** and **Close all** commands from the **CLIADD**, **CLIEDIT** and **CLIDEL** modules.

4   Remove the **Close all** command from the **CLIREP** module. Insert the code, **USE CLIENTS ORDER TAG ACNO** before returning to the menu.

5   When the modifications are complete, test the system.

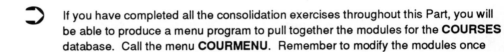

27.4   Consolidation exercise

If you have completed all the consolidation exercises throughout this Part, you will be able to produce a menu program to pull together the modules for the **COURSES** database. Call the menu **COURMENU**. Remember to modify the modules once they are called from the menu (*see* 27.3 Creating the menu program on page 209).

If working from disk, you can copy the course modules by typing:

!COPY A:\C27\COUR*.PRG

You will still need to write a menu to pull these modules together and to modify the modules in line with the examples in 27.3.

See Appendix 3, page 272 for solutions.

Part 4

Advanced programming

28 Overview

28.1 Objectives

In Part 3 you looked at the basic structures used by the dBASE programming language. In many ways you have just scratched the surface. In fact we could fill a book twice the size of this just outlining the dBASE commands and methodologies. Bearing this mind, note the following points before continuing.

Checklist

❶ It is recommended that you become fully conversant with all the commands used in Part 3 before continuing. Ideally you should have worked through the example system and created at least one other system of your own. The examples given in this Part are fairly complex and will only confuse if you have not practiced the programming structures introduced in Part 3.

❷ There are always a number of ways to approach a problem. In this Part the approach taken will be determined by the new concepts that need to be introduced. At all stages, feel free to experiment with different methods of achieving the same end.

❸ Although there are suggested exercises included for some chapters, detailed solutions are not included. By this stage, you should be able to draw upon the examples given in the chapter to form your own solutions to the problems.

❹ The scope of this book makes it infeasible to cover all the dBASE commands and programming structures available within the dBASE language. It is recommended that you work through the remainder of the examples and exercises using the manuals that accompany the dBASE product as reference.

28.2 Preparing for this Part

The database files required for this Part are listed at the beginning of Part 3 (Chapter 22, page 172). If you have not worked through Part 3, refer back to Chapter 22 and either create or load the necessary files. This Part modifies a number of program files created in Part 3. The appropriate files will be listed as required.

29 Database relationships

The report created in Part 3 (CLIREP) produces a list of all clients who have placed one or more orders during the month. The values of those orders are totalled giving a monthly invoice value.

Computer And Training Services
Invoice details for the month of February

| Customer Number: | BRO01 | Monthly Invoice Total: | 2390 |
| Customer Number | FRE01 | Monthly Invoice Total: | 1120 |

etc

You will enhance the report to include the client name and address as well as the account number.

Computer And Training Services
Invoice details for the month of February

Customer Number:	BRO01	Monthly Invoice Total:	2390
Name	Mary Brown		
Address	45 Main Street		
	Leeds		

In order to produce this report, it is necessary to extract data from the summarised ORDERS file, ORDCLIEN and the CLIENTS file. To do this, a relationship must be set up between the two files.

29.1 Building a relationship

In dBASE there are two ways to build a relationship, either by creating a dBASE query file (*see* 18.5 Queries from multiple databases, page 140) or by writing the program code.

In general, the code required to produce a two file relationship is as follows:

USE <secondary file> ORDER TAG <tagname> IN 2
USE <master file>
SET RELATION TO <common field> INTO <secondary file>

In this example there are two database files, referred to as *master* file and *secondary* file. The master file is related to the secondary file, the link being a common field. The two databases are opened at the same time in two different areas of memory. The secondary file is opened in area 2 and the master file in area 1. When stating the **Set relation** command the master file must be the active file (indicated on the status bar).

A relationship cannot be formed without a common field and the secondary file must be indexed on the common field so that the files can be related. The following example will show this more clearly.

1   If you do not have the summary file **ORDCLIEN** on disk, (if you are not sure, type **DIR** at the dot prompt to get a list of databases), type the following commands to create the file (*see* 26.6 Total command, page 202 for further details):

USE ORDERS ORDER TAG ACNO
TOTAL ON ACNO TO ORDCLIEN

2   At the dot prompt, type the following code to create a relationship between the **CLIENTS** and **ORDCLIEN** files.

CLOSE ALL
USE CLIENTS ORDER TAG ACNO IN 2
USE ORDCLIEN
SET RELATION TO ACNO INTO CLIENTS

The relationship is based on the common field, **ACNO**. The master file, **ORDCLIEN**, is related into the **CLIENTS** file.

3   Type **DISPLAY STATUS** to show which files are open and the area of memory they are stored in.

29.2   Using related databases

In order to manipulate fields that are not in the master file, prefix the fieldname by either the filename or an alias. An alias is used as shorthand instead of the filename. The default alias is a character in the range A - J depending on the memory area (there are ten memory areas available, numbered 1 to 10). For example, the alias for area 1 is A, area 2 is B etc. To list any fields from the secondary file, the fieldname must be prefixed by the filename or the alias and a dash and a greater than symbol (->).

Having related the **ORDCLIEN** and **CLIENTS** databases, type the following examples at the dot prompt:

LIST ACNO, CLIENTS->SURNAME, TOT_COST
LIST ACNO, B->SURNAME, TOT_COST

Both examples produce the same result. In the second example, an alias has been used. As **SURNAME** is a field in the secondary file it must be prefixed by the filename or alias. The alias is B because the **CLIENTS** file is located in memory area **2**. For clarity, it is advisable to use the filename rather than the alias in a program file.

Reporting from two databases

By including the relationship commands in the report file you will have completed the objectives.

If working with the disk, put the disk for Parts 3 and 4 in drive A, type the following commands at the dot prompt. Then continue from instruction 2 below:

!COPY A:\C29\CLI*.PRG
!COPY A:\C29\RESET.PRG

If working without the disk, update the program **CLIREP** (*see* 26.6 Total command, page 202). The comments are designed to aid clarity and can be excluded.

1   Modify the **CLIREP** program file as shown in the following example:

USE ORDERS ORDER TAG ACNO

*The order file needs to be summarised to produce one record for
*each customer, totalling the TOT_COST field.

TOTAL ON ACNO TO ORDCLIEN

*Creates a new database containing one record per customer
USE ORDCLIEN

*Select another work area, open the CLIENTS file and relate the
*ORDCLIEN and the CLIENTS file on the common field.

USE CLIENTS ORDER TAG ACNO IN 2
SET RELATION TO ACNO INTO CLIENTS

CLEAR
STORE "N" TO MANS
@3,0 TO 19,79
@10,10 SAY "Do you want to print the report? Y/N...." GET MANS;
    FUNCTION "M Y,N"
READ

IF MANS = "Y"
    SET PRINT ON
ENDIF

```
*Print a page heading including the date.
?"          Computer And Training Services"
?
?"          Invoice details for the month of "+CMONTH(ODATE)
?
DO WHILE .NOT. EOF()
   ?"Customer Number: "+ACNO
   ?? "          Monthly Invoice Total:  "+STR(TOT_COST,6,2)
   ?"Name          "+TRIM(CLIENTS->FIRST)+" "+CLIENTS->SURNAME
   ?"Address       "+CLIENTS->ADD1
   ?"              "+CLIENTS->ADD2
   ?
   SKIP
ENDDO

IF MANS = "Y"
   EJECT
   SET PRINT OFF
ELSE
   WAIT
ENDIF

CLEAR
CLOSE ALL
USE CLIENTS ORDER TAG ACNO
RETURN
```

2   Run the report from the menu program, **CLIMENU** (*see* Chapter 27, page 207).

29.4   Suggested exercises

1   Produce a report that will list the following fields:

From the **COURSES** database file, **COURSE, LEVEL**
From the **TRAINERS** database file, **FNAME, SNAME & PHONE**.

2   If you created a report called **COURREP** in Part 3 you can modify this program. If not, create a new program file **COURREP**. You will need to build a relationship between the **COURSES** and **TRAINERS** files. The common field is the trainer code.

3   Use the listing of **CLIREP.PRG** as a guideline.

30 Procedure files and parameter passing

As a system grows routines are included which are similar or even identical to existing routines. Repetition of code should be avoided if possible. As well as causing extra typing, it also results in more disk space being needed and it can result in the slowing down of the system.

A *procedure file* can be used to hold the routines that are repeated within the system. Each routine is referred to as a **procedure**. Alternatively, routines can be held as separate program files. A procedure file is usually preferred for reasons of speed. Each time a program file is called, dBASE has to go to the disk and open the file. When a procedure file is used, the file is opened before the first procedure is called and remains open until no longer needed. As the file remains open, this method reduces disk access time and delay. A procedure file can contain up to 1,170 procedures although the size of a procedure file is also limited by the available RAM. Only one procedure file can be open at one time.

30.1 Creating a procedure file

A procedure file is created in the same way as a program file using the **Modify command** command. It is given the extension PRG.

It is advisable to create each routine independently. When tested; each routine can be added to the procedure file using the **Read file** option from the **Word** menu.

Each procedure within the procedure file should start with the **Procedure <name>** command, where <name> is the name of the procedure file, and end with the **Return** command. For example:

```
*PROC1.PRG

PROCEDURE MESSAGE1

@10,10 SAY "Please wait, processing request"
RETURN

PROCEDURE MESSAGE2

@10,10 SAY "Request rejected"
RETURN
```

Calling a procedure

The procedure file should be opened before the first procedure is called. This could be in the first program in the system, usually the menu program or it could be opened in a specific program if only needed within that program.

The command to open a procedure file is **Set procedure to**. The command is followed by the name of the procedure file. A procedure is then called by the **Do** command. When dBASE encounters a **Do** command it will first look for a procedure with the specified name (if a procedure file is open). If a procedure cannot be found, it will then look on the disk for an independent program file with the specified name.

*MENU.PRG

SET PROCEDURE TO PROC1

```
<commands>
IF MCOUNT = 1
   DO MESSAGE1
ELSE
   DO MESSAGE2
ENDIF

<commands>
```

With the above example, dBASE will look in the procedure file PROC1 for procedures called MESSAGE1 and MESSAGE2 before looking to disk for programs with those names.

A procedure file can be closed by the **Close procedure** command or the **Close all** command. If another procedure file is opened the current procedure file is automatically closed.

30.3   Using parameters

On many occasions, the routines within a system are similar but not exactly the same. If this is the case, the procedure can be called with one or more parameters. The use of parameters is best demonstrated by example. The following exercise is used purely to demonstrate the principle behind the use of parameters and can be omitted. (A copy of this program can be loaded from A:\C30 if required.)

Create the program as **BOX.PRG**:

```
* BOX.PRG - this program is designed to draw a box. The size of
*         the box is determined by the coordinates given as
*         parameters.

PARAMETERS BEGROW, BEGCOL, ENDROW, ENDCOL
```

```
SET STATUS OFF
CLEAR
@BEGROW,BEGCOL TO ENDROW,ENDCOL DOUBLE
SET COLOR TO W/R
@BEGROW+1,BEGCOL+1 CLEAR TO ENDROW-1,ENDCOL-1
@BEGROW+(ENDROW-BEGROW)/2+1,BEGCOL+(ENDCOL-BEGCOL)/2;
    SAY "BOX"
SET COLOR TO W+/B, B/W,N
STORE " " TO MANS
@22,10 SAY "Press any key to continue.." GET MANS
READ
SET STATUS ON
CLEAR
RETURN
```

The program draws a box on the screen-colours it in and displays the word box in the centre; a relatively useless routine but it demonstrates the use of parameter passing. The first command in the program file is **Parameters** followed by a list of memory variables. The memory variables will obtain values when the program is called.

The following command calls a program and passes values to that program:

DO <name> WITH <a1, a2....etc>

where <name> is the name of the program or procedure and a1,a2 etc the data to be passed to the parameters declared at the beginning of the program or procedure. With the next example, the value 8 is stored in the memory variable BEGROW, 10 in BEGCOL and so on.

 Issue the command **DO BOX WITH 8,10,18,50** and observe the outcome. Any key will exit the program. Try running the program several times providing different parameter values.

30.4   Public and private memory variables

When a memory variable is created within a program it is automatically given the status *private*. This means that the variable is private to the current program and programs or procedures called by that program. When the sub-routine is completed and control is returned to the calling program, the variable is released (deleted). In many cases this is what is required. However, if a variable is given a value in a sub-routine and that value is needed in the calling program, it is important that the variable is not released. If this is the case, the memory variable must be declared as *public*. It can then be accessed in all programs and modules. This is often the case when calling procedures with parameters.

1   To illustrate the use of public memory variables create the following small programs, **PROG1** and **PROG2**:

```
*PROG1
CLEAR
SET TALK OFF
STORE 0 TO MPRICE
@10,10 SAY "How much does 1 item cost? " GET MPRICE
READ
DO PROG2
?"Total cost is £"+STR(MPRICE*MNUM,6,2)
SET TALK ON
CLEAR ALL
RETURN

*PROG2
CLEAR
STORE 0 TO MNUM
@10,10 SAY "How many do you want? " GET MNUM
READ
CLEAR
RETURN
```

2   Run the programs by typing **DO PROG1**. An error message is given because **MNUM** was released when returning from **PROG2** to **PROG1**. In this situation the code **PUBLIC MNUM** should be included in **PROG1**.

3   Amend **PROG1** by including **PUBLIC MNUM** following **SET TALK OFF**.

4   Run **PROG1** again. The program should run without error.

30.5   Parameter passing to a procedure

Procedures should be used in a system wherever code is repeated. By using parameters, procedures can be used to replace routines that are similar if not identical in structure. For example, a procedure can be used to display messages on the screen and capture user response to Yes/No questions. By calling the procedure with a parameter, the message associated with the routine can vary depending upon the situation. If you are capturing a user response in a memory variable and taking that response back to the calling program you must declare that memory variable as public.

If you are going to use procedures in a system you must remember to include the command **Set procedure to <procedure name>** and the command **Public** followed by the memory variables that are going to be used between programs.

The following example illustrates the use of a simple procedure that can be used with the current system.

If working with the disks, copy the program files from **A:\C30**. Read through the code and comments below. Examine the changes to the modules and run the modules from the menu program.

1   Create a program file called **PROC.PRG**:

*** PROC.PRG *****

PROCEDURE FOOTER   &&footer with Y/N capture

PARAMETERS NOTE
@22,0 CLEAR
STORE "N" TO MANS
@22,(80-LEN(NOTE))/2 SAY NOTE
@23,38 GET MANS FUNCTION "M N,Y"
READ
@22,0 CLEAR

RETURN

FOOTER - the **FOOTER** procedure is called with one parameter, **NOTE**. The **NOTE** parameter holds a message which is displayed in the centre of line 23. The user response is captured to a memory variable called **MANS**. The value in **MANS** is then returned to the calling program.

2   To call this procedure file from the system you will need to include the following commands at the beginning of the **CLIMENU** program:

SET PROCEDURE TO PROC
PUBLIC MANS

3   As this procedure uses the bottom of the screen to display the message, you will need to turn the status bar off during the running of the system. Include **SET STATUS OFF** at the beginning of **CLIMENU.PRG** and **SET STATUS ON** in **RESET.PRG**.

4   Modify the modules to include the **FOOTER** procedure wherever a yes/no response is required. The following is an example from the **CLIEDIT** module:

Replace:

STORE "Y" TO MANS
@3,0 TO 19,79
@10,10 SAY "Account number does not exist re-enter? Y/N";
GET MANS FUNCTION "M Y,N"
READ

with:

DO FOOTER WITH "Account number does not exist re-enter? Y/N"

Similar code can be used in the report module; replace the existing code with:

DO FOOTER WITH "Do you want to print the report? Y/N"

Modify the deletion module in the same way.

30.6   Parameter passing to a program

In Part 3 you created an edit and delete module for the CLIENTS database. If you completed the consolidation exercises you will have created similar modules for the COURSES database. Where you have programs that are similar, you may find that you can create one program and call that program with a number of parameters rather than repeating code. The following edit program will be used to demonstrate this. It can be used to edit both the CLIENTS and COURSES databases.

If working with the disks you should find that you have copied a program called **GENEDIT**. Refer to the listing and comments below before testing the program.

1   Copy the **CLIEDIT** program to a new program called **GENEDIT**. Modify **GENEDIT** in the following way:

```
PARAMETERS MLENGTH, MPROMPT, MPICT, MSCREEN

SET TALK OFF
SET BELL OFF
SET CONFIRM ON
SET STATUS OFF
SET PROCEDURE TO PROC
PUBLIC MANS

DO WHILE .T.
    STORE SPACE(MLENGTH) TO MITEM
    CLEAR
    @3,0 TO 19,79
    @10,10 SAY "Please enter the " + MPROMPT GET MITEM;
        PICTURE MPICT
    READ

    SEEK TRIM(MITEM)
    CLEAR

    IF .NOT. EOF()
        SET FORMAT TO &MSCREEN
        EDIT RECORD RECNO()
        CLOSE FORMAT
```

```
              ELSE
                      DO FOOTER WITH "Record does not exist, re-enter? Y/N.."
                      IF MANS = "Y"
                              LOOP
                      ENDIF
              ENDIF

              CLEAR
              DO FOOTER WITH "Edit another record? Y/N.."
              IF MANS = "Y"
                      LOOP
              ENDIF

              CLOSE ALL
              CLEAR
              SET TALK ON
              SET BELL ON
              SET CONFIRM OFF
              SET STATUS ON
              RETURN
      ENDDO
```

MLENGTH - the length of the search string - used to define the memory variable.

MPROMPT - the text needed to complete the prompt "Please enter the".

MPICT - the picture needed to validate the entry of the search string.

MSCREEN - the name of the screen form. This parameter is preceded by the **&** character when used in the program. The **&** character is used to denote *macro substitution* and indicates that dBASE should use the contents of the memory variable and not the actual memory variable name when interpreting the code. Without the use of the **&** command, dBASE would assume the form name to be MSCREEN rather than CLIENTS, the content of the MSCREEN memory variable. For further information on macro substitution refer to the dBASE manuals.

2   To call the general edit module for the **CLIENTS** database, type the following at the dot prompt:

    USE CLIENTS ORDER TAG ACNO
    DO GENEDIT WITH 5,"Client Account Number: ","@! AAA99","CLIENTS"

3   Update **COUREDIT** to include the **FOOTER** procedure and then type:

    USE COURSES ORDER TAG C_CODE
    DO GENEDIT WITH 6 "Course Code: ","@!A","COURSES"

4   To call the general edit module from the menus (**CLIMENU** and **COURMENU**), replace the commands **DO CLIEDIT** and **DO COUREDIT** with **DO GENEDIT WITH** followed by the appropriate parameters (*see* 2 and 3 above).

1. Copy **CLIADD.PRG** to a new file called **GENADD.PRG**. Modify the code so that it can be called by both the **CLIENTS** and **COURSES** databases.

2. Create a general deletion module.

3. Modify **GENEDIT** so that it can also be called by the **ORDERS** and **TRAINERS** databases. This is more difficult and should only be attempted with reference to the dBASE manuals.

31   Multiple file validation

When adding a record to a database file within a database system it is often necessary to check some of the details with other files in the system. This is referred to as *cross file validation*. When this is the case, the use of screen forms for data input becomes inadequate. When adding data to a database, the data needs to be read into memory variables and validated. When the data has been validated a blank record is appended to the appropriate database and the fields replaced by the data held in the memory variables.

31.1   Routine to add an order

This routine is designed to add an order to the ORDERS database file. Cross validation is needed to check that the account number entered is in the CLIENTS file and that course code is in the COURSES file. This will prevent an order being entered for a client not included in the CLIENT file and will also prevent an order being taken for a non-existent course. The routine also needs to automatically generate the order number.

If working with the disk, type the following at the dot prompt:

!COPY A:\C31*.PRG

If working without the disk complete the following.

1   Modify **PROC.PRG** to include the following procedure:

PROCEDURE FOOTER1   &&places messages on screen, row 24

PARAMETERS NOTE
@22,0 CLEAR
@23,(80-LEN(NOTE))/2 SAY NOTE

RETURN

2   Create a new program **ORDADD.PRG** as shown below. Include the standard **Set** commands (including **SET PROCEDURE TO PROC**) at the beginning of the program. The comments (in light text) should be excluded.

```
PUBLIC MANS

DO WHILE .T.
     USE ORDERS ORDER TAG ORDNO
```

The order number is generated automatically. The first check is for an empty file using the BOF() (beginning of file) function and the EOF() (end of file) function. If both functions return a True value the file is empty and a memory variable is set to 1. If the file is not empty the pointer is moved to the bottom of the file and the order number incremented by one.

```
IF EOF() .AND. BOF()
     STORE 1 TO MORDNO
ELSE
     GO BOTTOM
     STORE VAL(ORDNO)+1 TO MORDNO
ENDIF
```

Memory variables are initialised to hold the account number of the client placing the order, the course code of the course they want to attend, the date of the course and the number of places required on the course. The order date is set to the system date (this can be changed if necessary).

```
STORE SPACE(5) TO MACNO
STORE DATE() TO MODATE
STORE SPACE(6) TO MC_CODE
STORE {  /  /  } TO MC_DATE
STORE 0 TO MNUMBER
```

This routine displays an entry screen prompting the user to enter the Customer Account Code for the client placing the order.

```
DO WHILE .T.
     CLEAR
     @1,0 TO 20,79
     @3,30 SAY "CUSTOMER ORDER FORM"
     @2,29 TO 4,49 DOUBLE
     @6,23 SAY "Enter Customer Account Code: "
     @6,COL() GET MACNO PICTURE "@!  AAA99"
     READ
```

The CLIENTS database file is opened indexed on account number. The entered account number is searched for. If found, the first name and surname are copied to the appropriate memory variables. If the account number does not exist a message is displayed. The user is given the option to re-enter the data or exit the module. An enhancement that could be included at this stage is the option to add the new client to the CLIENTS database. This is included as a suggested exercise at the end of this chapter.

```
USE CLIENTS ORDER TAG ACNO
SEEK MACNO
```

```
                        IF FOUND()
                                STORE FIRST TO MFIRST
                                STORE SURNAME TO MSURNAME
                                EXIT
                        ELSE
                                DO FOOTER WITH "This account number does not exist;
                                        re-enter? Y/N "
                                IF MANS = "N"
                                        DO RESET
                                        RETURN
                                ELSE
                                        STORE SPACE(5) TO MACNO
                                        LOOP
                                ENDIF
                        ENDIF
                ENDDO
```

The name of the client, the order number and the order date are displayed. The
order date can be edited if required.

```
STORE "Enter Order for "+TRIM(MFIRST)+" "+MSURNAME TO MPROMPT
DO FOOTER1 WITH MPROMPT

@10,8 SAY "Order Number: "
@10,COL() SAY LTRIM(STR(MORDNO))
@10,COL()+25 SAY "Order Date: "
@10,COL() GET MODATE
```

The user is prompted to enter the course code and course date.

```
DO WHILE .T.
 @13,28 SAY "Enter Course Code: "
 @13,COL() GET MC_CODE PICTURE "@!A"
 @15,28 SAY "Enter Course Date: "
 @15,COL() GET MC_DATE
 READ
```

The program then checks with the COURSES database that the course code
entered is valid.

```
USE COURSES ORDER TAG C_CODE

 SEEK  MC_CODE
 IF FOUND()
      STORE COURSE TO MCOURSE
      STORE LEVEL TO MLEVEL
      STORE PRICE TO MPRICE
      STORE DAYS TO MDAYS
      EXIT      && exits from the current DO WHILE loop
 ELSE
      DO FOOTER WITH "This is not a valid course re-enter Y/N "
      IF MANS = "N"
```

```
                    DO RESET
                    RETURN
           ELSE
                    STORE SPACE(6) TO MC_CODE
                    STORE { / / } TO MC_DATE
                    LOOP
           ENDIF
     ENDIF
ENDDO
```

The course description is displayed and the user prompted to enter the number of places required.

```
STORE "Taking order for "+TRIM(UPPER(MLEVEL))+" ";
   +TRIM(UPPER(MCOURSE)) TO MPROMPT
DO FOOTER1 WITH MPROMPT
@17,8 SAY "Enter Number of Places: "
@17,COL() GET MNUMBER PICTURE "@Z 99"
READ
```

The total cost is calculated by multiplying the number of days by the number of places by the price.

```
STORE MDAYS*MNUMBER*MPRICE TO MT_COST
@17,COL()+50 SAY "TOTAL COST: £"
@17,COL() SAY MT_COST
```

A routine could be added here to ask the user whether they wish to proceed and add the order to the ORDERS database. A blank record is appended to the ORDERS database and the fields in this file replaced by the values held in the appropriate memory variables.

```
DO FOOTER1 WITH "Please wait....."

USE ORDERS ORDER TAG ORDNO
APPEND BLANK
REPLACE ACNO WITH MACNO, ORDNO WITH STR(MORDNO,4,0)
REPLACE ODATE WITH MODATE
REPLACE C_CODE WITH MC_CODE, C_DATE WITH MC_DATE
REPLACE NUMBER WITH MNUMBER, TOT_COST WITH MT_COST
```

The option is given to add another order.

```
DO FOOTER WITH "ADD ANOTHER ORDER? Y/N "
IF MANS ="N"
    DO RESET
    RETURN
ENDIF
ENDDO
```

Run the program by typing **DO ORDADD** at the dot prompt.

```
                        ┌──────────────────┐
                        │CUSTOMER ORDER FORM│
                        └──────────────────┘

                  ENTER CUSTOMER ACCOUNT CODE: SMI01


     ORDER NUMBER: 16                          ORDER DATE: 22/09/92

                        ENTER COURSE CODE: ▮▮▮▮▮▮
                        ENTER COURSE DATE:  /   /




                     ENTER ORDER FOR Peter Smith
```

```
                        ┌──────────────────┐
                        │CUSTOMER ORDER FORM│
                        └──────────────────┘

                  ENTER CUSTOMER ACCOUNT CODE: SMI01


     ORDER NUMBER: 16                          ORDER DATE: 22/09/92

                        ENTER COURSE CODE: LOTADU
                        ENTER COURSE DATE: 12/10/92
     ENTER NUMBER OF PLACES: 2



                   TAKING ORDER FOR ADVANCED LOTUS 1-2-3
```

31.2   Suggested exercises

 1 Modify the program so that if an order is being placed for a new client, the user has the option to add that client to the **CLIENTS** database before continuing to add the order.

2 Modify the program so that the user has the option to abandon the operation before adding the new record to the **ORDERS** database. This routine should be included before the **Append blank** command.

32 Creating and using menus and windows

You have already created menus by using the Applications Generator and by coding the menu using the **@Say Get** command to display the menu and the **Do case** command to act on the menu option chosen. This chapter will look at ways to code more sophisticated menus and will introduce the concept of dBASE Windows.

32.1 Windows

The dBASE **Window** command can be used to display information within a window. The window can be displayed on top of the information currently on the screen. This feature is ideal for many applications including error messages, help information and user prompts.

The following example shows the use of a window to display help information on the screen. The user is informed that the record they have selected to be marked for deletion is, in fact, already marked for deletion.

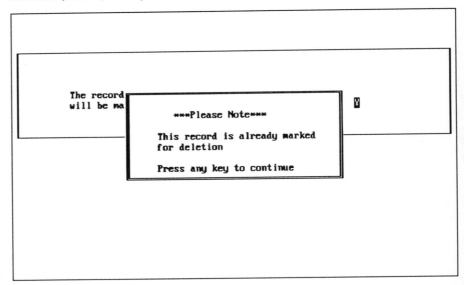

 If you are working with the disks, copy the program **CLIDEL.PRG** from **A:\C32**. Study the code before running the program.

Modify **CLIDEL.PRG** in the following way:

1   Type the **Define** command as the first line of the program:

DEFINE WINDOW MSG1 FROM 12,20 TO 20,59 DOUBLE

2   Modify the deletion part of the module in the following way:

```
IF .NOT. EOF()
        STORE " " TO MANS
        @8,0 TO 16,79
        @12,10 SAY "The record containing details on "+TRIM(FIRST)
                +" "+SURNAME
        @13,10 SAY "will be marked for deletion. Is this correct? Y/N ";
                GET MANS FUNCTION "M Y,N"
        READ
        IF MANS="Y"
                IF DELETED()
                        ACTIVATE WINDOW MSG1
                        @2,05 SAY "   ***Please Note***"
                        @4,05 SAY "This record is already marked"
                        @5,05 SAY "for deletion"
                        @6,1 SAY " "
                        WAIT "    Press any key to continue"
                        DEACTIVATE WINDOW MSG1
                ELSE
                        DELETE
                ENDIF
        ENDIF
ENDIF
```

DEFINE WINDOW - The **Define window** command specifies the size and position of the window and the border type.

ACTIVATE WINDOW - The **Activate window** command is followed by the text that is to appear in the window. The coordinates are relative to the window not the screen.

DEACTIVATE WINDOW - Clears the window from the screen.

Run the modified module from the **CLIMENU** program. Mark the same record for deletion twice. The second time you mark the record, the window should display.

32.2   Vertical bar menus

A vertical bar menu contains options placed vertically on the screen. Although the menu can be placed anywhere, vertical bar menus are usually placed in the centre of the screen, if used independently, or placed under an option if used with a horizontal bar menu. In this case they are often referred to as pop-up menus (*see* 32.4 Bar menus with pop-up sub menus, page 237).

```
                    Add information
                    Change information
                    Remove information
                       Print report
                      Exit to dBASE
```

```
VERT_BAR C:\dbase\data\CLIENTS    Rec 2/16        File          Num
                    Please select from menu
```

The following code will produce an independent vertical bar (pop-up) menu. An explanation of the different commands follows the code.

If you are working with the disks, copy the program **VERT_BAR.PRG** from **A:\C32**. Study the code before running the program.

Create the following program as **VERT_BAR.PRG**:

setup procedure

```
SET TALK OFF
SET BELL OFF
SET SAFETY OFF
*SET ESCAPE OFF     &&COMMENTED OUT UNTIL TESTING COMPLETE
SET CONFIRM ON
SET STATUS OFF
SET PROCEDURE TO PROC

PUBLIC MANS

CLEAR
USE CLIENTS ORDER TAG ACNO

*PRESENT MENU AND PROMPT FOR CHOICE*

SET BORDER TO SINGLE
DEFINE POPUP CLIMENU FROM 7,25 TO 13,48 ;
MESSAGE "Please select from menu"
DEFINE BAR 1 OF CLIMENU PROMPT " Add information   "
DEFINE BAR 2 OF CLIMENU PROMPT " Change information "
DEFINE BAR 3 OF CLIMENU PROMPT " Remove information "
```

```
DEFINE BAR 4 OF CLIMENU PROMPT "   Print report   "
DEFINE BAR 5 OF CLIMENU PROMPT "   Exit to dBASE    "
ON SELECTION POPUP CLIMENU DO POPMENU

ACTIVATE POPUP CLIMENU
PROCEDURE POPMENU
  DO CASE
    CASE BAR()=1
      DO CLIADD
    CASE BAR()=2
      DO CLIEDIT
    CASE BAR()=3
      DO CLIDEL
    CASE BAR()=4
      DO CLIREP
    CASE BAR()=5
      DO RESET
      DEACTIVATE POPUP
      CLEAR POPUPS
      RETURN
  ENDCASE

  CLEAR
  RETURN
```

SET BORDER - The **Set border** command draws a border around the defined menu. It can include the options:

> **NONE** - to give a menu without a border
> **SINGLE** - for a single line border
> **DOUBLE** - for a double line border
> **PANEL** - for a reverse video border

DEFINE POPUP - Defines the menu name, the size of the menu and the message that will appear at the bottom of the screen.

DEFINE BAR - The **Define bar** command needs to be included for each bar in the menu. A prompt must be included for each bar.

ON SELECTION - The **On selection** command tells dBASE what to do when a menu option is selected. In this example the procedure **POPMENU** is called.

ACTIVATE POPUP - When this command is encountered, the menu is displayed.

Run the program **VERT_BAR** from the dot prompt.

A horizontal bar menu can be used to display the available choices across the top of
the screen.

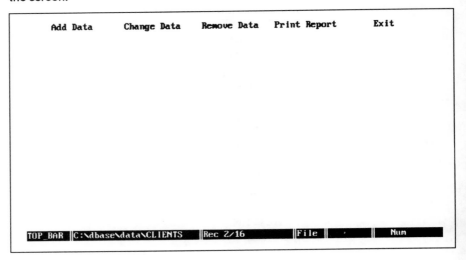

If you are working with the disks, copy the program **TOP_BAR.PRG** from **A:\C32**.
Study the code before running the program.

Create the following program as **TOP_BAR.PRG**:

```
*SETUP PROCEDURE*
SET TALK OFF
SET BELL OFF
SET SAFETY OFF
*SET ESCAPE OFF      &&COMMENTED OUT UNTIL TESTING COMPLETE
SET CONFIRM ON
SET STATUS OFF
SET PROCEDURE TO PROC

PUBLIC MANS
USE CLIENTS ORDER TAG ACNO

*PRESENT MENU AND PROMPT FOR CHOICE*
  CLEAR
  DEFINE MENU MAINMENU MESSAGE "Please select a menu choice"

  DEFINE PAD PAD_1 OF MAINMENU PROMPT " Add Data  " AT 1,3
  ON SELECTION PAD PAD_1 OF MAINMENU DO CLIADD
  DEFINE PAD PAD_2 OF MAINMENU PROMPT " Change Data" AT 1,18
  ON SELECTION PAD PAD_2 OF MAINMENU DO CLIEDIT
  DEFINE PAD PAD_3 OF MAINMENU PROMPT " Remove Data" AT 1,33
```

```
ON SELECTION PAD PAD_3 OF MAINMENU DO CLIDEL
DEFINE PAD PAD_4 OF MAINMENU PROMPT "Print Report" AT 1,48
ON SELECTION PAD PAD_4 OF MAINMENU DO CLIREP
DEFINE PAD PAD_5 OF MAINMENU PROMPT "   Exit   " AT 1,63
ON SELECTION PAD PAD_5 OF MAINMENU DO EXIT

ACTIVATE MENU MAINMENU

PROCEDURE EXIT
 DO RESET
 DEACTIVATE MENU
 RETURN
```

DEFINE MENU - The **Define menu** command defines the bar type menu and the message that will appear centred at the bottom of the screen.

DEFINE PAD - The **Define pad** command is used to define each menu choice on the bar menu. The command includes the prompt to appear on the menu. The pad name is limited to 10 characters and the first character must be a letter (A-Z). The **At** command can be included to specify the coordinates of the menu prompt.

ON SELECTION - The **On selection** command is used to tell dBASE what to do if the menu option is chosen.

ACTIVATE MENU - This command calls up the menu.

Run the program **TOP_BAR** from the dot prompt.

32.4   Bar menus with pop-up sub menus

Pop-up menus can be used as sub menus for a bar menu. The example below displays a horizontal bar menu with a pop-up menu linked to the first option on the bar. In practice, each option on the bar menu would have an associated pop-up menu.

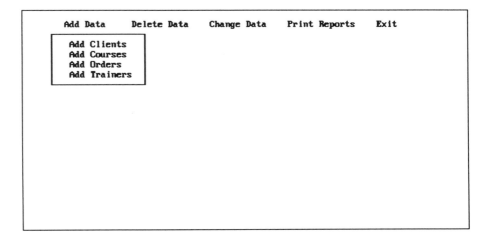

If you are working with the disks, copy the program **POPUP.PRG** from **A:\C32**. Study the code and complete steps 2 to 4 below.

1   Create the following program as **POPUP.PRG**:

```
*SETUP PROCEDURE*
SET TALK OFF
SET BELL OFF
SET SAFETY OFF
*SET ESCAPE OFF    &&COMMENTED OUT UNTIL TESTING COMPLETE
SET CONFIRM ON
SET STATUS OFF
SET PROCEDURE TO PROC
PUBLIC MANS
*PRESENT MENU AND PROMPT FOR CHOICE*

  CLEAR
  DEFINE MENU MAINMENU MESSAGE "Please select a menu choice"
  DEFINE PAD PAD_1 OF MAINMENU PROMPT " Add Data " AT 1,3
  ON PAD PAD_1 OF MAINMENU ACTIVATE POPUP ADDMENU
  DEFINE PAD PAD_2 OF MAINMENU PROMPT "Delete Data " AT1,18
  ON SELECTION PAD PAD_2 OF MAINMENU DO NOT_AV
  DEFINE PAD PAD_3 OF MAINMENU PROMPT "Change Data " AT 1,33
  ON SELECTION PAD PAD_3 OF MAINMENU DO NOT_AV
  DEFINE PAD PAD_4 OF MAINMENU PROMPT "Print Reports" AT 1,48
  ON SELECTION PAD PAD_4 OF MAINMENU DO NOT_AV
  DEFINE PAD PAD_5 OF MAINMENU PROMPT "  Exit    "
  ON SELECTION PAD PAD_5 OF MAINMENU DO EXIT

  DEFINE POPUP ADDMENU FROM 2,2 TO 7,20 ;
  MESSAGE "Select database to add to"
  DEFINE BAR 1 OF ADDMENU PROMPT "  Add Clients "
  DEFINE BAR 2 OF ADDMENU PROMPT "  Add Courses "
  DEFINE BAR 3 OF ADDMENU PROMPT "  Add Orders "
  DEFINE BAR 4 OF ADDMENU PROMPT "  Add Trainers "
  ON SELECTION POPUP ADDMENU DO POPMENU

  ACTIVATE MENU MAINMENU

  PROCEDURE POPMENU

  DO CASE
    CASE BAR() = 1
        USE CLIENTS ORDER TAG ACNO
        DO CLIADD
    CASE BAR() = 2
        USE COURSES ORDER TAG C_CODE
        DO COURSADD
```

```
        CASE BAR() = 3
            DO NOT_AV
        CASE BAR() = 4
            DO NOT_AV
    ENDCASE
    RETURN


PROCEDURE NOT_AV
    STORE " " TO MANS
    @15,15 SAY "This option is not available..."
    @16,15 SAY "Press any key to continue......" GET MANS
    READ
    CLEAR
RETURN


PROCEDURE EXIT
    DEACTIVATE MENU
    DEACTIVATE POPUP
    DO RESET
RETURN
```

2   Run **POPUP.PRG** from the dot prompt.

3   Having run the program you will notice that the bar menu does not automatically display on returning from an addition routine. To rectify this, you need to display the sub menu within a window.

Modify the program by adding the following code before defining the menu called **MAINMENU**:

DEFINE WINDOW SUBMENU FROM 2,0 TO 24,79 NONE

Include the code to activate the window before calling the addition module. Deactivate the window on completion of the module. For example:

**ACTIVATE WINDOW SUBMENU
USE CLIENTS ORDER TAG ACNO
DO CLIADD
DEACTIVATE WINDOW SUBMENU**

4   Run the program again.

33   Testing and debugging a program

The advantages of writing a system in a modular form have already been outlined. These advantages certainly become apparent when the program contains errors.

Program errors can roughly be broken down into four categories:

Typing errors - Typing errors can be easily spotted and corrected. Sometimes it is a good idea to get someone else to scan through the program if the errors cannot easily be found.

Syntax errors - Syntax errors are more difficult to spot and come in several guises. The following are some of the more common syntax errors.

- incorrect spacing between commands

- incorrect fieldnames, filenames or memory variable names

- memory variables not declared public

- data type mismatches

- incorrect command format

- no closing bracket or quote mark

- no **Endif** or **Enddo** command

Syntax errors become easier to spot with practice.

Environmental errors - Environmental errors are more difficult to find. An example of such as error might be a call to a program that has not yet been generated.

Logic errors - The worst kind of error is the error that does not return an error message. Logic errors only appear when the program is run. The program appears to run correctly but the results are not what is expected.

Before trying to correct a run time error, make a copy of the program so if the debugging takes you too far astray you can always recall the original version.

Once you have discovered that a program has a problem there are several ways to discover what the problem is.

If dBASE finds the error in the program, the program will stop and the following three choices given:

CANCEL - By cancelling the program you exit back to the dot prompt. You can then modify the program in the usual way and run the program again. Be careful when cancelling a program as the environment may have been changed by the program; files may be open and **Set** commands changed. It is advantageous to have a program that resets the environment, closes all files, sets options off that may have been set on and vice versa. You have used a program called RESET.PRG in earlier chapters.

IGNORE - If you know that the error will not cause further problems later in the program, you can choose to ignore the problem and continue running the program.

SUSPEND - The **Suspend** command stops the program running until the **Resume** command is given. You are returned to the dot prompt where you can issue various commands to try and pin-point the error, for example:

LIST MEMORY TO PRINT
LIST STATUS TO PRINT

These commands will show you what files are open and the current values of memory variables.

Once the error has been found you can correct the error at the dot prompt and then type RESUME to continue running the program. It is important to note that by correcting the error at the dot prompt you have not corrected the program. When the program has finished running you will need to modify it in the usual way.

If the error cannot easily be solved you can type CANCEL to exit from the program.

33.1   Using the dBASE debug command

The dBASE debug facility is designed to help the programmer locate and correct program errors. Debug has four windows:

- a window to display the program code

- a window to display the break points

- a window to display values of variables and expressions

- the **Debug action** window

You can leave the debug windows at any stage to view the screen as the user would see it. You can also return to the dot prompt to issue commands whilst in suspend mode.

To enter debug, issue the command at the dot prompt in place of the **Do** command:

DEBUG <prog name>

For example, assuming that the CLIENTS database is open with ACNO as the master index, **DEBUG CLIDEL** will debug the deletion routine. When you enter debug you are automatically suspended at the first program statement.

```
┌─ C:\DBASE\DATA\CLIDEL.PRG ──────┬──────────────────────────────────┐
│ 1 DEFINE WINDOW MSG1 FROM 12,20 │        ─── Debug Commands ───     │
│ 2                               │                                   │
│ 3 DO WHILE .T.                  │ B    - Change Breakpoint entries  │
│ 4                               │ D    - Change Display entries     │
│ 5   STORE SPACE(5) TO MACNO     │ E    - Edit program file          │
│ 6   CLEAR                       │ L    - Continue from given line   │
│ 7   @3,0 TO 19,79               │ [n]M - As 'S' but on same or above level│
│ 8   @12,10 SAY "Please enter th │ P    - Show program traceback info│
│ 9     GET MACNO PICTURE "@! AA  │ Q    - Quit debugger              │
│ 10  READ                        │ R    - Run until interrupt or error│
│ 11                              │ [n]S - Execute next statement     │
│                                 │ U    - Suspend program & go to dot prompt│
│ ┌─ DISPLAY ────────────────┐    │ [n]↵ - Repeat last step or next   │
│ │                        :  │    │ [n]↑ - Show previous line         │
│ │                        :  │    │ [n]↓ - Show next line             │
│ │                        :  │    │ F1   - Toggle Command Help On/Off │
│ │                        :  │    │ F9   - Show user screen           │
│ └──────────────────────────┘    │                                   │
│ ┌─ DEBUGGER ──────────────────────────────────────────────────────┐│
│ │ Work Area: 1     Database file:        Program file: clidel.prg  ││
│ │ Record:    0     Master Index:         Procedure:    CLIDEL      ││
│ │ ACTION:                                Current line: 1           ││
│ └──────────────────────────────────────────────────────────────────┘│
│ Stopped for step.                                                     │
└──────────────────────────────────────────────────────────────────────┘
```

F1   Function key 1 displays and hides the available debug actions (it works as a toggle key).

B   The first thing to do is set up the break points by selecting the B action. A break point is the point in the program where you want execution to be suspended (the program stopped). For example, you may want the program to stop when a certain record is reached, a certain line in the program is reached or when a memory variable reaches a certain value.

You define a break point by entering a valid dBASE expression. For example:

MANS = "Y"
LINENO() = 30
RECNO() = 6

Once the break points have been entered press $\boxed{\text{Ctrl + End}}$ to save.

R   Once the break points have been entered the R action can be used to run the program. The program will run until the first break point is reached. You can start the program by typing R again. The program will run until the next break point is encountered.

D   Once the break point is reached the program will halt (suspend). At this point the D action can be used to display the contents of variables. The display window is opened and variable names and expressions can be entered to the left of the colon. The values will be displayed to the right of the colon.

E   If the program needs editing you can select the E action to enter the dBASE editor (Modify command). The changes you make will not have any effect until the program is re-compiled. To re-compile the program you must stop the current execution and re-run the program. Basically, this option is only useful if you want to edit the program while the error is fresh in your mind otherwise you are probably best to exit and modify the code in the usual way.

F9   Function key 9 can be used to zoom in and out of the program. By pressing function key 9 once you will see the screen as the user sees it. For example, if, at the current point in the program, a menu is displayed you will see the menu. By pressing function key 9 again, you will return to the dBASE code.

X   The X action will take you back to the dot prompt. You can then use any dBASE command and return to debug by typing RESUME.

Q   The Q action quits debug, cancelling the program. Use your **reset** program to re-set the environment.

S   The S action will execute the next instruction. If preceded by a number, for example 5, dBASE will execute the next 5 commands before stopping. The N action works in a similar way except commands calling sub-routines will be ignored. dBASE will just step through the current program.

Appendix 1: Consolidation exercises Part 1

Chapter 4: Creating a database system

Creating a database to hold staff records

1 Suggested structure for the **STAFF** database.

Num	Field Name	Field Type	Width	Dec	Index
1	AGENT	Character	4		N
2	SURNAME	Character	20		N
3	FNAME	Character	20		N
4	TITLE	Character	4		N
5	STREET	Character	25		N
6	AREA	Character	25		N
7	TOWN	Character	15		N
8	POSTCODE	Character	10		N
9	DOB	Date	8		N
10	PHONE	Character	10		N
11	SALARY	Numeric	5	0	N
12	COMMISSION	Numeric	5	2	N
13	HOLIDAY	Numeric	2	0	N

2 To create the new database select the **Create** option from the **Data** panel, enter the field information and save the structure using the **Exit** menu.

3 Add the records to the **STAFF** database by selecting the database from the data panel, selecting the **Modify structure/order** option followed by the **Enter records from keyboard** option from the **Append** menu.

4 Select the **Exit** menu twice, to exit from **Append** saving the records.

Creating a personal catalog and database

1 To create a new catalog, access the **Catalog** menu and select the **Use different catalog** option. Select the **Create** option from the pop-up menu. Type a suitable name for the catalog and press ⟨ Enter ⟩.

2 Define the structure of your database and follow instructions 2, 3 and 4 in the previous solution to create the database and add records.

3 To change the catalog back to **ESTATE**, access the catalog menu, select the **Use a different catalog** option and select **ESTATE** from the list.

Chapter 5: Viewing the database

1 To create a new database select the **Create** option from the **Data** panel. Type in the field information as shown in the exercise illustration (*see* Chapter 5). Save the structure using the **Exit** menu.

2 Add the eight given records to the **CUSTOMER** database by selecting the database from the Data panel, selecting the **Modify structure/order** option followed by the **Enter records from keyboard** option from the **Append** menu.

3 Add four more records and select the **Exit** menu twice to exit from **Append**.

4 To view the records in browse mode, highlight the **CUSTOMER** database in the Data panel and press ⟦Enter⟧ and select the **Use file** option. Press ⟦F2⟧ to access browse mode (if in edit mode press ⟦F2⟧ again to toggle to browse mode).

   Move to the **SURNAME** column of the first record and select the **Forward search** option from the Goto menu. Type **Smith** as the search information and press ⟦Enter⟧. The cursor should move to the record for Mr Smith. Press ⟦F2⟧ to toggle to edit mode to view the record in detail. Press ⟦F2⟧ again to return to browse mode.

5 Move to the **AGENT** column of the first record. Select the **Forward search** option from the Goto menu. Type **A1** as the search information and press ⟦Enter⟧. Press ⟦Shift + F4⟧ to see if there are any other properties managed by Agent 1.

6 With the cursor in the **SURNAME** column, select the **Lock fields on left** option from the **Fields** menu. Type **2** as the number of fields to be locked (**SURNAME** and **FIRSTNAME**). Scroll across so that the **TELEPHONE** and **ENROLED** fields are displayed.

7 Select the **Lock fields on left** option from the **Fields** menu. Type **0** as the number of fields to be locked. This will unlock the locked fields. Access the **Exit** menu to leave browse mode. Highlight **CUSTOMER** in the **Data** panel and press ⟦Enter⟧. Select the **Close file** option to close the **CUSTOMER** database.

Chapter 8: Query by example

1 Make sure all databases are closed (below the line in the **Data** panel). Move to the **Queries** panel and select the **Create** option. Select the **Add file to query** option from the Layout menu. Select **PROPERTY**. Move, in turn, to the **PROP_ADD**, **TYPE**, **AGE** and **PRICE** fields and press ⟦F5⟧ to add them to the view skeleton.

2 Press ⟦F2⟧ to activate the query. Press ⟦Shift + F2⟧ to return to query design.

3 Move to under the **TYPE** field in the database skeleton and type "T" (you must include the quotes and type an upper-case T). Press `F2` to activate the query and `Shift + F2` to return to query design.

4 Move to the **TYPE** field and press `Ctrl + Y` to delete the criterion. Move to the **AREA** field and type **"Lumley"**. Activate the query and then return to query design.

Follow the instruction above to complete the rest of the exercises. The following illustrations show the criteria needed . Choose appropriate fields to display in each case.

5 Set up the following query:

Property.dbf	AGE	NO_BEDS	RECEPT	GARDEN	GARAGE	FREEHOLD	↓PRICE	DAT
							<80000	

PROP_ADD	AREA	TYPE	PRICE
5 Hall Road		T	61000.00
89 Cliff Road	Lumley	F	51000.00
6 Brook Road	Farley	T	55000.00
76 Ruin Grove	Old Town	T	63000.00
9 Bookers Avenue	Lumley	S	65000.00
6 Kirk Way		F	48000.00
4 Garden Terrace	Old Town	T	67000.00
6 Taper Ave	Old Town	F	67000.00

6 Set up the following query:

Property.dbf	RECEPT	GARDEN	GARAGE	FREEHOLD	PRICE	↓DATE_TAKEN	OWNER
						<{1/1/92}	

PROP_ADD	AREA	TYPE	DATE_TAKEN
5 Hall Road		T	05/12/91
4 Hever Court	Old Town	D	11/11/91
43 Trewitt Ave	Farley	D	21/10/91
32 Leder Road	Old Town	C	08/01/91
8 Oak Lane	Farley	S	21/01/91
76 Ruin Grove	Old Town	T	02/12/91
9 Bookers Avenue	Lumley	S	17/11/91
56 Rainforest Way	Farley	D	19/03/91
7 Kelly Park Drive	Lumley	S	05/10/91
12 Lewis Mount	Lumley	S	12/12/91

7 Set up the following query:

Property.dbf	↓TYPE	AGE	NO_BEDS	RECEPT	↓GARDEN	GARAGE	FREEHOLD	PRIC
					.T.			

PROP_ADD	AREA	TYPE	GARDEN
4 Hever Court	Old Town	D	T
90 Primly Rise	Lumley	C	T
43 Trewitt Ave	Farley	D	T
23 Yew Bank Drive	Lumley	D	T
32 Leder Road	Old Town	C	T
8 Oak Lane	Farley	S	T
9 Bookers Avenue	Lumley	S	T
56 Rainforest Way	Farley	D	T
7 Kelly Park Drive	Lumley	S	T
90 Otway Road	Farley	D	T

8 Set up the following query:

Property.dbf	↓AREA	TOWN	POST	↓TYPE	AGE	NO_BEDS	RECEPT	↓GARDEN
	"Old Town"							.T.

PROP_ADD	AREA	TYPE	GARDEN
4 Hever Court	Old Town	D	T
32 Leder Road	Old Town	C	T
4 Garden Terrace	Old Town	T	T
6 Taper Ave	Old Town	F	T

9 Set up the following query:

Property.dbf	TOWN	POST	↓TYPE	AGE	NO_BEDS	RECEPT	↓GARDEN	↓GARAGE	FR
			"S"				.T.	.T.	

PROP_ADD	TYPE	GARDEN	GARAGE
3 Oak Lane	S	T	T
12 Lewis Mount	S	T	T

10 Set up the following query:

Property.dbf	TOWN	POST	↓TYPE	AGE	↓NO_BEDS	RECEPT	GARDEN	GARAGE	FR
			"S"		>1				
			"T"		>1				

PROP_ADD	TYPE	NO_BEDS
5 Hall Road	T	2
6 Brook Road	T	4
6 Elm Road	T	3
8 Oak Lane	S	3
76 Ruin Grove	T	5
9 Bookers Avenue	S	3

Chapter 9: Producing simple reports

1   Make sure the **CUSTOMER** database is in use (above line in **Data** panel).
    Move to the **Query** panel and select the **Create** option. If all the fields are
    already included in the view, press F5 whilst the cursor is under the database
    name in the database skeleton. Move across to each specified field in turn and
    press F5 to add them to the view skeleton.

2   Access the **Exit** menu and select the **Save changes** and **Exit** option. Type
    COMMENTS as the query name .

3   Making sure that the query file, **COMMENTS**, is still active (above the line in the
    Queries panel), move across to the **Reports** panel and select **Create**.

4   Select the **Quick layouts** option from the **Layout** menu. Select **Column layout**.

```
 Layout    Fields    Bands    Words    Go To    Print    Exit            11:01:55
 [.......▼.1.....▼...2..▼.....3.▼.......▼.......▼.5.....▼...6...▼.....7.▼.....
 Page        Header   Band

 Page No.  999
 DD/MM/YY

 FIRSTNAME             SURNAME                     TELEPHONE    COMMENTS

 Report    Intro     Band
 Detail              Band
 XXXXXXXXXXXXXX     XXXXXXXXXXXXXXXXXXXXX  XXXXXXXXXXXXX UUUUUUUUUUUUUUUUUUUUUUUU
 Report    Summary  Band

 Page      Footer   Band
```

5   Move the cursor to underneath the field heading **FIRSTNAME** in the header
    band. Access the **Layout** menu and select the **Line** option. Select **Double
    line**. Press Enter to indicate start of line. Use → to draw line across width
    of report (to the end of the V's in the Details band). Press Enter again to
    confirm end of line.

```
 Layout    Fields    Bands    Words    Go To    Print    Exit            11:05:45
 3.▼.......▼.......▼.5.....▼...6...▼.......7.▼.......▼.......▼.9.....▼...10..▼..
 Page        Header   Band

            TELEPHONE     COMMENTS

 Report    Intro     Band
 Detail              Band
 XXXXXXX  XXXXXXXXXXXX  UUUUUUUUUUUUUUUUUUUUUUUUUUUUUUUUUUUUUUUUUUUUUUUUUU
 Report    Summary  Band

 Page      Footer   Band
```

6   Access the **Print** menu and select the **View report screen** option. The text is wrapping around due to a report width greater than 80 characters. Access the **Print** menu again. Select the **Control of printer** option and change the text pitch to **Condensed**. Print the report by selecting the **Begin printing** option.

7   Access the **Exit** menu and select the **Save changes and exit** option. Call the report **COMMENTS**. Save the changes to the print settings using the default name.

Chapter 10: Organising the database

---

1   Move the cursor to the **PROPERTY** database in the **Data** panel and press ⬚F2⬚. Access the **Organise** menu and select the **Create new index** option. Press ⬚Enter⬚ to access the **Name of index** option and type **DATE_TAKEN**. Press ⬚Enter⬚ to confirm. Repeat this process to enter the **Index expression** as **DATE_TAKEN**. Make sure that the **Order of index** is set to **Ascending**. Press ⬚Ctrl + End⬚ to save.

2   Access the **Organise** menu and select **Order records by index** option. Select **Natural** order.

3   Repeat instruction 2 but select the **PRICE** tag as the index order. Select the **Exit** option from the **Exit** menu.

4   Move the cursor to the **CUSTOMER** database in the **Data** panel and press ⬚F2⬚. Select the **Create new index** option from the **Organise** menu. Enter the index information as shown in the following illustration:

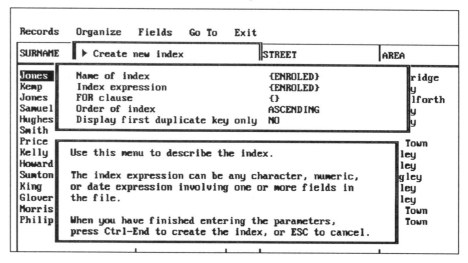

Press ⬚Ctrl + End⬚ to save.

AREA	TOWN	POSTCODE	TELEPHONE	ENROLED	TYPE	AGE
Chapelforth	Leeds	LS4 5TO	(0532)33921	12/09/91	T S C	ANY
Lumley	Greenoak	GR5 6TY	987341	17/11/91	D	ANY
Farley	Grecoak	GR8 5RT	875643	03/12/91	F	M N
Old Town	Greenoak	GR3 6UP	456365	15/12/91	F T S	ANY
Lumley	Greenoak	GR4 5SD	986300	21/12/91	S T	ANY
Lumley	Greenoak	GR5 6RW	982176	01/01/92	F	M N
Lumley	Greenoak	GR4 6TD	567432	01/01/92	D S	PO M
	Bradford	BD4 5TB	(0274)976491	05/01/92	C D	O U
Old Bridge	London	EC2 5TY	(081)345621	01/02/92	C D S	O U
Kingley	Lowston	LO5 2HY	(065)326589	23/02/92	T	O U
Farley	Greenoak	GR8 9RP	872190	07/03/92	S T	PR P
Old Town	Greenoak	GR2 8PL	219543	12/03/92	F T	ANY

The records are displayed in order of date enroled.

5 Select the **Organise** menu and select the **Order records by index** option. Select **NAME**.

6 Select the **Exit** option from the **Exit** menu and close the **CUSTOMER** database.

Chapter 12: Data entry forms

1 Open the **CUSTOMER** database and move to the **Forms** panel. Select the **Create** option. Press Esc to remove the **Layout menu form** screen.

2 Move down to row 3 (*see* status bar) and type **CUSTOMER DETAILS**. Access the **Words** menu and select the **Position** option. Select **Center**.

3 Move to row 2, column 30. Access the **Layout** menu and select the **Box, Double line** options. Press Enter to confirm start of box. Use the arrow keys to draw a box around the text and press Enter to complete.

4 Move to row 6, column 14 and type **CUSTOMER NAME**. Move to row 6, column 24 and press F5. Select the **TITLE** field from the list (you will need to use the ↓ key to see fields not displayed).

CUSTOMER	CALCULATED
ENROLED	<create>
FIRSTNAME	
MAX_PRICE	
MIN_BEDS	
POSTCODE	
REQ_AREA	
STREET	
SURNAME	
TELEPHONE	
TITLE	
TOWN	
TYPE	

Press Ctrl + End to accept the display attributes.

5 Use the same procedure to add the **FIRSTNAME** field at row 6, column 29 and the **SURNAME** field at row 6, column 45.

6   Type the prompt **CUSTOMER ADDRESS** underneath the **Customer name:** prompt. Add the **STREET** field at row 7, column 24; **AREA** at row 8, column 24; **TOWN** at row 9, column 24 and **POSTCODE** at row 9, column 36. Add the following helpful prompts:

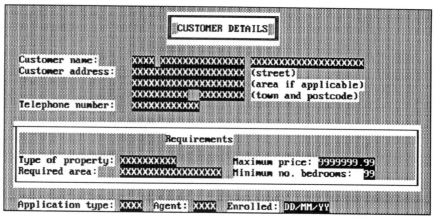

7   Add the telephone number below the address.

8   Save the form at this stage by selecting the **Save this form** option from the **Layout** menu. Name the form **CUSTOMER**.

9   Type the title requirements at row 13, column 1. Centre the title.

10 Add the following prompts and fields:

11 Type the prompt **Comments:** at row 19, column 72 and add the **COMMENTS** field in the usual way. Draw the memo window to take up the bottom half of the screen (read the instructions at the bottom of the screen). Enter the memo marker at row 19, column 72.

12 Access the **Exit** menu and select the **Save changes and exit** option.

13 Test the form by firstly making sure the **CUSTOMER** database is open. Move to the **Form** panel, highlight **CUSTOMER** and press F2. Toggle to edit mode if necessary. Access the memo field.

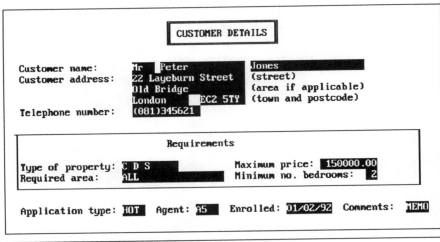

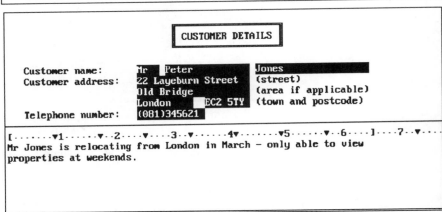

14 Exit from edit mode and close all files.

Chapter 13: The dBASE Application Generator

1 Move to the **Applications** panel and select the **Create** option. Select the **Applications generator** option.

2 Fill in the details as shown below.

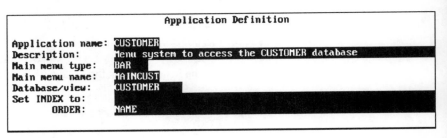

Press [Ctrl + End] when complete.

3   Use $\boxed{\text{Ctrl + Y}}$ to delete the information in the banner and add your own sign on information. Access the **Application** menu and select the **Display sign-on banner** option. Select **Yes**.

4   Select the **Generate quick application** option and fill in the details as shown below.

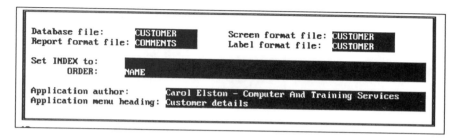

5   Press $\boxed{\text{Ctrl + End}}$ when complete. Select **yes** to generate the application. Press any key when prompted. Access the **Exit** menu and select the **Save changes and exit** option.

6   Select the **CUSTOMER** application from the **Application** panel and select **Run application**. At the prompt, select **Yes**.

7   Press any key to exit from the sign-on banner. The following menu will be displayed.

```
Add Information
Change Information
Browse Information
Discard Marked Records
Print Report
Mailing Labels
Reindex Database
Exit From Customer
```

8   Test each option in turn.

9   Close all files.

Chapter 14: Consolidation of Part 1

14.2: Creating the database

1   The following is a suggested structure for the new **RENTALS** database. Select the **Create** option from the **Data** panel and enter the following field information.

Num	Field Name	Field Type	Width	Dec	Index
1	OWNER	Character	35		N
2	STREET	Character	20		N
3	AREA	Character	20		N
4	TOWN	Character	20		N
5	POSTCODE	Character	10		N
6	TELE_HOME	Character	12		N
7	TELE_WORK	Character	12		N
8	RENT	Numeric	8	2	N
9	TYPE	Character	1		N
10	BEDROOMS	Numeric	2	0	N
11	RECEPTION	Numeric	2	0	N
12	GARDEN	Logical	1		N
13	GARAGE	Logical	1		N
14	AGENT	Character	3		N
15	COMM_RATE	Numeric	6	2	N
16	DATE_RENT	Date	8		N
17	COMMENTS	Memo	10		N

Access the **Exit** menu and select the **Save changes and exit** option. Name the database **RENTALS**.

2 Highlight **RENTALS** in the **Data** panel and press Enter. Select **Modify structure/order application**. Access the **Append** menu and select the **Enter records from keyboard** option. Add the following records as detailed in the exercise (*see* 14.2 Creating the database, page 109).

14.3: Viewing and changing the database data and structure

1 Move to the **RENTALS** database in the **Data** panel and press F2. Press F2 again if you are not in browse mode.

2 With the cursor in the first column containing the **OWNER** field, access the **Fields menu** and select **Lock fields on left** option. Set it to **1** to lock the first field. Press the Tab key until the work telephone number and rent information are in view. Unlock the first field by accessing the **Fields** menu and setting the **lock fields on left** option to **0**.

3 Move across to the **AGENT** column of the first record. Access the **Goto** menu and select the **Forward search** option. Type **A3** as the search criterion.

4 Press F2 if you would rather enter the new information in edit mode. Access the **Records** menu and select the **Add new records** option. Add **2** new records. Use the edit mode. Use Shift + F8, the ditto facility, to enter the property type for the second record.

5 Press F2 if you are not already in edit mode. Press Page Up until record **6** is displayed. Make sure Insert is off and overtype the old telephone number with the new.

6 Access the **Goto** menu and select the **Record number** option. Type **8**. Change the property area to **LUMLEY**. Undo this last change by accessing the **Records** menu and selecting **Undo change to record** option.

7 Access the **Goto** menu and select the **Last record** option. Access the **Records** option and select the **Mark record for deletion** option. To permanently remove this record, access the **Organise** menu and select the **Erase marked records** option. Access the **Exit** option from the **Exit** menu.

8 With **RENTALS** above the line in the **Data** panel press `Shift + F2`. Press `Esc` to remove the menu from the display. Move down to a suitable position in the database structure and press `Ctrl + N` to add a new field. Enter a suitable fieldname, type and width. For example:

Num	Field Name	Field Type	Width	Dec	Index
1	OWNER	Character	35		N
2	STREET	Character	20		N
3	AREA	Character	20		N
4	TOWN	Character	20		N
5	POSTCODE	Character	10		N
6	TELE_HOME	Character	12		N
7	TELE_WORK	Character	12		N
8	RENT	Numeric	8	2	N
9	TYPE	Character	1		N
10	BEDROOMS	Numeric	2	0	N
11	RECEPTION	Numeric	2	0	N
12	GARDEN	Logical	1		N
13	GARAGE	Logical	1		N
14	DATE_AV	Date	8		N
15	AGENT	Character	3		N
16	COMM_RATE	Numeric	6	2	N

Access the **Exit** menu and select the **Save changes and exit** option. Select **Yes** to confirm that this is what you wish to do. Press `F2` to enter browse mode and add suitable dates for the new field. Exit to the Control Centre via the **Exit** menu.

14.4: Querying the database

1 Make sure that the **RENTALS** database is in use (above the line in the **Data** panel). Move across to the **Queries** panel and select the **Create** option. If all the fields are displayed in the view skeleton, press `F5` to remove them all.

Move across to each specified field in turn (use the `Tab` and `Shift + Tab` keys), and press `F5` to add the field to the view skeleton. Move to the **TYPE** field and type "F". Move to the **BEDROOMS** field and type **1**.

Rentals.dbf	↓TELE_HOME	TELE_WORK	↓RENT	TYPE	BEDROOMS	RECEPTION	GARD
				"F"	1		

OWNER	TELE_HOME	AREA	RENT
Mr Brian Douglas	876983		275.00
Mrs Frances Dover	985621	Old Town	250.00

Press F2 to activate the query and Shift + F2 to return to query design.

2   Use Ctrl + Y to delete the criteria entered into the database skeleton. Move to the **AREA** field and type **"Lumley"**. Move to the **RENT** field and type **< 450**. Add the required fields to the view skeleton.

Rentals.dbf	↓AREA	TOWN	POSTCODE	↓TELE_HOME	TELE_WORK	↓RENT	TYPE
	"Lumley"					<450	

Activate the query and return to query design.

3   Remove the existing criteria, move to the **GARAGE** field and type .T.. Activate the query and return to query design.

4   Remove the existing criteria. Add the **DATE_AV** field to the view skeleton. Move to the **DATE_AV** column and type **{01/03/92}**, assuming that to be today's date. Activate the query and return to query design.

5   This is an OR query. The customer wants a flat *or* terrace property. Set up the query as shown below. Unless you have added extra records that meet this criteria, you should find that you receive no matches.

Rentals.dbf	↓AREA	TOWN	POSTCODE	TELE_HOME	TELE_WORK	↓RENT	↓TYPE
	"Farley"					▬▬▬	"F"
	"Farley"						"T"

6   As you do not know the full address you will need to use the **$** operator to search within a string. Remove any existing criteria and set up the query as shown below.

Rentals.dbf	OWNER	↓STREET	↓AREA	TOWN	POSTCODE	TELE_HOME	TELE_WOR
		$ "Jasmin"					

7   Remove any existing criteria and add the criteria **"C"** to the **TYPE** field. Select a range of fields and activate the query. Return to query design. If happy with the result, access the **Layout** menu and select the **Save this query** option. Type **COTTAGE** as the query name. Repeat this procedure for detached properties. Enter the criteria as **"D"**. Access the **Layout** menu, select the **Save this query** option, backspace out the current file name and type **DETACHED**. Repeat for the other types of properties. Exit from query design.

At the Control Centre. move to the **Queries** panel, highlight the required query and press F2 to view the records included in the query in either browse or edit mode.

14.5: Indexing, reports and labels

1 Move to the **Data** panel, highlight **RENTALS** and press [F2]. Access the **Organise** menu and select the **Create new index** option. Give the index a suitable name and set the index expression to **RENT**.

```
Name of index                        {RENT}
Index expression                     {RENT}
FOR clause                           {}
Order of index                       ASCENDING
Display first duplicate key only     NO
```

Press [Ctrl + End] to confirm. In browse mode, move across to the **RENT** field and check that the rents are in order, lowest to highest. Select the **Exit** option from the **Exit** menu.

2 With **RENTALS** still as the active database move to the **Reports** panel and select the **Create** option. Press [Esc] to remove the **Layout** menu from the display. For this example you will add the fields one by one rather than using the **Quick layout** option.

Move the cursor to line 0, column 0 in the header band and make sure that **Insert** is **On**. Press [Enter] to add a new line. Type **Report printed on:**, leave a space and press [F5] to add a field.

RENTALS	CALCULATED	PREDEFINED	SUMMARY
AGENT	<create>	Date	Average
AREA		Time	Count
BEDROOMS		Recno	Max
COMMENTS		Pageno	Min
COMM_RATE			Sum
DATE_AV			Std
DATE_RENT			Var
GARAGE			
GARDEN			

Move across to the **Predefined** column and select the **DATE** field. Press [Ctrl + End] to accept the display attributes. Type **at**, leave a space and repeat the process to add the **TIME** field. Press [Enter] twice to leave two blank lines.

```
Page        Header   Band────────────────────────────

Report printed on: DD/MM/YY at HH:MM:SS

Report      Intro    Band────────────────────────────
```

Type **Full property address** as a column heading at line 3, column 0. Move down to the detail band and press [F5] to load a field. Select **STREET** from the list. Press [Ctrl + End] to accept the display attributes. Leave a space and load the **AREA** field. Move to the header band and enter the column heading as **Property type**. Add the **TYPE** field to the detail band.

```
[·······▼·1····▼···2·▼·····3·▼······▼·······▼·5····▼···
Page      Header  Band
░░░░░░░░░░░░░░░░░░░░░░░░░░░░░░░░░░░░░░░░░░░░░░░░░░░░░░░░░░
Report printed on: DD/MM/YY at HH:MM:SS

Full Property Address░░░░░░░░░░░░░░░░░░░░░░░░Property Type
Report    Intro   Band
░░░░░░░░░░░░░░░░░░░░░░░░░░░░░░░░░░░░░░░░░░░░░░░░░░░░░░░░░░
Detail            Band
XXXXXXXXXXXXXXXXXXXX XXXXXXXXXXXXXXXXXXX    X
Report    Summary Band
░░░░░░░░░░░░░░░░░░░░░░░░░░░░░░░░░░░░░░░░░░░░░░░░░░░░░░░░░░
```

Add the **BEDROOMS** field and **RENT** field as shown below. When adding the
RENT field, change the **Picture function** so that the **Financial format** is **On**.

```
[·······▼·1····▼···2·▼·····3·▼······▼·······▼·5····▼···6··▼····7·▼·······
Page      Header  Band
░░░░░░░░░░░░░░░░░░░░░░░░░░░░░░░░░░░░░░░░░░░░░░░░░░░░░░░░░░░░░░░░░░░░░░░░░
Report printed on: DD/MM/YY at HH:MM:SS

Full Property Address░░░░░░░░░░░░░░░Property Type Bedrooms   Rent
Report    Intro   Band
░░░░░░░░░░░░░░░░░░░░░░░░░░░░░░░░░░░░░░░░░░░░░░░░░░░░░░░░░░░░░░░░░░░░░░░░░
Detail            Band
XXXXXXXXXXXXXXXXXXXX XXXXXXXXXXXXXXXXXXX    X            99       999999.99
Report    Summary Band
░░░░░░░░░░░░░░░░░░░░░░░░░░░░░░░░░░░░░░░░░░░░░░░░░░░░░░░░░░░░░░░░░░░░░░░░░
Page      Footer  Band
░░░░░░░░░░░░░░░░░░░░░░░░░░░░░░░░░░░░░░░░░░░░░░░░░░░░░░░░░░░░░░░░░░░░░░░░░
```

Access the **Print** menu and select the **View report on screen** option.

```
Report printed on: 03/09/92 at 10:53:19

Full Property Address                         Property Type Bedrooms    Rent

56b High Street       Old Town                   F             1        £250.00
26 High Street                                   F             1        £275.00
Flat 2, 9 Buck Lane   Old Town                   F             2        £300.00
12a Princes Lane      Lumley                     F             2        £350.00
56 High Street        Old Town                   F             2        £375.00
10 Hanover Lane       Lumley                     C             2        £400.00
12 The Avenue                                    T             3        £400.00
32 Greebank Road      Lumley                     S             3        £500.00
21 Jasmin Lane        Farley                     D             3        £600.00
21 Littlebrook Ave    Farley                     D             4        £670.00
```

Select the **Save changes and exit** option from the **Exit** menu. Name the report
RENTALS.

3   With **RENTALS** as the active database, move to the Labels panel and select the
    Create option. Press F5 to add a field. Select **OWNER** from the list and
    press CTRL + End to accept the display attributes. Add the rest of the fields
    as shown in the following illustration.

OWNER

STREET

AREA

TOWN

POSTCODE

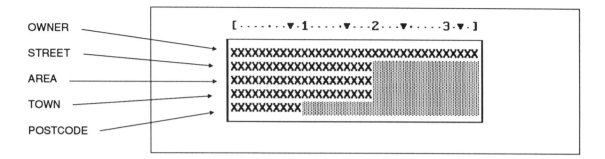

Access the **Dimensions** menu and select the **Predefined size** option. Select a suitable label size, for example, option **2**, **15/16 x 3 1/2 by 2**.

Access the **Print** menu and select the **View labels on screen** option.

```
Mrs Frances Dover          Mr Brian Douglas
56b High Street            26 High Street
Old Town                   Greenoak
Greenoak                   GR1 8YT
GR2 6GH

Mrs J Clare                Miss Karen Harris
Flat 2, 9 Buck Lane        12a Princes Lane
Old Town                   Lumley
Greenoak                   Greenoak
GR2 8JK                    GR4 7TF
```

Access the **Exit** menu and select the **Save changes and exit** option. Name the labels file **RENTALS**.

14.6: Forms and applications

1   Highlight **RENTALS** in the **Data** panel and press ⎸**Shift + F2**⎹. Move to the **Layout** menu and select the **Print database structure** option. Select **Begin printing**. Use the structure to design a layout for the form. The following is just one example.

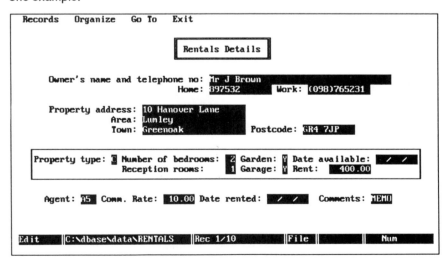

Exit to the Control centre. With **RENTALS** as the active database, move to the **Forms** panel and select the **Create** option. Press `Esc` to remove the **Layout** menu from the display. Move down to row 3 and type the form heading, **Rentals Details**. Access the **Words** menu and select the **Position** option. Select the **Center** option.

Move to row 2, column 30, access the **Layout** menu and select the **Box**, **Double line** options. Press `Enter` to confirm the position of the upper left of the box. Draw the box around the heading and press `Enter` to complete.

Move to row 6, column 6 and type the prompt Owner's name and telephone number:. Leave a space. Press `F5` and select the **OWNER** field from the list. Press `Ctrl + End` to accept the display attributes. Use the same procedure to add the work and home telephone numbers.

```
                              ╔════════════════╗
                              ║ Rentals Details ║
                              ╚════════════════╝

Owner's name and telephone no: XXXXXXXXXXXXXXXXXXXXXXXXXXXXXXXXXXXX
                         Home: XXXXXXXXXXX  Work: XXXXXXXXXXX
```

Add the remaining fields as shown in the following illustration adding a single line box around the property information.

```
                          ╔════════════════╗
                          ║ Rentals Details ║
                          ╚════════════════╝

    Owner's name and telephone no: XXXXXXXXXXXXXXXXXXXXXXXXXXXXXXXXXXXX
                             Home: XXXXXXXXXXX  Work: XXXXXXXXXXX

        Property address: XXXXXXXXXXXXXXXXXXXX
                    Area: XXXXXXXXXXXXXXXXXXXX
                    Town: XXXXXXXXXXXXXXXXXXXX  Postcode: XXXXXXXXXX

  ┌──────────────────────────────────────────────────────────────────┐
  │ Property type: X Number of bedrooms: 99 Garden: X Date available: DD/MM/YY │
  │                  Reception rooms:     99 Garage: X Rent:    99999.99 │
  └──────────────────────────────────────────────────────────────────┘

  Agent: XXX Comm. Rate: 999.99 Date rented: DD/MM/YY
```

The only remaining field is **COMMENTS**, a memo field. Add the prompt **Comments:** following the date rented and a space and load the **COMMENTS** field in the usual way. When prompted for the memo window size, move to the top left corner of the screen and press `Enter`. Draw the window to fill the whole screen and press `Enter` again to complete. Move the cursor to the position following the prompt, **Comments**, and press `Enter` to confirm the marker position.

Access the **Exit** menu and select the **Save changes and exit** option. Call the form **RENTALS**.

2   Move to the **Applications** panel and select the **Create** option. Select the
    Applications generator option and complete the application definition:

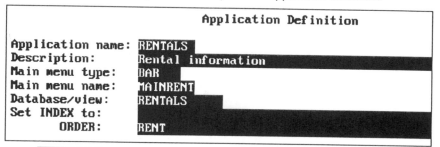

Application Definition

Application name:	RENTALS
Description:	Rental information
Main menu type:	BAR
Main menu name:	MAINRENT
Database/view:	RENTALS
Set INDEX to:	
ORDER:	RENT

Press `Ctrl + End` to complete.

If you want to include a banner, use `Ctrl + Y` to delete the current information
and add your own text. Access the **Application** menu and select the **Display
sign-on banner** option. Select **Yes**.

Select the **Generate quick application** option from the **Application** menu. Add
the following details:

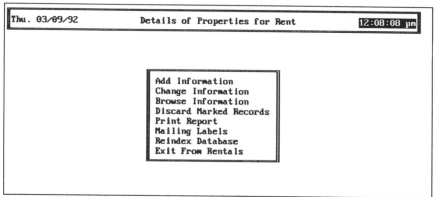

Database file:	RENTALS	Screen format file:	RENTALS
Report format file:	RENTALS	Label format file:	RENTALS
Set INDEX to:			
ORDER:	RENT		
Application author:	Carol Elston – Computer And Training Services		
Application menu heading:	Details of Properties for Rent		

Press `Ctrl + End` to confirm. Select **Yes**. Press any key when generation is
complete.

Access the **Exit** menu and select **Save all changes and exit** option.

Test the application by highlighting the **RENTALS** database in the **Application**
panel and pressing `Enter`. Select the **Run application** option. Select **Yes**.
Press any key when the banner displays.

Thu. 03/09/92   Details of Properties for Rent   12:08:08 pm

```
Add Information
Change Information
Browse Information
Discard Marked Records
Print Report
Mailing Labels
Reindex Database
Exit From Rentals
```

Test each option in turn and return to the Control Centre.

Appendix 2: Consolidation exercises Part 2

Chapter 16: Commands at the Dot Prompt

1 Type the following at the dot prompt:

   USE PROPERTY
   SET FORMAT TO PROPERTY

2 Type the following at the dot prompt:

   EDIT 5

   Change the **DATE_TAKEN** field. Access the **Exit** menu and select the **Exit** option.

3 Type the following at the dot prompt:

   APPEND

   Add a record. Access the **Exit** menu and select the **Exit** option.

4 Type the following at the dot prompt:

   GO BOTTOM
   DELETE
   PACK

5 Type the following at the dot prompt:

   USE CUSTOMER
   CREATE VIEW GRCUSTS

   Add the specified fields to the view skeleton.

6 Enter the criteria **"Greenoak"** in the **TOWN** column.

Customer.dbf	FIRSTNAME	↓TITLE	↓STREET	↓AREA	↓TOWN	↓POSTCODE	TELEPH
					"Greenoak"	▉▉▉▉	

7 If the query file **GRCUSTS** is not already open type:

   SET VIEW TO GRCUSTS

To create a new report type:

CREATE REPORT GRCUSTS

8 Access the **Layout** menu and select the **Quick layout** option. Select the **Mailmerge layout** option.

11 Press F5 to add a field. Select the **TITLE** field from the list and press Ctrl + End to accept the display attributes. Add a space and then load the **SURNAME** field in the same way. Load the **STREET**, **AREA**, **TOWN** and **POSTCODE** fields to make up the address block. Load the predefined **DATE** field below the address.

GRCUSTS	CALCULATED	PREDEFINED	SUMMARY
AREA POSTCODE STREET SURNAME TITLE TOWN	\<create\>	Date Time Recno Pageno	Average Count Max Min Sum Std Var

Type **Dear** and then add the **TITLE** and **SURNAME** fields.

```
 Layout   Fields   Bands   Words   Go To   Print   Exit
[·······▼·1·····▼··2····▼·····3·▼·······▼·······▼·5·····▼·
 Page     Header   Band────────────────────────────────
 Report   Intro    Band────────────────────────────────
 Detail            Band────────────────────────────────
 XXXX XXXXXXXXXXXXXXXXXXXXX
 XXXXXXXXXXXXXXXXXXXXX
 XXXXXXXXXXXXXXXXXXXXX
 XXXXXXXXXX XXXXXXXX

 DD/MM/YY

 Dear XXXX XXXXXXXXXXXXXXXXXXX
```

Type the body of the letter. Access the **Exit** menu and select the **Save changes and exit** option.

13 To display the report, type the following at the dot prompt.

REPORT FORM GRCUSTS

Most of the letters scroll past too quickly to read but you can check the last letter in the file. To view the letters more carefully, view the report from within the Report Generator.

14 Type the following at the dot prompt:

REPORT FORM GRCUSTS FOR AREA = "Lumley" TO PRINT

2   With **CUSTOMER** as the active database, type the following at the dot prompt:

DISP ALL FIRSTNAME, SURNAME, TELEPHONE

3   Type the following at the dot prompt (all on the same line):

DISP FIRSTNAME, SURNAME, TELEPHONE, AGENT FOR APP_TYPE="HOT"

4   Type the following at the dot prompt:

DISP FIRSTNAME, SURNAME, MAX_PRICE FOR MAX_PRICE>=100000

5   Type the following at the dot prompt (all on the same line):

**DISP FIRSTNAME, SURNAME, REQ_AREA FOR "1" $ REQ_AREA .OR.
REQ_AREA="ALL"**

6   Type the following at the dot prompt (all on the same line):

**DISP FIRSTNAME, SURNAME, TYPE, MAX_PRICE FOR TYPE="T" .AND.
MAX_PRICE<60000**

7   Type the following at the dot prompt (all on the same line):

**DISP FIRSTNAME, SURNAME, TYPE, MIN_BEDS FOR TYPE = "S" .AND.
MIN_BEDS>=3**

8   Type the following at the dot prompt:

**DISP FIRSTNAME, SURNAME, ENROLED FOR ENROLED>{31/12/91} .AND.
ENROLED<{1/4/92}**

9   Type the following at the dot prompt (all on the same line):

**DISP FIRSTNAME, SURNAME, REQ_AREA, MIN_BEDS FOR
("7" $ REQ_AREA .OR. "8" $ REQ_AREA .OR. "9" $ REQ_AREA .OR.
REQ_AREA="ALL") .AND. MIN_BEDS>=3**

10 Type the following at the dot prompt:

**USE PROPERTY
LIST STRUCTURE TO PRINT**

11 Type the following at the dot prompt:

**LOCATE FOR PRICE>100000
CONTINUE**

In the sample database the records 4, 7, 8,13 and 16 are found. This may be
different if you have added different or extra records.

12 Type the following at the dot prompt:

INDEX ON OWNER TAG OWNER
SEEK "Mr D Swan"
EDIT

Press Esc to exit.

13 Type the following at the dot prompt:

REPLACE ADVERTS WITH ADVERTS+25 FOR AGENT="A1"

Chapter 19: Validation with a screen form

1 Close all databases. Highlight **CUSTOMER** in the **Forms** panel and press
 Enter . Select the **Modify layout** option.

2 Move to the **TITLE** field (refer to the bottom of the screen to make sure you are
on the correct field).

```
Form       C:\dbase\data\CUSTOMER   Row:6 Col:24     File:Customer    Num    Ins
           Add field:F5   Select:F6   Move:F7   Copy:F8   Size:Shift-F7
           CUSTOMER->TITLE     Type: Character   Width:   4   Decimal:   0
```

Press F5 to modify the display attributes for this field. Move to the **Picture
functions** option and press Enter . Select the **Multiple choice** option. Type
the following as the choices, each separated by a comma (,) but no spaces:

Mr,Mrs,Ms,Miss,Dr

Press Enter to confirm followed by CTRL + End to save.

Select the **Edit** options. Move down to the **Message** option, press Enter and
type the following message:

Mr, Mrs, Ms, Miss, Dr - Press spacebar to choose

Press Enter to confirm.

Press Ctrl + End to save the **Edit** options and Ctrl + End again, to complete
the changes to the display attributes.

The validation of the remaining fields follows a similar pattern. Move to the field,
press F5 and then change the **Template, Picture function** and/or **Edit** options.
Always use Ctrl + End to complete an operation.

The following are some suggestions as to the validation that could be included for
each field on the form. It is suggested that you use the **Edit** options to include a
suitable message for each field. Not all fields have suggested validation.

FIRSTNAME, SURNAME and AREA:

Template   first character convert to upper case (!)

TOWN:

Edit   as most customers live in Greenoak this could be set as the default
(this can always be overtyped for customers outside of Greenoak) -
set the **Default value** option to **"Greenoak"** (the quotes are needed)

POSTCODE:

Function   turn **Upper-case conversion** to **On**

TYPE:

Edit   use the **Multiple choice** option - enter the available types of
properties as codes separated by commas - remember to include **ANY**

REQ_AREA:

Edit   use the **Multiple choice** option - enter the available areas as codes
separated by commas - remember to include **ALL**

MAX_PRICE

Template   remove the decimal places from the template

Function   turn **Financial format** to **On**

APP_TYPE:

Edit   use the **Multiple choice** option to select choices

AGENT

Template   set the **Template** as **A999**

Function   set **Upper-case conversion** to **On**

Save the changes using the **Exit** menu. Add a record to the database to test the
validations.

Appendix 3: Consolidation exercises Part 3

Chapter 23: Programming with dBASE

1 To create a new program file called **COURSADD**, type the following at the dot prompt:

MODI COMM COURSADD

2 Read in the heading by accessing the **Word** menu and selecting the **Write/read text file** option. Select the **Read text from file** option and type **HEADING.PRG**. Fill in the relevant details.

3 Type in the code, the following is one solution:

SET BELL OFF
SET CONFIRM ON
USE COURSES
SET FORMAT TO COURSES
APPEND
CLOSE FORMAT
CLOSE ALL
CLEAR
SET BELL ON
SET CONFIRM OFF
RETURN

4 Access the **Exit** menu and select the **Save changes and exit** option.

5 Run the program by typing **DO COURSADD** at the dot prompt.

This sample solution can be copied from disk by typing **!COPY A:\C23\COURSADD.PRG**.

Chapter 24: Program interaction

1 The following code is one solution to the exercise:

SET TALK OFF
SET BELL OFF
SET CONFIRM ON

```
USE COURSES ORDER TAG C_CODE

STORE SPACE(6) TO MC_CODE
CLEAR
@3,0 TO 19,79
@10,10 SAY 'Please enter the Course Code..' GET MC_CODE;
    FUNCTION '!A'
 READ

SEEK MC_CODE          && SEARCH FOR THE COURSECODE
CLEAR
SET FORMAT TO COURSES
EDIT
CLOSE FORMAT

CLOSE ALL
CLEAR
SET BELL ON
SET CONFIRM OFF
SET TALK ON
RETURN
```

Chapter 25: Testing user response and using program loops

Changing the COUREDIT program

The following is one solution:

```
SET TALK OFF
SET BELL OFF
SET CONFIRM ON
USE COURSES ORDER TAG C_CODE

DO WHILE .T.
    STORE SPACE(6) TO MC_CODE
    CLEAR
    @3,0 TO 19,79
    @10,10 SAY 'Please enter the Course Code..' GET MC_CODE;
            FUNCTION '!A'
    READ

    SEEK MC_CODE
    CLEAR
    IF .NOT. EOF()
            SET FORMAT TO COURSES
            EDIT RECORD RECNO()
            CLOSE FORMAT
```

```
                ELSE
                        STORE "Y" TO MANS
                        @3,0 TO 19,79
                        @10,10 SAY "Course code does not exist re-enter?Y/N";
                                GET MANS FUNCTION "M Y,N"
                        READ
                        IF MANS = "Y"
                                LOOP
                        ENDIF
                ENDIF
                CLEAR
                STORE "Y" TO MANS
                @3,0 TO 19,79
                @10,10 SAY "Edit another record? Y/N";
                        GET MANS FUNCTION "M Y,N"
                READ
                IF MANS = "Y"
                        LOOP
                ENDIF

                CLOSE ALL
                CLEAR
                SET BELL ON
                SET CONFIRM OFF
                SET TALK ON
                RETURN
        ENDDO
```

A deletion module for the CLIENTS database

The following is one solution:

```
SET TALK OFF
SET BELL OFF
SET CONFIRM ON
USE CLIENTS ORDER TAG ACNO

DO WHILE .T.
   STORE SPACE(5) TO MACNO
   CLEAR
   @3,0 TO 19,79
   @12,10 SAY "Please enter the Account Number..";
      GET MACNO PICTURE "@! AAA99"
   READ

   SEEK MACNO
   CLEAR
   IF .NOT. EOF()
        STORE " " TO MANS
        @8,0 TO 16,79
```

```
                              @12,10 SAY "The record containing details on"+TRIM(FIRST)
                                      +" "+SURNAME
                              @13,10 SAY "will be marked for deletion.  Is this correct? Y/N ";
                                      GET MANS FUNCTION "M Y,N"
                  READ
                  IF  MANS="Y"
                  DELETE
                  ENDIF
          ELSE
                  STORE " " TO MANS
                  @3,0 TO 19,79
                  @10,10 SAY "Account Number does not exist re-enter? Y/N";
                          GET MANS FUNCTION "M Y,N"
                  READ
                  IF  MANS="Y"
                              LOOP
                  ENDIF
          ENDIF

          CLEAR
          STORE " " TO MANS
          @3,0 TO 19,79
          @10,10 SAY "Delete another record? Y/N";
              GET MANS FUNCTION "M Y,N"
          READ
          IF  MANS="Y"
              LOOP
          ENDIF

          CLEAR
          STORE " " TO MANS
          @3,0 TO 19,79
          @10,10 SAY "Do you want to pack the database Y/N";
              GET MANS FUNCTION "M Y,N"
          READ
          IF  MANS="Y"
              PACK
          ENDIF

          CLOSE ALL
          CLEAR
          SET BELL ON
          SET CONFIRM OFF
          SET TALK ON
          RETURN
ENDDO
```

A deletion module for the COURSES database

The deletion module for the **COURSES** database is similar to the module written for
for the **CLIENTS** database. Modify the **CLIDEL** program, access the **Layout** menu

and select the **Save as** option. Change the program name to **COURDEL.PRG**.
The code that needs to be changed is listed below:

```
USE COURSES ORDER TAG C_CODE

STORE SPACE(6) TO MC_CODE

@12,10 SAY "Please enter the Course Code..";
    GET MC_CODE FUNCTION "@!A"

 SEEK MC_CODE

@12,10 SAY "The record containing details on "+TRIM(LEVEL)+" "+COURSE
@13,10 SAY "will be marked for deletion. Is this correct? Y/N ";
    GET MANS FUNCTION "M Y,N"

@10,10 SAY "Course Code does not exist re-enter? Y/N";
    GET MANS FUNCTION "M Y,N"
```

Chapter 26: Programming a report

The following is just one solution:

```
SET TALK OFF
SET SAFETY OFF

USE COURSES ORDER TAG C_CODE
CLEAR
STORE 'N' TO MANS
@3,0 TO 19,79
@10,10 SAY 'Do you want to print the report? Y/N....' ;
    GET MANS FUNCTION "M Y,N"
READ

IF MANS = 'Y'
    SET PRINT ON
ENDIF

*Print a page heading including the date.
?'              Computer And Training Services'
?
?'              Current List of Available Courses'
?


DO WHILE .NOT. EOF()
    ?
    ?TRIM(LEVEL)+" "+TRIM(COURSE)+" - "+STR(DAYS,2)
    ??" day(s) @ £"+STR(PRICE,3,0)+" per day"
```

```
        ?
        SKIP
    ENDDO

    IF MANS = "Y"
        EJECT
        SET PRINT OFF
    ELSE
        WAIT
    ENDIF

    CLOSE ALL
    CLEAR
    SET SAFETY ON
    SET TALK ON
    RETURN
```

Chapter 27: The menu system

The program code for **COURMENU** should be similar in structure to the code listed for **CLIMENU** (*see* 27.3, Creating the menu program, page 209).

1   Copy the **CLIMENU** program by typing **COPY FILE CLIMENU.PRG TO COURMENU.PRG** at the dot prompt.

Make changes to the following:

2   Change the menu heading to **@3,22 SAY "COURSE INFORMATION"**.

3   Change the choice for:

MCHOICE=1 to **DO COURSADD**
MCHOICE=2 to **DO COUREDIT**
MCHOICE=3 to **DO COURDEL**
MCHOICE=4 to **DO COURREP**.

Index

ORDER FORM

wish to purchase the following book(s) and /or disks in the From Start to Finish *Series:*

Qty	ISBN	Title	Price
_	0 273 03814 1	**Microsoft Word 2.0 for Windows**	£12.99
_	0 273 03883 4	**Microsoft Word 2.0 for Windows** Disk pack containing three 3.5"disks and three 5.25" disks	£12.99 + VAT
_	0 273 03816 8	**dBASE IV 1.1**	£12.99
_	0 273 03881 8	**dBASE IV 1.1** Disk pack containing three 3.5"disks and three 5.25" disks	£12.99 + VAT
_	0 273 03817 6	**Lotus 1, 2, 3 for Windows**	£12.99
_	0 273 03879 6	**Lotus 1, 2, 3 for Windows** Disk pack containing three 3.5"disks and three 5.25" disks	£12.99 + VAT
_	0 273 03815 X	**WordPerfect 5.1 for Windows**	£12.99
_	0 273 03885 0	**WordPerfect 5.1 for Windows** Disk pack containing three 3.5"disks and three 5.25" disks	£12.99 + VAT

- -

NB Please add £2.35 to your order for Postage & Packing
in the UK.

ayment should be made in £ Sterling.

enclose a cheque (payable to **Pitman Publishing**)

or £ _____

Alternatively, please debit my credit card:

VISA ☐ ☐ ☐ ☐

Please supply cardholder's address below if paying by
credit card.

Card No:

☐☐☐☐☐☐☐☐☐☐☐☐☐☐☐☐☐☐

Expiry Date _____

Signature _____

PLEASE USE CAPITALS
Mr/Mrs/Miss/Ms
Initials   Surname

My job title is

Institute

Address

Town

County   Postcode

Return this form with your remittance to
Customer Services Dept, Pitman Publishing
Southport Book Distributors, 12-14 Slaidburn Crescent
Southport PR9 9YF

OR Tel: 0704 26881   OR Fax: 0704 231970

Prices and availability are subject to change without notice.
Pitman Publishing, part of the Longman Group UK Limited Registered office: 5 Bentinck Street, London W1M 5RN